UNFREEDOM

OF THE

PRESS

MARK R. LEVIN

Threshold Editions

NEW YORK   LONDON   TORONTO   SYDNEY   NEW DELHI

Threshold Editions
An Imprint of Simon & Schuster, Inc.
1230 Avenue of the Americas
New York, NY 10020

Copyright © 2019 by Mark Levin

First Threshold Editions hardcover edition May 2019

THRESHOLD EDITIONS and colophon are trademarks
of Simon & Schuster, Inc.

For information about special discounts for bulk purchases,
please contact Simon & Schuster Special Sales at 1-866-506-1949
or business@simonandschuster.com.

The Simon & Schuster Speakers Bureau can bring authors to your
live event. For more information, or to book an event, contact
the Simon & Schuster Speakers Bureau at 1-866-248-3049
or visit our website at www.simonspeakers.com.

Manufactured in the United States of America

1 3 5 7 9 10 8 6 4 2

Library of Congress Cataloging-in-Publication Data is available.

ISBN 978-1-4767-7309-4
ISBN 978-1-4767-7348-3 (ebook)

Dedicated to and in memory of my wonderful parents,
Jack and Norma Levin
Loving and beloved, American patriots,
and together forever

Jack E. Levin	*Norma R. Levin*
June 11, 1925	*February 13, 1931*
October 15, 2018	*February 10, 2019*

CONTENTS

UNFREEDOM

OF THE

PRESS

UNFREEDOM OF THE PRESS

UNFREEDOM OF THE PRESS is about how those entrusted with news reporting in the modern media are destroying freedom of the press from within: not government oppression or suppression, not President Donald Trump's finger-pointing, but present-day newsrooms and journalists. Indeed, social activism, progressive groupthink, Democratic Party partisanship, opinion and propaganda passed off as news, the staging of pseudo-events, self-censorship, bias by omission, and outright falsehoods are too often substituting for old-fashioned, objective fact gathering and news reporting. A self-perpetuating and reinforcing mindset has replaced independent and impartial thinking. And the American people know it. Thus the credibility of the mass media has never been lower.

This book could easily have been ten times its current length, but that would make it unreadable for most. Nonetheless, much

1

ground is covered and research undertaken, and many authors and
scholars consulted, as the history of the American press and the
evidence of its decades-long demise are carefully examined. The
purpose of *Unfreedom of the Press* is to jump-start a long-overdue
and hopefully productive dialogue among the American citizenry
on how best to deal with the complicated and complex issue of the
media's collapsing role as a bulwark of liberty, the civil society, and
republicanism, ranging from the early newspapers and pamphlets
promoting the principles set forth in the Declaration of Independence and the Constitution, to the subsequent party-press and
transparent allegiance to one party or the other, to the progressive
approach of so-called professional reporting, and the ideologically
driven advocacy press of today.

Unlike the early patriot press, today's newsrooms and journalists are mostly hostile to America's founding principles, traditions,
and institutions. They do not promote free speech and press freedom, despite their self-serving and self-righteous claims. Indeed,
they serve as societal filters attempting to enforce uniformity of
thought and social and political activism centered on the progressive ideology and agenda. Issues, events, groups, and individuals
that do not fit the narrative are dismissed or diminished; those
that do fit the narrative are elevated and celebrated. Of course, this
paradigm greatly influences the culture, the government, and the
national psyche. It defines a media-created "reality" whether or
not it has a basis in true reality, around which individuals organize
their thoughts, beliefs, and, in some cases, their lives.

Yet there is mystery and opacity that surround all of it. And if
one dares to question or criticize the motives and work product
of this enterprise or aspects of it—that is, the reporting by one

or more newsrooms—the response is often knee-jerk and emotionally charged, with the inquirer or critic portrayed as hostile to press freedom and the collective media circling the wagons around themselves.

It bears remembering that the purpose of a free press, like the purpose of free speech, is to nurture the mind, communicate ideas, challenge ideologies, share notions, inspire creativity, and advocate and reinforce America's founding principles—that is, to contribute to a vigorous, productive, healthy, and happy individual and to a well-functioning civil society and republic. Moreover, the media are to expose official actions aimed at squelching speech and communication. But when the media function as a propaganda tool for a single political party and ideology, they not only destroy their own purpose but threaten the existence of a free republic.

It is surely not for the government to control the press, and yet the press seems incapable of policing itself. We must remember, we are not merely observers, we are the citizenry. "We the People," for whom this nation was established and for whom it exists, "in Order to form a more perfect Union, establish Justice, insure domestic Tranquility, provide for the common defense, promote the general Welfare, and secure the Blessings of Liberty to ourselves and our Posterity,"[1] must demand a media worthy of our great republic. And we begin the process by informing ourselves about those institutions and individuals (and their practices and standards) who, by their own anointment, proclaim the high-minded obligation of informing us.

ONE

NEWS AS POLITICAL AND IDEOLOGICAL ACTIVISM

WHAT DO WE mean by a "free press," "press," or "freedom of the press"?

What is the purpose of a free press? Is it to report information?

What kind of information? Is it to interpret or analyze information?

What is "the news"? How are decisions made about what is newsworthy and what is not?

What is a "news organization"? One person (a blogger), a group of people (a weekly newspaper), a corporate conglomerate (a television network)?

What is a "journalist"? What qualifies someone as a journalist? Experience, education, position, self-identification?

What is the job of a journalist? Is journalism a profession?

Are there standards?

Are journalists able to be "fair" or "objective"?

What is the purpose of reporting? To reinforce the founding and fundamental principles of the republic? To challenge public officials and authority? To give voice to certain individuals, groups, and causes? To influence politics and policy? To alter the status quo of a society? To promote "the common good" of the community?

What is the common good? Who decides?

What is the difference between freedom of the press and "free speech"? And does the current media revolution, spurred by technological advances such as the internet and social media, change any of this?

Do these questions even matter anymore to news outlets? The questions are rarely asked today let alone rationally discussed. They are infrequently the subject of open or public media circumspection or focused and sustained national debate. It seems "the media" are loath to investigate or explore "the media." However, when the conduct of the media is questioned as biased, politically partisan, or otherwise irresponsible, they insist that they are of one mission: fidelity to the news and all that stems from it—protecting society from autocratic government, defending freedom of the press, and contributing to societal civility and justice. Moreover, they typically claim to pursue and report the news free from any personal or political agenda.

Is that true of the modern media?

More than seventy years ago, there was a serious self-examination of the media. The Commission on Freedom of the Press (also known as the Hutchins Commission) was organized in 1942 by *Time* and *Life* magazine publisher Henry Luce to explore whether freedom of the press was in danger and the proper function of the media in a modern democracy. Its report was issued in 1947 and concluded, in part, that freedom of the press was indeed in danger, and for three basic reasons: "First, the importance of the press to the people has greatly increased with the development of the press as an instrument of mass communication. At the same time the development of the press as an instrument of mass communication has greatly decreased the proportion of the people who can express their opinions and ideas through the press. Second, the few who are able to use the machinery of the press as an instrument of mass communication have not provided a service adequate to the needs of the society. Third, those who direct the machinery of the press have engaged from time to time in practices which the society condemns and which, if continued, it will inevitably undertake to regulate or control."[1]

The commission warned: "The modern press itself is a new phenomenon. Its typical unit is the great agency of mass communication. These agencies can facilitate thought and discussion. They can stifle it. They can advance the progress of civilization or they can thwart it. They can debase and vulgarize mankind. They can endanger the peace of the world; they can do so accidentally, in a fit of absence of mind. They can play up or down the news and its significance, foster and feed emotions, create complacent fictions and blind spots, misuse the great words, and uphold empty slogans. Their scope and power are increasing every day as new instruments become available to them. These instruments can spread lies faster and farther than our forefathers dreamed when they enshrined the freedom of the press in the First Amendment to our Constitution."[2]

The commission cautioned that "[w]ith the means of self-destruction that are now at their disposal, men must live, if they are to live at all, by self-restraint, moderation, and mutual understanding. They get their picture of one another through the press. The press can be inflammatory, sensational, and irresponsible. If it is, it and its freedom will go down in the universal catastrophe. On the other hand, the press can do its duty by the new world that is struggling to be born. It can help create a world community by giving men everywhere knowledge of the world and of one another, by promoting comprehension and appreciation of the goals of a free society that shall embrace all men."[3]

Is this how the modern media conduct themselves? Self-restrained, measured, and temperate? Are the media providing knowledge and insight useful to the public and a free society, or are they obsessed with their own personal, political, and progressive predilections and piques? Have the media earned the respect and esteem of their readers, viewers, and listeners as fair and reliable purveyors of information, or are large numbers of the citizenry suspicious and distrustful of their reporting? Are the media on a trajectory of self-destruction, unofficially identifying with one political party (Democratic Party) over the other (Republican Party)?

In point of fact, most newsrooms and journalists have done a very poor job of upholding the tenets of their profession and, ultimately, have done severe damage to press freedom. Many millions of Americans do not respect them or trust them as credible, fair-minded, and unbiased news sources.

For example, on October 12, 2018, Gallup reported: "Republicans have typically placed less trust in the media than independents and especially Democrats, but the gap between Republicans and Democrats has grown. The current 55-percentage-point gap is among the largest to date, along with last year's 58-point gap. President Donald Trump's attacks on the 'mainstream media' are likely a factor in the increasingly polarized views of the media. Republicans agree with his assertions that the media unfairly cover his administration, while Democrats may see the media as the institution primarily checking the president's power."[4]

Furthermore, "Democrats' trust surged last year and is now at 76%, the highest in Gallup's trend by party, based on available data since 1997. Independents' trust in the media is now at 42%, the highest for that group since 2005. Republicans continue to lag well behind the other party groups—just 21% trust the media—but that is up from 14% in 2016 and last year."[5] Another way to look at these statistics is that nearly 80 percent of Republicans distrust the media, while nearly 80 percent of Democrats trust the media. This would seem to underscore the close ideological and political association and tracking between Democrats and the press.

Lara Logan, who was a CBS News journalist and war correspondent from 2002 to 2018, spoke frankly in a February 15, 2019, podcast interview about the media's professional demise, preference for the Democratic Party and progressive advocacy, and intolerance of independent and diverse perspectives in reporting. "Visually—anyone who's ever been to Israel and been to the Wailing Wall has seen that the women have this tiny little spot in front of the wall to pray and the rest of the wall is for the men. To me that's a great representation of the American media, is that, you know, in this tiny little corner where the women pray, you've got Breitbart and Fox News and, you know, a few others. And then from that—from there on you have CBS, ABC, NBC, 'Huffington Post,' Politico, whatever, right, all of them. And that's a problem for me. Because even if it was reversed, if it was, you know, vastly—mostly, you know, right—on the right and a little bit, that would also be a problem for me. What I—my experience has been that the more—the more opinions you have, the more ways that you look at everything in life, everything in life is complicated, everything is gray, right. Nothing is black and white."[6]

Logan continued that this is not about politics or partisanship to her. It is not about pro-Trump or anti-Trump. It is about news reporting. "It's got nothing to do with whether I like Trump or I don't like Trump. Right? Or whether I believe him or identify with him, don't. Whatever. I don't even want to have that conversation because I approach that the same way I approach anything. I find that is not a popular way to work in the media today because although the media has always been historically left-leaning, we've abandoned our pretense or at least the effort to be objective today. . . . The former executive editor of the *New York Times* has a book coming out, Jill Abramson. And she says, 'We would do, I don't know, dozens of stories about Trump every single day and every single one of them was negative.' Abramson said, 'We have become the anti-Trump paper of record.' Well, that's not our job. That's a political position. That means we've become political activists in a sense. And some could argue, propagandists, right? And there's some merit to that. We have a few conventions—because they are not really rules—but you need at least two firsthand sources for something, right? Those things help keep your work to a certain standard. Those standards are out the window. I mean, you read one story or another and hear it and it's all based on one anonymous administration official, former administration official. That's not journalism. . . ."[7]

When a journalist breaks from the rest of the media pack, which is quite rare, their careers are typically threatened or ruined by the rest of the press. Indeed, after the Logan interview went viral, she was ostracized or worse, personally attacked by individuals in her own profession. In a subsequent interview on Fox's *Hannity,* Logan related that "if there were any independent voices out there, any journalists who are not beating the same drum and giving the same talking points, then we pay the price. What is interesting . . . they cannot take down the substance of what you're saying. They cannot go after the things that matter. So they smear you personally. They go after your integrity. They tear after your reputation as a person and a professional. They will stop at nothing. I am not the only one. And I am just, I am done, right, I am tired of it. And they do not get to write my story anymore. They do not get to speak for me. I want to say loudly and clearly to anybody who is listening, I am not owned. Nobody owns me. I'm not owned by the left or the right."[8]

Indeed, the Commission on Freedom of the Press had specifically emphasized that the media must pay special attention to the difference between fact and opinion. "Of equal importance with reportorial accuracy are the identification of fact as fact and opinion as opinion, and their separation, so far as possible. This is necessary all the way from the reporter's file, up through the copy and makeup desks and editorial offices, to the final, published product. The distinction cannot, of course, be made absolute. There is not fact without a context and no factual report which is uncolored by the opinions of the reporter. But modern conditions require greater effort than ever to make the distinction between fact and opinion. . . ."[9]

Having ignored the blaring warning of the commission, the media have knowingly commingled fact and opinion and have, in fact, regularly taken up the policies and causes of the Democratic Party. Consequently, the public's attitude toward the modern media is divided largely along ideological and party lines.

In January 2018, Knight Foundation–Gallup published its survey of 19,000 U.S. adults. It found that "Americans believe that the media have an important role to play in our democracy—yet they don't see that role being fulfilled."[10] "Eighty-four percent of Americans believe the news media have a critical or very important role to play in democracy, particularly in terms of informing the public—yet they don't see that role being fulfilled and less than half (44 percent) can name an objective news source."[11]

As in the Gallup survey, analysts found that "[w]hile the majority of Americans clearly recognized the importance of media in a democracy, there were clear differences between Democrats and Republicans in their views of the media. While 54 percent of Democrats have a very or somewhat favorable opinion of the media, 68 percent of Republicans view the news media in an unfavorable light."[12]

"Democrats," Gallup reported, "largely trust the media and Republicans largely distrust it. The divergence based on political affiliation was also seen in perceptions of bias in the news. Forty-five percent of Americans say there is a 'a great deal' of political bias in news coverage (up from 25 percent in 1989); 67 percent of Republicans say they see 'a great deal' of political bias in the news, versus only 26 percent of Democrats."[13]

As will become clear, the perceptions revealed in these surveys are realities, and the evidence is overwhelming that journalists as a group reject, in one form or another, the commission's admonition that reporters should strive to separate fact from opinion; rather, in varying ways and to different degrees, they embrace the idea of news "interpretation" or news "analysis" in the selection, gathering, and reporting of news, influenced by and filtered through the progressive mentality.

While there is much more to the commission's report, its closing summary is especially noteworthy: "The character of the service required of the American press by the American people differs from the service previously demanded, first, in this—that it is essential to the operation of the economy and to the government of the Republic. Second, it is a service of greatly increased responsibilities both as to the quantity and as to the quality of the information required. In terms of quantity, the information about themselves and about their world made available to the American people must be as extensive as the range of their interests and concerns as citizens of the self-governing, industrialized community in the closely integrated modern world. In terms of quality, the information provided must be provided in such a form, and with so scrupulous a regard for the wholeness of the truth and the fairness of its presentation, that the American people may make for themselves, by the exercise of reason and of conscience, the fundamental decisions necessary to the direction of their government and of their lives."[14]

A more recent effort to define modern journalism was undertaken by former journalists Bill Kovach and Tom Rosenstiel, who claim to have "distilled from our search, some clear principles that journalists agree on—and that citizens have a right to expect. . . . These are the principles that have helped both journalists and the people in self-governing systems to adjust to the demands of an ever more complex world. They are the elements of journalism. The first among them is that the purpose of journalism is to provide people with information they need to be free and self-governing."[15] Kovach and Rosenstiel list the elements of journalism as follows:

- Journalism's first obligation is to the truth.
- Its first loyalty is to citizens.
- Its essence is a discipline of verification.
- Its practitioners must maintain an independence from those they cover.
- It must serve as an independent monitor of power.
- It must provide a forum for public criticism and compromise.
- It must strive to make the significant interesting and relevant.
- It must keep the news comprehensive and in proportion.
- Its practitioners have an obligation to exercise their personal conscience.
- Citizens, too, have rights and responsibilities when it comes to news.[16]

These elements of journalism appear noncontroversial when taken at face value. But are they, in truth, the working guidelines for most modern newsmen?

Kovach and Rosenstiel fear that the great challenge—if not threat—to journalism today, as differentiated from past press transitions, results from the nature of the ownership of news outlets. "For the first time in our history, the news increasingly is produced by companies outside journalism, and this new economic organization is important. We are facing the possibility that independent news will be replaced by rumor and self-interested commercialism posing as news. If that occurs, we will lose the press as an independent institution, free to monitor the other powerful forces and institutions in society."[17] "In the new century, one of the most profound questions for a democratic society is whether an independent press survives. The answer will depend on whether journalists have the clarity and conviction to articulate what an independent press means and whether, as citizens, the rest of us care."[18]

While the consolidation of news outlets may or may not threaten the independence of news reporting, depending on the relationship between the particular conglomerate and the acquired news company, perhaps of greater moment is the advent of social media and its influence on news reporting. In either case, regardless of platform, format, or structure, the more important issue relates to *content*—that is, what is the nature and purpose of the modern newsroom and journalism.

Kovach and Rosenstiel raise the issue of "diversity" in the newsroom, which they argue is a vital priority to ensure the integrity of the news product and the credibility of those who produce it. They write, among other things, that "[t]he goal of diversity should be to assemble not only a newsroom that might resemble the community but also one that is as open and honest so that this diversity can function. This is not just racial or gender diversity. It is not just ideological diversity. It is not just social class or economic diversity. It is not just numerical diversity. It is what we call intellectual diversity, and it encompasses and gives meaning to all the other kinds."[19]

Is not the greater danger to an independent press "ideology" in the newsroom? Whether a monopoly of ideologically based reporting, which plainly exists today, or "intellectual diversity," should not ideology be reserved for the opinion-editorial pages of newspapers or the commentary segments of broadcasts? Whatever happened to "professional journalism" and the promise or at least suggestion that the press ought to pursue the *objective truth* in the gathering and reporting of news?

But apparently even the notion of objectivity in reporting is subject to dispute and debate. During the turn of the last century, particularly in the early 1920s, as the Progressive Era began to take hold, the "scientific" approach to journalism—that is, a press held to certain professional standards and processes—spread through newsrooms, as it spread through government. Kovach and Rosenstiel give voice to the arguments made in 1919 by Walter Lippmann, a venerated reporter and commentator at the time, and Charles Merz, an associate editor of the *New York World*, in which they condemned the *New York Times'* coverage of the Russian Revolution. Lippmann and Merz wrote, in part, that "[i]n the large, the news about Russia is a case of seeing not what was, but what men wished to see." The solution, argued Lippmann and Merz, exists in "the scientific spirit. . . . There is but one kind of unity possible in a world as diverse as ours. It is unity of method, rather than aim; the unity of disciplined experiment." In this, Lippmann and Merz are projecting the progressive approach to most things onto the profession of journalism and the press generally.[20]

Kovach and Rosenstiel elaborated: "When the concept of objectivity originally migrated to journalism, it was not meant to imply that journalists were free of bias. Quite the contrary. The term began to appear as part of journalism early in the last century, particularly in the 1920s, out of a growing recognition that journalism was full of bias, often unconscious. The call for journalists to adopt objectivity was an appeal for them to develop a consistent method of testing information—a transparent approach to evidence—precisely so that personal and cultural biases would not undermine the accuracy of their work."[21]

"In the nineteenth century," write the authors, "journalists talked about something called realism. This was the idea that if reporters simply dug out the facts and ordered them together, the truth would reveal itself rather naturally. Realism emerged at a time when journalism was separating from political parties and becoming more accurate. It roughly coincided with the invention of what journalists called the inverted pyramid, in which a journalist lines the facts up from the most important to the least important, thinking it helps audiences understand things naturally."[22]

But "good intentions" and "honest efforts" are not enough.

Thus the journalist's objectivity is not an issue, they argue. The focus must be on an objective process and standard by which the journalist must gather, digest, and report the news. "In the original concept . . . the journalist is not objective, but his method can be. The key was in the discipline of the craft, not the aim. . . . Most people think of objectivity in journalism as an aim, not a method. And many citizens scoff at this intention, since they have little idea of the methods journalists might be employing. Yet the notion that the aim of objectivity is insufficient without a unity of method to put it into practice is as valid today as ever. . . ."[23]

It is not clear, then, why Kovach and Rosenstiel raise the issue of newsroom diversity as an imperative unless they understand that an objective method and standard for vetting news is unlikely to occur in a newsroom populated by ideologues and party partisans. The aims then become the goal. Kovach and Rosenstiel as much as admit it. Even so, if the measure of modern journalism is, at least in part, determined by the intellectual diversity of newsrooms, it is apparent if not obvious that news outlets and journalists are overwhelmingly progressive in their thinking and attitudes and share the ideological mindset characteristic of the present-day Democratic Party—the same progressive mindset that has devoured so many of the nation's cultural and societal institutions during the last century, as I explain at length in *Rediscovering Americanism: And the Tyranny of Progressivism.*

George Mason professor Tim Groseclose, formerly of the University of California, Los Angeles, developed an "objective, social-scientific method" in which he calculates how the progressive political views of journalists and media outlets distort the natural views of Americans. It "prevents us from seeing the world as it actually is. Instead, we see only a distorted version of it. It is as if we see the world through a glass—a glass that magnifies the facts that liberals want us to see and shrinks the facts that conservatives want us to see. The metaphoric glass affects not just what we see, but how we think. That is, media bias really does make us more liberal. Perhaps worst of all, media bias feeds on itself. That is, the bias makes us more liberal, which makes us less able to detect the bias, which allows the media to get away with more bias, which makes us even more liberal, and so on."[24]

Groseclose continues: "U.S. newsrooms are extremely one-sided. One consequence of this is what I call the *first-order problem* of an unbalanced newsroom. This is the simple fact that if you read a newspaper article or watch a television news clip, then almost surely it will have been written or produced by a liberal. But another consequence, which I call the *second-order problem*, may be worse. Two effects of the second-order problem are the *minority-marginalization* principle, in which members of the majority group sometimes treat members of the minority group as if they don't exist. And on the occasions when they do remember that the minority group exists, they sometimes treat the members as if they are mildly evil or subhuman."[25]

Groseclose argues that another effect is the "*extremism-redefined* principle," in which "the terms 'mainstream' and 'extreme' take on new meaning within the group. When the group is, say, very liberal, mainstream Democratic positions begin to be considered centrist, and positions that would normally be considered extremely left-wing become commonplace."[26]

The American Press Institute cautions that there is such a bias that "used to be called 'pack journalism.' It has also been called 'group think.' It is the story-line that the press corps *en masse* is telling or repeating. A modern term for it is the *master narrative*. . . . These master narratives can become a kind of trap or rut. The journalist picks facts that illustrate a master narrative, or current stereotype, and ignores other facts."[27]

Let us examine some significant evidence—reports, surveys, and studies—that does a good job of underscoring Groseclose's observations and assessing the ideological and political nature of the modern media, and which raise serious questions about the diversity, objectivity, and/or impartiality of reporting.

A 2014 study conducted by Indiana University professors Lars Willnat and David H. Weaver, based on online interviews with

1,080 American journalists that were conducted during the fall of
2013, reveals that although 50.2 percent of journalists identified as
independent and 14.6 percent as "other," the number identifying
as Democratic was 28.1 percent compared to merely 7.1 percent
as Republican.[28] "In 1971, the first time the survey was conducted
(this was its fifth incarnation), some 25.7 percent of journalists
polled said they identified as Republican."[29] Moreover, the fact
that approximately 65 percent of these journalists self-identify as
either political independents or other does not necessarily mean
they are without a partisan or ideological outlook, which may
well motivate or influence their reporting. Indeed, during the
last several decades alone, poll after poll and survey after survey
have demonstrated the media are more liberal than the public at
large.[30]

A November 2018 survey of 462 financial journalists by professors at Arizona State University and Texas A&M University, of
which more than 70 percent of those surveyed were affiliated with
the *Wall Street Journal*, *Financial Times*, Bloomberg News, Associated Press, *Forbes*, the *New York Times*, Reuters, or the *Washington Post*, revealed that even most financial journalists are political
progressives. When asked, "Generally speaking, how would you
describe your political views?" the journalists responded: very
liberal (17.63 percent); somewhat liberal (40.84 percent); moderate (37.12 percent); somewhat conservative (3.94 percent); and,
very conservative (.046 percent). Thus nearly 60 percent of financial journalists surveyed were liberal and less than 5 percent were
conservative.[31]

The Center for Public Integrity, a left-of-center organization,
reports that "[c]onventional journalistic wisdom holds that re-

porters and editors are referees on politics' playing field—bastions of neutrality who mustn't root for Team Red or Team Blue, either in word or deed. . . . [However, in the 2016 presidential election], people identified in federal campaign finance filings as journalists, reporters, news editors or television news anchors—as well as other donors known to be working in journalism—have combined to give more than $396,000 to the presidential campaigns of Clinton and Trump. Nearly all of that money—more than 96 percent—. . . benefited Clinton: About 430 people who work in journalism have, through August [2016], combined to give about $382,000 to the Democratic nominee."[32]

And what of the incestuous relationship between journalists and the last Democratic administration? On September 12, 2013, the *Atlantic,* a progressive media outlet, reported that there were at least twenty-four journalists who transitioned from media jobs to working in the Obama administration.

Here is some of what the *Atlantic's* Elspeth Reeve uncovered:

- *Time* managing editor Rick Stengel moved to the State Department as undersecretary of state for public diplomacy and public affairs;
- Douglas Frantz, who wrote for the *New York Times* and the *Los Angeles Times,* was an assistant secretary of state for public affairs;
- *Boston Globe* online politics editor Glen Johnson was a senior adviser at the State Department;
- *Washington Post* writer Stephen Barr moved to the Labor Department as senior managing director of the Office of Public Affairs;

- *Washington Post* congressional reporter Shailagh Murray became Vice President Joe Biden's communications director and later senior adviser to President Obama;
- Rosa Brooks was a columnist for the *Los Angeles Times* before taking a position with the undersecretary of defense for policy;
- The *Washington Post*'s Desson Thomson left the paper to serve as a speechwriter for the U.S. ambassador to Britain;
- Roberta Baskin, a onetime CBS News investigative reporter, joined the Department of Health and Human Services as a senior communications adviser;
- The *Washington Post*'s Warren Bass, an Outlook section deputy editor, joined then–United Nations ambassador Susan Rice as director of speechwriting and senior policy adviser;
- *Education Week* reporter David Hoff moved to the Education Department;
- CNN senior political producer Sasha Johnson joined the Department of Transportation and later became chief of staff at the Federal Aviation Administration;
- The *Chicago Tribune*'s Jill Zuckman moved to the Department of Transportation as communications director;
- Rick Weiss, who had worked for the *Washington Post*, became communications director and senior policy strategist for the White House Office of Science and Technology;
- Former CBS and ABC reporter Linda Douglass joined the Obama campaign and was later communications director for the White House Office of Health Reform;
- *New York Times* reporter Eric Dash moved to the Treasury Department's public affairs office, as did MSNBC producer Anthony Reyes;

- CNN's Aneesh Raman worked for the Obama campaign and later as speechwriter for President Obama;
- CNN's national security reporter Jim Sciutto, formerly with ABC News, served as chief of staff to United States Ambassador to China Gary Locke;
- and *San Francisco Chronicle* environment reporter Kelly Zito joined the Environmental Protection Agency's public affairs office.[33]

Notably, *Time* magazine Washington bureau chief Jay Carney became communications director for Vice President Biden and subsequently press secretary to President Obama.

You would be hard-pressed to find a similar extensive relationship between numerous major media organizations and recent Republican administrations. Moreover, what of family ties between the press and the Obama administration? On June 12, 2013, the *Washington Post*'s Paul Farhi found the following: "ABC News President Ben Sherwood . . . is the brother of Elizabeth Sherwood-Randall, a top national security adviser to President Obama. His counterpart at CBS, news division president David Rhodes, is the brother of Benjamin Rhodes [deputy national security adviser for strategic communications]. CNN's deputy Washington bureau chief, Virginia Moseley, is married to Tom Nides, [formerly] deputy secretary of state under Hillary Rodham Clinton. Further, White House press secretary Jay Carney's wife is Claire Shipman, a veteran reporter for ABC. And [National Public Radio's] White House correspondent, Ari Shapiro, is married to a lawyer, Michael Gottlieb, who joined the White House counsel's office." Vice President Biden's onetime communications director

"Shailagh Murray . . . is married to Neil King, one of the Wall Street Journal's top political reporters."[34] Nonetheless, Farhi cites numerous media executives who insist that protections of various sorts are in place to prevent conflicts.

There are other former Democratic staffers who now work in the media and some have long family ties to the Democratic Party. For example:

- MSNBC's Chris Matthews previously worked for, among others, President Jimmy Carter and Democratic House Speaker Tip O'Neill.
- CNN's Chris Cuomo is brother to New York's Democratic governor, Andrew Cuomo.
- CNN's Jake Tapper worked for Democratic congresswoman Marjorie Margolies-Mezvinsky and Handgun Control Inc.
- ABC's Cokie Roberts's father was Hale Boggs, the House Democratic majority leader.
- Of course, ABC's George Stephanopoulos worked for President Bill Clinton.

There are others, including some Republicans, but this provides a sense of the coziness between the national Washington, D.C., media and the Democratic Party.

There are also other influences on reporting, including a "geographic bubble." *Politico*, a progressive media website, notes that "[t]he national media really does work in a bubble," which it contends is "something that wasn't true as recently as 2008. And the bubble is growing more extreme. Concentrated heavily along the coasts, the bubble is both geographic and political. If you're a working journalist, odds aren't just that you work in a pro-Clinton county—odds are that you reside in one of the nation's *most* pro-Clinton counties." Blaming the decline on the newspaper business and the rise of internet-based online reporting for this bubble, correspondents Jack Shafer and Tucker Doherty write that "[t]his isn't just a shift in medium. It's also a shift in socio-politics, and a radical one. Where newspaper jobs are spread nationwide, internet jobs are not: Today, 73 percent of all internet publishing jobs are concentrated in either the Boston–New York–Washington–Richmond corridor or the West Coast crescent that runs from Seattle to San Diego and on to Phoenix. The Chicago-land area, a traditional media center, captures 5 percent of the jobs, with a paltry 22 percent going to the rest of the country. And almost all the real growth of internet publishing is happening outside the heartland, in just a few urban counties, all places that voted for Clinton. So when your conservative friends use 'media' as a synonym for 'coastal' and 'liberal,' they're not far off the mark."[35]

Shafer and Doherty conclude that "[n]early 90 percent of all internet publishing employees work in a county where Clinton won, and 75 percent of them work in a county that she won by more than 30 percentage points. When you add in the shrinking number of newspaper jobs, 72 percent of all internet publishing or newspaper employees work in a county that Clinton won. By this measure, of course, Clinton was the national media's candidate.... The people who report, edit, produce and publish news can't help being affected—deeply affected—by the environment around them."[36]

Given these various studies and analyses, are journalists nonetheless able to put aside their progressive ideological mindset and political partisanship in a relatively objective or impartial pursuit of news?

Is that even still a goal of modern journalism?

A recent study by the nonpartisan Harvard Kennedy School's Shorenstein Center on Media, Politics and Public Policy suggests not—certainly with regard to the presidency of Donald Trump. On May 18, 2017, the Shorenstein Center issued a comprehensive analysis of news coverage of the first one hundred days of the Trump administration. Among its conclusions:

> Trump's attacks on the press have been aimed at what he calls the "mainstream media." Six of the seven U.S. outlets in our study—CBS, CNN, NBC, *The New York Times*, *The Wall Street Journal*, and *The Washington Post*—are among those he's attacked by name. All six portrayed Trump's first 100 days in highly unfavorable terms. CNN and NBC's coverage were the most unrelenting—negative stories about Trump outpaced positive ones by 13-to-1 on the two networks. Trump's coverage on CBS also exceeded the 90 percent [negative] mark. Trump's coverage exceeded the 80 percent level in *The New York Times* (87 percent negative) and *The Washington Post* (83 percent negative). *The Wall Street Journal* came in below that level (70 percent negative), a difference largely attributable to the *Journal's* more frequent and more favorable economic coverage. Fox was the only outlet where Trump's overall coverage nearly crept into positive territory—52 percent of Fox's reports with a clear tone were negative, while 48 percent were positive. Fox's coverage was 34 percentage points less negative than the average for the other six outlets. . . . Trump's coverage

during his first 100 days was not merely negative in overall terms. It was unfavorable on every dimension. There was not a single major topic where Trump's coverage was more positive than negative.[37]

These findings, particularly as they relate to Fox, are telling. The prevailing criticism of Fox, especially by its media competition, is that it is in the tank for Trump. While some Fox hosts and programs are more supportive of the president than others—and the distinction at Fox between the news programming and opinion programming is much better delineated than at CNN and MSNBC—the statistics gathered by the Shorenstein Center suggest that the Fox coverage overall is much more evenhanded than at other news outlets, which are overwhelmingly negative.

This may seem surprising given all the stories about Fox in the print and broadcast media portraying Fox as unfair and unbalanced in its coverage. Indeed, Fox and its executives and hosts are frequent targets of other press operations, such as the *New Yorker*, *Vanity Fair*, the *New York Times*, the *Washington Post*, *Politico*, CNN, MSNBC, etc., in which journalists and progressive commentators for these news outlets seem fixated with diminishing Fox's public standing and reputation and, in some instances, even promote commercial boycotts against certain Fox hosts and shows. The reason seems apparent: Fox defies the near ideological and political uniformity of the other media outlets, in which their coverage of Trump is "unfavorable on every dimension."[38]

The Shorenstein Center provides a thoughtful piece of advice to newsrooms and journalists. "Journalists would . . . do well to spend less time in Washington and more time in places where policy intersects with people's lives. If they had done so during the presidential campaign, they would not have missed the story that keyed Trump's victory—the fading of the American Dream for millions of ordinary people. Nor do all such narratives have to be a tale of woe. America at the moment is a divided society in some respects, but it's not a broken society and the divisions in Washington are deeper than those beyond the Beltway."[39]

By comparison, on April 28, 2009, the Pew Research Center issued its study of media reports on the Obama administration's first one hundred days. Pew reported that "President Barack Obama has enjoyed substantially more positive media coverage than either Bill Clinton or George Bush during their first months in the White House, according to a new study of press coverage. Overall, roughly four out of ten stories, editorials and op-ed columns about Obama have been clearly positive in tone, compared with 22% for Bush and 27% for Clinton in the same mix of seven national media outlets during the same first two months in office, according to a study by the Pew Research Center's Project for Excellence in Journalism. The study found positive stories about Obama have outweighed negative by two-to-one (42% vs. 20%) while 38% of stories have been neutral or mixed."[40]

There are numerous other examples of the media's progressive political and ideological bias, including more studies and surveys, illustrating its widespread existence.[41] Yet the evidence is often dismissed, denied, spun, or made righteous. But it is unequivocal. Indeed, in a growing number of circles, the ideological mission of news organizations and journalists is no longer subterranean. Their advocacy and mission are open and unambiguous.

For example, New York University professor Jay Rosen is a leading voice in the idea of so-called public or civic journalism—that is, the purpose-driven, community-based social activism journalism movement spreading throughout America's newsrooms for the last several decades. A harsh critic of then-candidate Donald Trump, Rosen wrote in the *Washington Post*: "Imagine a candidate who wants to *increase* public confusion about where he stands on things so that voters give up on trying to stay informed and instead vote with raw emotion. Under those conditions, does asking 'Where do you stand, sir?' serve the goals of journalism, or does it enlist the interviewer in the candidate's chaotic plan? I know what you're thinking, journalists: 'What do you want us to do? Stop covering a major party candidate for president? That would be irresponsible.' True. But this reaction short-circuits intelligent debate. Beneath every common practice in election coverage there are premises about how candidates will behave. I want you to ask: Do these still apply? Trump isn't behaving like a normal candidate; he's acting like an unbound one. In response, journalists have to become less predictable themselves. They have to come up with novel responses. They have to do things they have never done. They may even have to shock us."[42]

"They may need to collaborate across news brands in ways they have never known," Rosen adds. "They may have to call Trump out with a forcefulness unseen before. They may have to risk the breakdown of decorum in interviews and endure excruciating awkwardness. Hardest of all, they will have to explain to the public that Trump is a special case, and the normal rules do not apply."[43]

The news reporting about candidate Trump, President Trump, the Trump administration, and Trump supporters certainly gives every indication that Rosen's public or civic social activism approach to journalism has a firm grip on modern newsrooms and journalists. But it can also be discerned more broadly in the topics the news media ignore, report, or report repeatedly, as well as the manner in which they are reported and the selection of "experts" or public officials to support certain positions, etc.

Twenty-five years ago, teacher and journalist Alicia C. Shepard explained that Rosen's approach to journalism and "[t]he goal of public journalism—a.k.a. civic journalism, public service journalism or community-assisted reporting—is to 'reconnect' citizens with their newspapers, their communities and the political process, with newspapers playing a role not unlike that of a community organizer. According to the gospel of public journalism, professional passivity is passé; activism is hot. Detachment is out; participation is in. . . ."[44]

At the time, Marvin Kalb, then director of the Shorenstein Center and a former journalist, said, "I think the movement is one of the most significant in American journalism in a long time. This is not a flash in the pan phenomenon. It's something that seems to be digging deeper roots into American journalism and ought to be examined very carefully." Kalb went on to warn, "A journalist who becomes an actor, in my view, is overstepping the bounds of his traditional responsibility. When the journalist literally organizes the change and then covers it, I'm uncertain about such traditional qualities as detachment, objectivity, toughness. . . . The whole point of American journalism has always been detachment from authority so that critical analysis is possible."[45]

Rosen and other like-minded social activists of public and civic journalism reject the traditional standards and notions of a free press for, instead, a radical approach to reporting, where the media become an essential instrument for the Progressive Movement. They borrow from the philosophy of, among others, sociologist Amitai Etzioni. Etzioni describes his approach as "people committed to creating a new moral, social and public order based on restored communities, without allowing puritanism or oppression."[46]

But Etzioni's philosophy, Rosen's teachings and writings, and the practices of journalists throughout America's newsrooms (the latter wittingly and unwittingly) essentially embrace and share the role of journalism set forth by John Dewey nearly a century ago. Indeed, one might justifiably refer to Dewey, one of the earliest and most influential progressive intellectuals in the nation, as one of the founding fathers of modern journalism. After all, it is abundantly obvious that the Progressive Movement could not and would not overlook or somehow bypass the most important tool of mass communication for advancing its immense ideological program—a radical break from America's heritage, culture, and founding, particularly the principle of individual freedom and market capitalism (hence the emphasis on "communitarianism").

Dewey declared: "When . . . I say that the first object of a renascent liberalism is education, I mean that its task is to aid in producing the habits of mind and character, the intellectual and moral patterns, that are somewhere near even with the actual movements of events. It is, I repeat, the split between the latter as they have externally occurred and the ways of desiring, thinking, and of putting emotion and purpose into execution that is the basic cause of present confusion in mind and paralysis in action. The educational task cannot be accomplished merely by working upon men's minds, without action that effects actual change in institutions. The idea that dispositions and attitudes can be altered by merely 'moral' means conceived of as something that goes on wholly inside of persons is itself one of the old patterns that has to be changed. Thought, desire and purpose exist in a constant give and take of interaction with environing conditions. But resolute thought is the first step in that change of action that will itself carry further the needed change in patterns of mind and character."[47]

"In short," Dewey said, "liberalism must now become radical, meaning by 'radical' perception of the necessity of thoroughgoing changes in the set-up of institutions and corresponding activity to bring the changes to pass. For the gulf between what the actual situation makes possible and the actual state itself is so great that it cannot be bridged by piecemeal policies undertaken *ad hoc*."[48]

Moreover, this "liberalism," while said to be representative of the community and the people, is the opposite. There is no practical way for the public to influence the substance of the news and reporting it receives. Furthermore, the progressive ideology, while claiming to be people oriented, preaches the wisdom of expert masterminds and administrators, and the application of scientific models and approaches to human behavior through centralized decision making. This was well expressed in 1922 by the highly influential newsman and commentator Walter Lippmann, in his classic book, *Public Opinion*. At the time, Lippmann was a disenchanted socialist, increasingly disillusioned by the public. Consequently, like many progressives, he believed the problem rested with the inability of the citizenry, in a large and complex modern society, to grasp events and rationally discuss or act on them.

Lippman wrote that the world is just too complicated for inattentive or busy individuals, focused on their own lives and pursuits, to comprehend events: "The amount of attention available is far too small for any scheme in which it was assumed that all the citizens of the nation would, after devoting themselves to the publications of all the intelligence bureaus, become alert, informed, and eager on the multitude of real questions that never do fit very well into any broad principle. I am not making that assumption. Primarily, the intelligence bureau is an instrument of the man of action, of the representative charged with decision, of the worker at his work, and if it does not help them, it will help nobody in the end. But in so far as it helps them to understand the environment in which they are working, it makes what they do visible. And by that much they become more responsible to the general public."[49]

Lippmann contended that the experts, doing their daily business, are to be relied on to improve society: "The purpose, then, is not to burden every citizen with expert opinions on all questions, but to push that burden away from him towards the responsible administrator. An intelligence system has value, of course, as a source of general information, and as a check on the daily press. But that is secondary. Its real use is as an aid to representative government and administration both in politics and industry. The demand for the assistance of expert reporters in the shape of accountants, statisticians, secretariats, and the like, comes not from the public, but from men doing public business, who can no longer do it by rule of thumb. It is in origin and in ideal an instrument for doing public business better, rather than an instrument for knowing better how badly public business is done."[50]

And Lippman exhorted that it is the process of expert synthesis and analysis that enables the citizen to make sense of things. "Only by insisting that problems shall not come up to him until they have passed through a procedure, can the busy citizen of a modern state hope to deal with them in a form that is intelligible. For issues, as they are stated by a partisan, almost always consist of an intricate series of facts, as he has observed them, surrounded by a large fatty mass of stereotyped phrases charged with his emotion. According to the fashion of the day, he will emerge from the conference room insisting that what he wants is some soul-filling idea like Justice, Welfare, Americanism, Socialism. On such issues the citizen outside can sometimes be provoked to fear or admiration, but to judgment never. Before he can do anything with the argument, the fat has to be boiled out of it for him."[51]

As many regular consumers of news can attest, this condescending elitism, a fundamental characteristic of progressivism, abounds in the attitude of journalists, and undoubtedly in the environment of newsrooms in all their platforms.

Professor Charles Kesler of Claremont McKenna College and the Claremont Institute summed up the media's transformation this way: "Early in the 20th century journalism began to think of itself as a profession. In the 19th century most newspapers had been outgrowths of political parties. Now the rising spirit was non-partisan, independent, and expert, guided by the example of the new social sciences, whether philosophical-historical or more scientific approach. Both recipes came from the same university kitchen, so it was common to find enlisted in the same political causes both the earnest, idealistic, progressive social reformers and the cool, scientific social inquirers of facts and nothing but the facts...."[52]

Kesler added: "The new journalism, too, grew up thinking of itself as liberal and 'objective' at the same time. It was objective insofar as it separated facts from values: reporting the facts, and relegating the values to the editorial pages. But to be objective or scientific in that way was itself a liberal value. Liberals of almost all stripes were confident that those separate facts would eventually line up together as 'history,' meta-fact confirming their own version of progress and hence their own values. . . . The front page and the editorial page were ultimately in synch. . . ."53

Lacking confidence in the intelligence and wisdom of his fellow citizens, Rosen insists on indoctrination and manipulation by media elites: "If the public is assumed to be 'out there,' more or less intact, then the job of the press is easy to state: to inform people about what goes on in their name and their midst. But suppose the public leads a more broken existence. At times it may be alert and engaged, but just as often it struggles against other pressures— including itself—that can win out in the end. Inattention to public matters is perhaps the simplest of these, atomization of society one of the more intricate. Money speaks louder than the public, problems overwhelm it, fatigue sets in, attention falters, cynicism swells. A public that leads this more fragile kind of existence suggests a different task for the press: not just to inform a public that may or may not emerge, but to improve the chances that it will emerge. John Dewey, an early hero of mine, had suggested something like this in his 1927 book, *The Public and Its Problems*."54

Rosen seems to be referencing Dewey's view of news as providing "meaning"—the "social consequences" of the information. Dewey wrote that "'[n]ews' signifies something which has just happened, and which is new just because it deviates from the old and regular. But its *meaning* depends upon relations to what it imports, to what its social consequences are."55 Therefore, reporting events without a social context, and their relationship to the past as part of a continuum, isolates them from their connections. "Even if social sciences as a specialized apparatus of inquiry were more advanced than they are," Dewey continued, "they would be comparatively impotent in the office of directing opinion on matters of concern to the public as long as they are remote from application in the daily and unremitting assembly and interpretation of 'news.' On the other hand, the tools of social inquiry will be clumsy as long as they are forged in place and under conditions remote from contemporary events."[56]

Again we are reminded that real news is information infused with progressive social theory.

Seton Hall assistant professor and former journalist Matthew Pressman makes a more nuanced case for abandoning fact-based journalism for social activism. He contends that "[t]o some observers, the overriding characteristic of American journalism is liberal bias. But that is inaccurate, because it suggests either a deliberate effect to slant the news or a complete obliviousness to the political implications of news coverage. What truly defines contemporary American journalism is a set of values that determine news judgments. Some are political values: mistrust of the wealthy and powerful, sympathy for the dispossessed, belief in the government's responsibility to address social ills. Others are journalistic values: the beliefs that journalists must analyze the news, must serve their readers, must try to be evenhanded. These values are not designed to serve any ideological agenda, but they help create a news product more satisfying to the center-left than to those who are right of center."[57] Pressman argues that as a result of certain horrific events in the 1960s and 1970s, no longer could journalists simply report news as objective news without interpretation influenced by progressive values.

In other words, journalists should not seek and report facts as news, but launder their news gathering priorities and the facts themselves through a progressive ideology to give them meaning and purpose. Of course, the meaning or purpose happens to promote the progressive policy and political agenda. Inasmuch as this approach mostly excludes the moral and political values of a large population of Americans, it cannot be accomplished in an "evenhanded" way, as Pressman urges. It can merely be said to be evenhanded when, in truth, such an assertion is preposterous and impossible as a matter of fact. This helps explain the modern-day near monopoly of ideologically slanted news reporting. Too often it is biased. Too often it is policy driven. And it is, therefore, "more satisfying to the center-left."

Pressman explains what had been, in his view, the lamentable state of the press a century ago. "Ever since major American newspapers began adopting the ideal of objectivity in the 1910s and 1920s, they had allowed only a select few journalists to interpret the news: editorial writers, opinion columnists, and those writing for special sections in the Sunday edition.... Workaday reporters, however, had to stick to the four W's and one H: who, what, when, where, and how. The 'why' question was beyond their purview. With interpretive reporting, that began to change."[58]

Consequently, the pursuit and conveyance of objective truth as news is not the journalist's real purpose or goal anymore, but instead "interpretive reporting" through progressive lenses. "The move toward interpretation," explains Pressman, "began in the 1950s and continues today, and it has had far-reaching implications. It caused journalists to redefine objectivity, contributed to the public's mistrust of the news media, and shifted the balance of power in news organizations from editors to reporters. But at the outset, it was—like most profound changes in big, established institutions—simply an attempt to keep pace with the competition [that is, radio, then television, and now the internet]."[59]

Hence, when the news consumer reads, hears, or sees progressive bias or even political partisanship in the press that appears to closely align with the pronouncements and policies of the Democratic Party and Democratic officials, given its progressive ideological schema, he is not imagining things.

A decade before Pressman's writing, former *Washington Post* reporter Thomas Edsall was even more blunt and took the argument even further. Edsall proclaimed that "journalism should own its liberalism—then manage it, challenge it, and account for it." "The mainstream press is liberal. Once, before 1965, reporters were a mix of the working stiffs leavened by ne'er-do-well college grads unfit for corporate headquarters or divinity school. Since the civil rights and women's movements, the culture wars and Watergate, the press corps at such institutions as *The Washington Post*, ABC-NBC-CBS News, the *NYT*, *The Wall Street Journal*, *Time*, *Newsweek*, the *Los Angeles Times*, *The Boston Globe*, etc. is composed in large part of 'new' or 'creative' class members of the liberal elite—well-educated men and women who tend to favor abortion rights, women's rights, civil rights, and gay rights. In the main, they find such figures as Bill O'Reilly, Glenn Beck, Sean Hannity, Pat Robertson, or Jerry Falwell beneath contempt."[60]

Of course, Edsall is correct about the contempt the modern press has for conservatives generally. But it is more than that. It bleeds into open hostility for conservative media institutions, such as conservative talk radio and the Fox News Channel, the latter of which does not even claim to be a conservative news outlet but, rather, a nonconforming media network that uses the moniker "fair and balanced." Moreover, the media's progressive mindset and interpretive approach results in the press calling into question virtually every cultural, traditional, and institutional norm, as one might expect. After all, it now functions as an outgrowth of the broader progressive ideological and political project. It also leads to a more myopic view of society and the evident increasing disdain and intolerance newsrooms and journalists openly display for fellow citizens who may not share their ideological attitudes, especially these days supporters of President Trump. Again, this helps explain the synergy between the press and the Democratic Party. Therefore, it logically follows that the Democratic Party mostly benefits from the media's interpretation of the news.

As Gallup reported on April 5, 2017, "[s]ixty-two percent of U.S. adults say the media has a favorite [political party], up from about 50% in past years. Just 27% now say the media favors neither major party. . . . Currently, 77% of Republicans say the media favors one party over the other; in 2003, 59% of Republicans said the same. By comparison, 44% of Democrats now say the media plays favorites, unchanged from the 44% who said so in 2003. . . . Gallup asked those who perceive political bias in the news media to say which party the news media favors. Almost two-thirds (64%) of those who believe the media favors a political party say it is the Democratic Party. Only about a third as many (22%) believe the media favors Republicans. This is not new. Americans who perceive media bias have always said the direction of that bias leaned in favor of the Democrats, although the percentage holding that view has varied."[61]

For Edsall, the problem is that "there are very few good conservative reporters. There are many intellectually impressive conservative advocates and opinion leaders, but the ideology does not seem to make for good journalists."[62]

Of course, as the studies demonstrate, there are very few conservative reporters in the first place, given the lack of diverse beliefs and attitudes in newsrooms. And the community of journalists is increasingly cloistered by ideology and geography. But Edsall then makes the self-serving assertion that "[i]n contrast, any examination of the nation's top reporters over the past half-century would show that, in the main, liberals do make good journalists in the tradition of objective news coverage. The liberal tilt of the mainstream media is, in this view, a strength, but one that in recent years, amid liberal-bias controversies, has been mismanaged."[63]

Hence liberals far outnumber others in news organizations, liberals are better reporters anyway, and the issue with liberal bias in the media is actually a problem of branding and marketing.

Edsall, like Pressman later, must resort to a both self-fulfilling and incoherent formulation of journalism's purpose to justify liberal media bias and simultaneously reject bias as a criticism. "While the personnel tend to share an ideological worldview," writes Edsall, "most have a personal and professional commitment to the objective presentation of information." Edsall's complaint is that "[t]he refusal of mainstream media executives to acknowledge the ideological leanings of their staffs has produced a dangerous form of media guilt in which the press leans over so far backward to avoid the charge of left bias that it ends up either neutered or leaning to the right."[64]

Furthermore, it seems the media's progressive ideological outlook has in some ways morphed into a moral crusade, as in other societal areas so inflicted with progressive sensibilities during the course of the last century. Kovach and Rosenstiel assert that most journalists "sense that journalism is a moral act and know that all of their background and values direct what they will do and not do in producing it. . . . For many journalists, this moral dimension is particularly strong because of what attracted them to the profession in the first place. When they initially became interested in the news, often as adolescents or teenagers, many were drawn to the craft by its most basic elements—calling attention to inequities in the system, connecting people, creating community. . . . These journalists feel strongly about the moral dimension of their profession because without it they have so little to help them navigate the gray spaces of ethical decisions."[65]

A moral imperative to one's life, let alone career, is certainly noble. It is not exclusive to journalism. It is something to which individuals from all walks of life, in all professions and areas of work, should possess or strive. But if and when morality is defined by or interpreted through a progressive ideology and related policy and political objectives, the outcome is a profession whose members form a class or aristocracy of strident, pretentious, arrogant, and self-righteously superior individuals, rarely capable of circumspection or improvement. This has most recently and particularly revealed itself in the media's coverage of President Trump. Charles Kesler explains: "President Trump exploits that vulnerability with his criticism of 'fake news.' He accuses them not merely of making it up, that is, of getting the facts wrong or concocting 'facts' to fit their bias, but also of inventing the very standards by which to conceal and justify their abuses: the fake authority of 'objectivity,' nonpartisanship, and progress. They are as partisan as journalists were two centuries ago, but can't, or won't, admit it, which means they can't begin to ask how to moderate themselves. In truth, they may be as much self-deluded as deluding."[66] Thus, for many in the press, the president is challenging their moral paramountcy.

And herein lies a major part of the problem: what is the prime objective of "journalism"? Is modern journalism supposed to be a project inculcated with a progressive mindset and value system yet somehow free of bias, as Professor Pressman argues; or, is modern journalism supposed to be a reporter's pursuit of social activism and a social overhaul, therefore and necessarily an anti-Western reformation, as Professor Rosen demands; or, is it an exclusive club of wise men and women through whom the world is to be explained to the plebes; or, is it supposed to be the gathering and reporting of objective truth and facts, where interpretation and analysis are left to the readers, viewers, and listeners; or, is it an institution that should strengthen the civil society by promoting the nation's founding principles?

The evidence indicates that when it comes to matters of politics and culture, among other things, journalism has become an overwhelmingly progressive enterprise, and the disingenuousness with which it is mostly denied, defended, or even celebrated often leads to a pack mentality, groupthink, repetition, and even propaganda presented as news. However, it must be said, as demonstrated earlier, that the attitude of an increasing number of influential media voices is less concerned with the veneer of objectivity and more open about the progressive ideological outlook that motivates their reporting. This is a project that has been under way for about a century.

Therefore the questions raised at the opening of this chapter are more or less answered by the values and mindset of the media's collective progressive ethos and attachment to social activism. Moreover, as foot soldiers for the Progressive Movement, newsrooms and journalists have also traveled far from the substantive principles and beliefs that animated the early printers, pamphleteers, and newspaper publishers who gave birth to press freedom and American independence.

Two

The Early Patriot Press

A BRIEF EXAMINATION of the early history of the American press provides critical context for comparison with its contemporary progeny and a standard by which to measure the current state and purpose of freedom of the press.

The history of the early press is thoroughly encumbered with the battle for individual liberty and free speech, both essential elements of the American Revolution for independence.

In 1810, Isaiah Thomas, a printer, newspaper publisher, author, and witness to the revolution, published a seminal two-volume book, *The History of Printing in America, with a biography of printers, and an account of newspapers.* Thomas was among a very few who preserved the records of the printers during the Revolutionary War period. Thomas wrote that "[a]mong the first settlers of New England were not only pious but educated men. They emigrated from a country [England] where the press had more license than in other parts of Europe, and they were acquainted with the usefulness of it. As soon as they had made those provisions that were necessary for their existence in this land . . . their next objects were, the establishment of schools, and a printing press; the latter of which was not tolerated, till many years afterward, by the elder colony of Virginia."[1]

A printing house was first established in 1638 at Cambridge, Massachusetts. Printing began in 1639. Thomas praises Rev. Mr. Glover for the early printing press in Massachusetts and America generally, Thomas referring to him as "a nonconformist minister . . . [who] left his native country with a determination to settle among his friends, who had emigrated to Massachusetts; because in this wilderness, he could freely enjoy, with them, those opinions which were not countenanced by the government and a majority of the people in England." Thus early printing in America mostly related to debates about religion and, later, promoting the gospel and other books to Native Americans (in their language).[2]

Thomas wrote that "[t]he fathers of Massachusetts kept a watchful eye on the press; and in neither a religious nor civil point of view, were they disposed to give it much liberty. Both the civil and ecclesiastical rulers were fearful that if it was not under wholesome restraints, contentions and heresies would arise among the people. In 1662, the government of Massachusetts appointed licensers of the press, and afterward, in 1664, passed a law that 'no printing should be allowed in any town with the jurisdiction, except in Cambridge;' nor should anything be printed there but what the government permitted through the agency of those persons who were empowered for the purpose. . . . It does not appear that the press, in Massachusetts, was free from legal restraints till about the year 1755. . . . For several years preceding the year 1730, the government of Massachusetts had been less rigid than formerly; and after that period, [no] officer is mentioned as having a particular control over the press."[3]

"Except in Massachusetts," Thomas wrote, "no presses were set up in the colonies till near the close of the seventeenth century. Printing then was performed in Pennsylvania, 'near Philadelphia,' and afterward in that city, by the same press, which, in a few years subsequent, was removed to New York. The use of type commenced in Virginia about 1681; in 1682 the press was prohibited. In 1709, a press was established at New London, in Connecticut; and, from this period, it was gradually introduced into the other colonies. . . ."[4] However, the press—that is, the printing of books, pamphlets, newspapers, etc.—would become free from license and prior restraint years before the revolution. "Before 1775, printing was confined to the capitals of the colonies; but the war occasioned the dispersion of presses, and many were set up in other towns. After the establishment of our independence, by the peace of 1783, presses multiplied very fast, not only in seaports, but in all the principal inland towns and villages."[5]

During the lead-up to and commencement of the revolution, and the eventual victory over Britain, Thomas was most impressed with Benjamin Edes, a printer who founded and published the *Boston Gazette* with John Gill. "When the dispute between Great Britain and her colonies assumed a serious aspect, this paper arrested the public attention, from the part its able writers took in the cause of liberty and their country; and it gained a very extensive circulation."[6] When the British troops arrived in force in Boston, Edes was able to escape "with a press and a few types," and began printing from Watertown. "In 1776, Edes returned to Boston, on the evacuation of the town by the British army." Thomas wrote that "[n]o publisher of a newspaper felt a greater interest in the establishment of the independence of the United States than Benjamin Edes; and no newspaper was more instrumental in bringing forward this important event than *The Boston Gazette*."[7]

David A. Copeland, professor at Elon University, writes that by 1768, Edes and others "synthesized all that had happened in terms of the importance of the press. . . . The press, they said, protects the liberties of the people. It keeps government in check. As the voice of the people, the press assures that officials will follow the consent of the governed."[8] Copeland describes how the *Gazette* declared, under the pseudonym Populus:

> THERE is nothing so *fretting* and *vexatious*; nothing so justly TERRIBLE to tyrants, and their tools and abettors, as a FREE PRESS. The reason is obvious; namely, Because it is, as it has been very justly observ'd . . . "the *bulwark of the People's Liberties*." For this reason, it is ever watched by those who are forming plans for the destruction of the people's liberties, with an *envious* and *malignant* eye. . . . *Your* Press has spoken to us the words of truth: It has pointed to this people, their danger and their remedy: It has set before them Liberty and Slavery; and with the most perswasive and pungent Language, conjur'd them, in the name of GOD, and the King, and for the sake of all posterity, to chuse Liberty and refuse Chains." [Capitalization, spelling, and italics as in the original.][9]

Professor Carol Sue Humphrey of Oklahoma Baptist University explains that "[h]istorians have long studied and discussed the factors that led to the American Revolution, and they have always given ample credit for the success of the revolt to the press, and particularly the newspapers, for their efforts during the conflict. Even those historians who wrote in the years immediately after the war praised the press for its many contributions to ultimate victory."[10]

"During the first half of the nineteenth century," explains Humphrey, "historians emphasized the patriotism of the printers in their efforts to help America establish its republican system of government as a model for the rest of the world to follow. These scholars are often classified as nationalist or romantic in their outlook and conclusions. For these historians, the American colonies had an important role to play in making the world a better place to live through the spread of democracy and freedom, and the newspapers served well in helping to bring about the break with Great Britain that led to these developments."[11] Humphrey argues that "[t]hese historians continually emphasized the importance of the newspapers in bringing on the revolt against British tyranny and praised the printers for their loyalty and patriotism in the fight for liberty and independence."[12]

Indeed, support for independence spread from New England to the rest of the colonies. David Ramsay, one of the first historians of the American Revolution, famously wrote in 1789 that "in establishing American independence, the pen and press had merit equal to that of the sword." In other words, most of the early printers, pamphleteers, and newspapers in the decades leading up to independence encouraged revolution, and they likewise were supportive of the revolution once war broke out.

As Ramsay noted, the role of the early pamphleteers and the relatively few newspapers—forty or fewer by 1775—that existed in the years before the revolution and the commencement of the war was profound. They were not only sources of information, but far and away provided the philosophical, substantive, and even polemical arguments for the causes and principles that animated the revolution and America's founding. Indeed, in many ways they fashioned the case for liberty, independence, and representative government.

Copeland explains that "[b]y the last half of the 1760s, the press had become a partisan tool. Writers regularly proclaimed their rights to a free press. Increasingly, however, the Patriots, those in favor of American independence from Great Britain, attempted to silence opposing voices. What seemed to be a contradiction of demands to speak freely for decades, even centuries among Britons, vanished for a time in the colonies, but there was a purpose. It could be found in the ideas of government as proposed by thinkers such as Locke. When Americans won the Revolution and freed themselves from tyranny and oppression, the press resumed its role as a partisan mouthpiece, and most citizens of the new United States adopted the motto . . . 'Freedom of speech is the great bulwark of liberty; they prosper and die together.'"[13] The groundwork had been set for what would later become the First Amendment to the Constitution.

Harvard professor and historian Bernard Bailyn, who has likely studied more of the early pamphlets than any other scholar, asserts that "influential in shaping the thought of the Revolutionary generation were the ideas and attitudes associated with the writings of Enlightenment rationalism—writings that expressed not simply the rationalism of liberal reform but that of enlightened conservatism as well." "In pamphlet after pamphlet the American writers cited Locke on natural rights and on the social and governmental contract, Montesquieu and later Delolme on the character of British liberty and on the institutional requirements for its attainment."[14]

The pamphlets, of which there were several hundred between 1750 and 1776, were, Bailyn writes, "[e]xplicit as well as declarative, and expressive of the beliefs, attitudes, and motivations as well as of the professed goals of those who led and supported the Revolution." They confirm that the Revolution was "above all else an ideological-constitutional struggle and not primarily a controversy between social groups undertaken to force changes in the organization of society. It confirmed . . . that intellectual developments in the decades before Independence led to a radical idealization and rationalization of the previous century and a half of American experience, and that it was this intimate relationship between Revolutionary thought and the circumstances of life in eighteenth-century America that endowed the Revolution with its peculiar force and made of it a transforming event."[15]

Therefore, while the revolution was undeniably a transforming event, it was not about the "fundamental transformation" of American *civil society* itself, as President Barack Obama would proclaim about his own election. Moreover, its purpose and principles were the antithesis of and incompatible with the philosophies that undergird the modern Progressive Movement, such as those espoused by German philosophers Georg Wilhelm Friedrich Hegel and Karl Marx, and later American progressive intellectuals including Herbert Croly, Woodrow Wilson, John Dewey, and Walter Weyl, among others.

Bailyn makes the critical point that "[w]hat was essentially involved in the American Revolution was not the disruption of society, with all the fear, despair, and hatred that entails, but the realization, the comprehension and fulfillment, of what was taken to be America's destiny in the context of world history. The great social shocks that in the French and Russian Revolutions sent the foundation of thousands of individual lives crashing into ruins had taken place in America in the course of the previous century, slowly, silently, almost imperceptibly, not as a sudden avalanche but as myriads of individual changes and adjustments which had gradually transformed the order of society. By 1763 the great land-marks of European life . . . had faded in their exposure to the open, wilderness environment of America. But until the disturbances of the 1760s these changes had not been seized upon as grounds for a reconsideration of society and politics." By the end of 1776, "Americans came to think of themselves as in a special category, uniquely placed by history to capitalize on, to complete and fulfill, the promise of man's existence. The changes that had overtaken their provincial societies, they saw, had been good: elements not of deviance and retrogression but of betterment and progress; not a lapse into primitivism, but an elevation to a higher plane of po-litical and social life than had ever been reached before." Bailyn writes, "It was the most creative period in the history of Ameri-can political thought. Everything that followed assumed and built upon its results."[16]

Bailyn states that the pamphlets published before and during the revolution and American independence were so important that "everything essential to the discussion of those years ap-peared, if not original then in reprints, in pamphlet form. The treatises, the sermons, the speeches, the exchanges of letters published as pamphlets—even some of the most personal polemics—all contain elements of this great, transforming debate."[17]

Indeed, Bailyn writes, "[e]xpressing vigorous, polemical, and more often than not considered views of the great events of the time; proliferating in chains of personal vituperation; and embodying to the world the highly charged sentiments uttered on commemorative occasions, pamphlets appeared year after year and month after month in the crisis of the 1760s and 1770s. More than 400 of them bearing on the Anglo-American controversy were published between 1750 and 1776; over 1,500 appeared by 1783.[18]

One of the great pamphleteers was, of course, Thomas Paine. Although a recent immigrant from Britain, coming to Philadelphia in October 1774, Paine became a decisive voice for American independence. On January 10, 1776, Paine's essay, *Common Sense*, was published as a pamphlet. Only forty-eight pages long and written in plain English, the pamphlet spread throughout the colonies. The Constitution Center points out that it sold an amazing 120,000 copies in its first three months, and an estimated 500,000 copies by the end of the revolution. An estimated 20 percent of colonists owned a copy of the pamphlet.[19] Numerous newspapers also reprinted it, in whole or part.

It is indispensable, therefore, when writing about the press then and now, to examine key elements of this enormously influential pamphlet and the ideas and principles it promoted, contrasted with the ideas and principles of the modern media and the progressive ideology.

Common Sense begins with a statement about the distinction

between society and government, and the latter's limitations in a
free society:

> Some writers have so confounded society with government,
> as to leave little or no distinction between them; whereas they
> are not only different, but have different origins. Society is
> produced by our wants, and government by our wickedness;
> the former promotes our happiness *positively* by uniting our
> affections, the latter *negatively* by restraining our vices. The
> one encourages intercourse, the other creates distinctions. The
> first is a patron, the last a punisher.[20]
>
> Society in every state is a blessing, but Government, even
> in its best state, is but a necessary evil; in its worst state an
> intolerable one; for when we suffer, or are exposed to the same
> miseries *by a Government*, which we might expect in a country
> *without Government*, our calamity is heightened by reflecting
> that we furnish the means by which we suffer. . . ." [Italics are
> in the original.][21]

As the colonies increase in population and distance grows between members of society, and as public concerns multiply, a government of representatives small in size and confined in power
becomes necessary, writes Paine, to "establish a common interest
with every part of the community, [and] they will mutually and
naturally support each other. . . ." "I draw my idea of the form of
government from a principle in nature which no act can overturn,
viz. that the more simple any thing is, the less liable it is to be disordered, and the easier repaired when disordered. . . ."[22]

Paine believed in the primacy of individual liberty; he was

hostile to large institutions and averse to taxation and government regulation. For the modern Progressive Movement, and its media voices and scribes, Paine's conception of government is too messy and too dispersed to allow for the required "expert" decision making and "scientific" planning required of a centralized administrative state.

Paine then attacks the British monarchy and hereditary succession:

[T]here is . . . a greater distinction for which no truly natural or religious reason can be assigned, and that is the distinction of men into KINGS and SUBJECTS. Male and female are the distinctions of nature, good and bad the distinctions of Heaven; but how a race of men came into the world so exalted above the rest, and distinguished like some new species, is worth inquiring into, and whether they are the means of happiness or of misery to mankind.[23]

Paine continues:

England, since the conquest, hath known some few good monarchs, but groaned beneath as much larger number of bad ones, yet no man in his senses can say that their claim under William the Conqueror is a very honorable one. A French bastard, landing with an armed banditti, and establishing himself king of England against the consent of the natives, is in plain terms a very paltry rascally original. It certainly hath no divinity in it. However, it is needless to spend much time in exposing the folly of hereditary right, if there are any so weak as to believe it, let them promiscuously worship the ass and lion, and welcome. I shall neither copy their humility, nor disturb their devotion.[24]

Of course, the progressive and modern media would agree with Paine's condemnation of monarchy and hereditary succession, but what of the enormous power exercised today by lifetime-appointed judges, who micromanage more and more of society; unelected bureaucrats employed by scores of government departments and agencies, who legislate not through elected members of Congress but by the issuance of untold regulations and rules; and, the surrendering of sovereign legal and policy authority to international organizations, thereby conferring governing decisions to organizations that exist outside the Constitution's framework? Is this a republican design of representative government of which Paine and his fellow countrymen would approve? Yet this is the design and increasing reality of progressive governance.

Paine follows with a call to arms for a revolution that had, in fact, already begun in Massachusetts, but had yet to rally all colonists to the cause.

Volumes have been written on the subject of the struggle between England and America. Men of all ranks have embarked in the controversy, from different motives, and with various designs; but all have been ineffectual, and the period of debate is closed. Arms as a last resource decide the contest; the appeal was the choice of the King, and the Continent has accepted the challenge....[25]

'Tis repugnant to reason, to the universal order of things,

to all examples from the former ages, to suppose, that this continent can longer remain subject to any external power. The most sanguine in Britain does not think so. The utmost stretch of human wisdom cannot, at this time, compass a plan short of separation, which can promise the continent even a year's security. Reconciliation is *now* a falacious dream. Nature hath deserted the connexion, and Art cannot supply her place. For, as Milton wisely expresses, "never can true reconcilement grow where wounds of deadly hate have pierced so deep."[26]

Every quiet method for peace hath been ineffectual. Our prayers have been rejected with disdain; and only tended to convince us, that nothing flatters vanity, or confirms obstinacy in Kings more than repeated petitioning—and nothing hath contributed more than that very measure to make the Kings of Europe absolute: Witness Denmark and Sweden. Wherefore, since nothing but blows will do, for God's sake, let us come to a final separation, and not leave the next generation to be cutting throats, under the violated unmeaning names of parent and child.[27]

The progressive historians were not about to let the early historians write the definitive history of the pamphleteers, printers, and newspaper publishers, despite the fact that the early historians were obviously closest to the actual events. The problem for the progressives was that the early historians tell the story of the revolution and America's founding in which the principles and ideas of Western enlightenment—individual, economic, and political liberty—lead to a mass movement, indeed a revolution. For America's beginning must be either reinterpreted to accommodate the progressive ideological project, or denounced as a fraud and a sham perpetrated by self-serving commercial interests.

Indeed, as Humphrey explains, over time, later historians provided different explanations of American history that parted from the early historians and their patriotic view of the role of the press. For example, she writes that "[a]fter 1900 [progressive] historians presented a new interpretation of American history. In an era concerned with inequities and the lack of unity in American society in the twentieth century, the progressive historians emphasized the presence of conflict from the initial settlement of the colonies down to the present. Most of the disagreements and arguments occurred between different classes of people or geographic sections of the American colonies, but the Revolutionary era represented a period of both internal and external troubles. Divisions existed both between groups within the colonies and between the colonies and Great Britain. In this environment, the press played an important role in encouraging and carrying out a crusade for change. In pushing for alterations in the relationship between the colonies and Great Britain, the mass media often helped to accentuate the differences and thus helped to make the divisions grow and become worse."[28]

But the historical evidence paints a picture of a colonial press that is courageous, vigorous, and openly partisan about America's principles in promoting and defending the cause and arguments for the revolution—and, in fact, reflecting the remarkable unity of Americans during the revolutionary period. Therefore, the colonial press itself is deplored by subsequent progressive historians—not for its activism but the wrong kind of activism. Humphrey writes: "With a growing interest in the role of economics in history, more recent progressive historians have questioned the motives for the actions of the Revolutionary printers. Several have concluded that most pressmen supported the Patriot cause for reasons of economic survival rather than any strong ideological commitment."[29] Hence, for these progressives, the press was part of a self-interested ruse that successfully bamboozled the masses into risking their livelihoods, lifestyles, and even their lives to go to war against the most powerful military force on the planet.

But facts are facts. And the fact is, as Humphrey observes, that "most Americans concluded that the efforts of Patriot newspaper printers to keep readers informed about the war helped ensure ultimate success by boosting people's morale and rallying Americans to the cause until victory was achieved. . . . For the Patriots involved in the American Revolution, the weekly news sheets published throughout America were an essential part of the fight. By keeping people informed about the war's progress, newspapers made winning independence possible. . . . Newspapers were essential in the fight to win independence and thus were essential in the creation of the United States."[30]

Consequently, the early printers, pamphleteers, and newspaper publishers were truly brave souls—they were patriots, pioneers, and entrepreneurs, both leaders of and reflective of the colonists and their commitment to liberty and revolution. They risked everything to advance and defend an independent nation and civil society based on the ancient truths and observations of Aristotle and later Cicero, among others; the Enlightenment principles and reasoning of John Locke and Montesquieu, among others; and specifically, the moral underpinnings of natural law and natural rights, the unalienable rights of the individual, liberty, equal justice, property rights, freedom of speech, and, yes, freedom of the press—in sum, this is the essence of the Declaration of Independence, the formal proclamation of the united colonies and America's founding.

While asserting their own support for freedom of the press, it is difficult to square the modern media's progressivism and social activism with the Declaration's principles, given that every prominent progressive intellectual at the turn of the twentieth century denounced the Declaration as an old and stale way of thinking about society, set in a preindustrialized, largely agrarian culture, thereby emphasizing the individual over the community, personal interests over the general welfare, and limited taxation and government over the government's need to be a dynamic force, led by experts, in order to better plan and organize society. For similar reasons, the early progressive intellectuals condemned the Constitution's separation of powers and deference to state sovereignty as conflicting with social engineering and collectivism.

In understanding the mentality of the modern media, it is crucial to understand the extent to which progressives reject so much of America's early history. For example, in 1907, in a Fourth of July address about the Declaration, Woodrow Wilson, a renowned progressive intellectual and historian, then president of Princeton University, and future president of the United States, wrote:

> It is common to think of the Declaration of Independence as a highly speculative document; but no one can think it so who has read it. It is a strong, rhetorical statement of the grievances against the English government. It does indeed open with the assertion that all men are equal and that they have certain in-

alienable rights, among them the right to life, liberty, and the pursuit of happiness. It asserts that governments were instituted to secure these rights, and can derive their just powers only from the consent of the governed; and it solemnly declares that "whenever any government becomes destructive of these ends, it is the right of the people to alter or to abolish it, and to institute a new government, laying its foundations on the principles, and organizing its powers in such forms, as to them shall seem most likely to effect their safety and happiness." But this would not afford a general theory of government to formulate policies upon. No doubt we are meant to have liberty, but each generation must form its own conception of what liberty is. No doubt we shall always wish to be given leave to pursue happiness as we will, but we are not yet sure where or by what method we shall find it. That we are free to adjust government to these ends we know. But Mr. Jefferson and his colleagues in the Continental Congress prescribed the law of adjustment for no generations but their own. They left us to say whether we thought the government they had set up was founded on "such principles," its powers organized in "such forms" as seemed to us most likely to effect our safety and happiness. They did not attempt to dictate the aims and objects of any generation but their own. . . .[31]

Wilson continued:

So far as the Declaration of Independence was a theoretical document, that is its theory. Do we still hold it? Does the doctrine of the Declaration of Independence still live in our principles of action, in the things we do, in the purposes we applaud, in the measures we approve? It is not a question of piety. We are not bound to adhere to the doctrines held by the signers of the Declaration of Independence; we are as free as they were to make and unmake governments. We are not here to worship men or a document. But neither are we here to indulge in a mere theoretical and uncritical eulogy. Every Fourth of July should be a time for examining our standards, our purposes, for determining afresh what principles, what forms of power we think most likely to effect our safety and happiness. That and that alone is the obligation the Declaration lays upon us. It is no fetish; its words lay no compulsion upon the thought of any free man; but it was drawn by men who thought, and it obliges those who receive its benefits to think likewise. . . ."[32]

Thus the absurdity of the progressive historians and their attempt to hijack and rewrite the history of America's founding becomes clear. More to the point, it can be fairly said that the modern media and most journalists who share this progressive attitude must also reject the principles of their press forefathers, the founders of the free press who urged rebellion against Britain—although they undoubtedly appreciate their wisdom in establishing a free press.

But what has become of freedom of the press? Have today's newsrooms and journalists lived up to their purposes?

THREE

THE MODERN DEMOCRATIC PARTY-PRESS

HISTORIANS WRITE OF the "party-press era," roughly from the 1780s to the 1860s, not long after the founding of the United States.

What was the party-press era? It was a time when most newspapers aligned themselves with a politician, campaign, or party, and did so openly. As described by California State University associate professor Charles L. Ponce De Leon: "Sparked by divergent plans for the future of the new republic, competing factions emerged within George Washington's administration and Congress, and by the mid-1790s each faction had established partisan newspapers championing its point of view. These publications were subsidized through patronage, and, though they had a limited circulation, the material they published was widely reprinted and discussed, and contributed to the establishment of the nation's first political parties, the Federalists and the Democratic-Republicans [or Republicans]."[1]

Ponce De Leon added: "Newspapers like Philip Freneau's *National Gazette*, writes the most prominent [Republican] organ, crafted distinctly partisan lenses through which readers were encouraged to view the world. Specializing in gossip, innuendo, and ad hominem attacks, these newspapers sought to make readers fearful about the intentions of their opponents. The strategy was quite effective at arousing support and mobilizing voters to go to the polls—after all, the fate of the republic appeared to be at stake. . . ."[2]

Virginia Tech associate professor Jim A. Kuypers explains that the *Gazette* was anti-Federalist and anti–George Washington, and it had the backing of Thomas Jefferson. "Jefferson's view was that Freneau merely provided balance to John Fenno's Federalist *Gazette of the United States*, arguing, 'The two papers will show you both sides of our politics.' Freneau later infuriated Washington with an editorial titled '*The Funeral of George Washington*'; that, and his attack on Alexander Hamilton's economic program, left the *National Gazette* as an unmistakable mouthpiece of Republican views. Jefferson himself was targeted for equally vicious slanders by journalist James T. Callender, who afflicted politicians of all stripes, including Jefferson's *bete noir* Alexander Hamilton and his old friend John Adams. . . ."[3]

According to University of Virginia professor Peter Onuf, the 1800 presidential election, which saw Jefferson challenging Adams, "reached a level of personal animosity seldom equaled in American politics. The Federalists attacked the fifty-seven-year-old Jefferson as a godless Jacobin who would unleash the forces of bloody terror upon the land. With Jefferson as President, so warned one newspaper, 'Murder, robbery, rape, adultery, and incest will be openly taught and practiced, the air will be rent with the cries of the distressed, the soil will be soaked with blood, and the nation black with crimes.' Others attacked Jefferson's deist beliefs as the views of an infidel who 'writes aghast the truths of God's words; who makes not even a profession of Christianity; who is without Sabbaths; without the sanctuary, and without so much as a decent external respect for the faith and worship of Christians.'"[4]

"The luckless Adams was ridiculed from two directions," writes Onuf. "By the Hamiltonians within his own party and by the Jeffersonian-Republicans from the outside. For example, a private letter in which Hamilton depicted Adams as having 'great and intrinsic defects in his character' was obtained by Aaron Burr and leaked to the national press. It fueled the Republican attack on Adams as a hypocritical fool and tyrant. His opponents also spread the story that Adams had planned to create an American dynasty by the marriage of one of his sons to a daughter of King George III. According to this unsubstantiated story, only the intervention of George Washington, dressed in his Revolutionary military uniform, and the threat by Washington to use his sword against his former vice president had stopped Adams's scheme."[5]

But it was the presidential campaign of 1828, between President John Quincy Adams and challenger Andrew Jackson, that many consider among the most brutal of the early contests. Once again, the party-press was in the thick of it.

As described by the Hermitage website: "By 1828, Jackson was ready to win the White House. First he would suffer through a bruising campaign still recognized today as one of the most malicious in American history. Adams's supporters accused Jackson of being a military tyrant who would use the presidency as a spring-board for his own Napoleonic ambitions of empire. For proof, they brought out every skeleton in Jackson's closet: his duels and brawls, his execution of troops for desertion, his declaration of martial law in New Orleans, his friendship with Aaron Burr and his invasions of Spanish Florida in 1814 and 1818. . . ."[6] "The most painful at-tack for Jackson, by far, was that on his and Rachel's character over their marriage. Technically, Rachel was a bigamist and Jackson her partner in it. Adams's supporters thus judged Jackson as morally unfit to hold the nation's highest office." Jackson's allies "struck back with attacks on corrupt officials in the Adams administration and labeled Adams an elitist who wanted to increase the size and power of government to benefit the aristocracy."[7]

But historian Robert Remini observes that the Jacksonians cre-ated "a vast, nationwide newspaper system."[8]

Kuypers explains that "at the time that 'newspapers' emerged as a driving force in American political life, they had little to do with objective news. Quite the contrary, they deliberately reported everything with a political slant, and were intended to be biased. Nor did they hide their purpose: it was in their names, such as the *Arkansas Democrat-Gazette,* or the *Arizona Republican.* . . . Parti-sanship was their primary raison d'etre. Editors viewed readers as voters who needed to be guided to appropriate views, then mobi-lized to vote."[9]

In fact, Kuypers asserts, so corrupt was the relationship be-tween the press and Jacksonians that "many editors owed their jobs directly and specifically to the Jacksonians. . . . Jackson himself appointed numerous editors to salaried political positions, includ-ing many postmasters, while nationally it is estimated that 50–60 editors had been given plum political jobs. Rewarding political friends was nothing new—the Federalists had appointed nearly 1,000 editors to postmaster positions over a 12-year period—but the Jacksonians transformed an ad hoc approach to appointments to a strategic plan. Under such circumstances, few readers of 'news' doubted where a paper stood on a particular position, nor did people think they were receiving objective facts upon which to make reasoned decisions."[10]

Historian Harold Holzer describes the impact of party-journalism and its power to influence politics and the electorate in the years before the Civil War: "By the 1850s . . . almost no independent voters were left in America, only Democrats and Whigs (most of whom later became Republicans), and nearly all of them avid readers of newspapers. Kept in a perpetual state of political arousal by journalism, and further stimulated by election cycles that drew voters to the polls several times each year, not just on the first Tuesdays of November, the overwhelming majority regarded politics with a fervor that approached religious awakening, evoking interest characteristic of modern sports or entertainment. With only a few notable exceptions, few unaligned newspapers prospered."[11]

Sadly, this sounds quite similar to the media environment today.

In point of fact, the party-press is back, and with a vengeance. Of course, there are certain differences between the party-press of old and its present-day incarnation, but there is no denying its reality.

While today's editors and journalists are not on the payroll of the post office or other federal departments, and are not subsidized by political parties, the revolving door of journalists and/or their family members serving primarily in Democratic administrations,

Democratic congressional offices, and Democratic campaigns—and vice versa—is a fact.

The evidence of a progressive ideological mindset sympathetic to and supportive of the Democratic Party, in which news is "interpreted" or "analyzed" or "given context," and where "social activism" is an essential and overarching framework for reporting, results in writing and broadcasting that mainly conform to the objectives, policies, and principles of the modern Democratic Party and the progressive agenda.

Importantly, unlike the early party-press era, where newspapers lined up fairly evenly behind one party or the other or one candidate or the other, and transparently proclaimed their partisanship, the current party-press also differs in that news outlets are overwhelmingly supportive of the Democratic Party and hostile to the Republican Party—particularly conservatives—and, these days, virulently antagonistic to President Donald Trump, his supporters, and his policies.

Indeed, on January 15, 2018, veteran newsman and columnist Andrew Malcolm summed up "the current sad state of American political journalism" as so thoroughly and obviously anti-Trump that it has inflamed and balkanized the public. In his opinion piece, titled "Media's Anti-Trump Addiction Amps Up the Outrage and Fuels the Public's Suspicion," Malcolm observes that "much of today's political journalism has fallen into advocacy, intentionally inflammatory, using or omitting selective details, quotes and background to make a case against President Donald Trump. The criticism generally centers on something he did or said he would do—or something someone, usually unidentified, said he might do or is considering possibly doing. And then in a kind of Kabuki dance,

journalists run to gather reaction from waiting opponents who provide a predictably outraged quote calling for counteraction."[12]

When media outlets and journalists conduct themselves this
way, they "den[y] Americans a set of generally-accepted facts to debate," writes Malcolm, "merely providing fodder for an anti-Trump
agenda and more argumentative ammo for both sides. . . . The
Washington media rightly claim the duty to check presidential
statements. Unfortunately, they couldn't find the time or inclina-
tion to apply the same regimen to former President Obama's words
as they have imposed on Trump's. Otherwise, Obama would have
been called out for the 36 times he promised we could keep our
doctor and health plan, the countless specious claims that al Qaeda
was on the run, the false suggestion that Russia was no longer a
strategic competitor and the laughable claim that his administration experienced no scandal during its 2,922 days."[13]

When reporting on a Democratic president and his progressive
agenda, the same newsrooms and reporters take a very different
approach. "That's because," writes Malcolm, "the D.C. media, by
and large, sympathized with Obama's election and policies. And
while the election of an African American was historic, it was
not the historically shocking upset that Trump's base delivered to
him—and us. An upset that far too many political journalists have
been unable to digest and have allowed to corrupt their professionalism. . . ."[14]

Moreover, press reports are filled with headlines and breaking
news akin to supermarket tabloids. The public is subjected to daily
if not hourly hype about "news" reports and "alerts" often based
on wishful thinking, speculation, partisan advocacy, anonymous
sources, and outright inaccuracies. Virtually anyone with a gripe

against President Trump is treated as a newsmaker and repeatedly provided multiple national media formats and platforms to air their criticisms. The list is too long and the examples too numerous to reproduce here, but a few will suffice:

Porn actress Stormy Daniels and her attorney Michael Avenatti, who was recently charged with multiple felonies by prosecutors in New York and Los Angeles, became overnight media stars and appeared endlessly on news programs and in news reports; reality personality Omarosa Onee Manigault Newman, a disgruntled former White House staffer who was removed from her government job, was given numerous media platforms to promote her "tell-all" book about the Trump White House; Michael Wolff, whose writing was filled with references to anonymous interviews and questionable claims, was given numerous media platforms to promote his "tell-all" book about the Trump White House; Bob Woodward, whose writing was also filled with references to anonymous interviews, which earned public denials by present and former White House staff, was given numerous media platforms to promote his "tell-all" book about the Trump White House; and so on.

And there is the endless press drumbeat about—or more like cheerleading for—President Trump's imminent demise. As the *Free Beacon*'s Matthew Continetti put it: "The litany has been repeated so often that it's easy to recite: The walls are closing in on Donald Trump, person x or y or z is going to bring him down, it's only a matter of time before he is caught or exposed or loses his base of support and driven from public life. The phrases sound out from our cable channels. We see them in newspaper headlines and in our Twitter timelines. This time Trump has gone too far. The end is near. Take that, Drumpf!"[15]

The press has been campaigning alongside Democratic politicians, officials, consultants, and surrogates for President Trump's impeachment since even before his nomination. Jennifer Harper of the *Washington Times* has commented that "the press mulled the impeachment of President Trump even before he became the Republican nominee for president. That is a rough guide to how long the 'I-word' has been floated before the public. 'Could Trump be impeached shortly after he takes office?' asked *Politico*. 'Impeachment is already on the lips of pundits, newspaper editorials, constitutional scholars, and even a few members of Congress.' The date of that report was April 17, 2016; Mr. Trump only became the official nominee on July 19 of that year. . . . Journalists continue to bandy about the term with gusto, then posture on-camera like it's a foregone conclusion. Many appear convinced that if they package impeachment speculation like fact enough, the American public will believe that the president should be shamed, blamed, defamed and shown the door. Democrats reinforce the effort with appropriate commentary, even as the persuasive press offers only scanty coverage of Mr. Trump's authentic accomplishments."[16]

In fact, on one day in August 2018, the Media Research Center analyzed an eighteen-hour period on CNN and MSNBC and found that reporters, anchors, and paid contributors used the word "impeachment" an incredible 222 times. "MRC analysts examined all CNN and MSNBC coverage between 6:00 a.m. and 11:59 p.m. on August 22, counting every use of the word 'impeach,' 'impeachment,' or some permutation thereof. Analysts found 114 instances of the term on MSNBC and 108 on CNN, for a total of 222 total uses of the word."[17]

Now impeachment is reported as a foregone conclusion, with a long line of anti-Trump Democratic members of Congress, college professors, former Watergate prosecutors, Never Trumpers, etc., carefully chosen as news guests and commentators to provide the patina of "expert" opinion and "objective" analysis for President Trump's impeachment.

There was also nonstop media speculation about, indeed advocacy for, the indictment of President Trump by either the special counsel, Robert Mueller, or now the United States Attorney's Office for the Southern District of New York (SDNY), for a laundry list of supposed violations. Might the president be indicted for obstruction of justice resulting from his firing of former FBI director James Comey; his discussion with Comey about retired lieutenant general Michael Flynn; allegations in a discredited dossier funded by the Hillary Clinton campaign and the Democratic National Committee; a meeting at Trump Tower about which the president was unaware; alleged campaign violations said to result from nondisclosure agreements with Stormy Daniels and Karen McDougal; etc.?

Of course, two Department of Justice (DOJ) memoranda, initially dating back nearly half a century, explicitly provide that the official position of the DOJ is that a sitting president cannot be indicted. The Special Counsel's Office was—and the SDNY is—bound by those memoranda as a matter of DOJ regulation. Therefore, the constant reporting—"analysis" and "interpretation"—seems intended by the Democratic party-press to build political and public support for the president's impeachment. Indeed, in the end, Mueller found no evidence of collusion between the Trump campaign and Russia, and he did not seek any charges for obstruction of justice. More on this later.[18]

But even the tone of the press in reporting on President Trump has reached a level of invective rarely seen in politics. The president is repeatedly referred to or impliedly compared to a fascist dictator, neo-Nazi, white supremacist, racist, Hitler, Stalin, or Mussolini in various news outlets and on media platforms by their journalists, paid commentators, and invited guests. These unhinged and shameful characterizations and rants are so numerous, they are easily searchable and profuse on the internet. However, a generous sampling, compiled by the Media Research Center, is sufficient to prove the point:

- When Trump "goes out there and whips people up, it's like a Mussolini rally. And yes, that's what I said."—MSNBC host Joe Scarborough, 3/12/18
- "[I]t's our responsibility to call out those times when constitutional norms are being challenged, those times when the president of the United States actually channels Joseph Stalin and calls the media 'the enemy of the people.'"—MSNBC host Joe Scarborough, 3/8/18
- "Donald Trump talks like a racist, thinks like a racist, makes statements like a racist. Conjures emotions that give succor and support to white supremacists and white nationalists. . . . He has emboldened white supremacists to come forward."—MSNBC political analyst Michael Eric Dyson, 7/5/2018
- "Our president is a disturbed person, and he's behaving in ways that are simply inexplicable. . . ."—*New York Times* columnist Thomas Friedman, 2/21/18
- "The world witnessed a betrayal the likes of which we've never seen. America's president sided with its enemy today."—CNN host Chris Cuomo, 7/16/18

- "[T]he spirit of what Trump did is clearly treasonous. It's a betrayal of the United States. He threw our U.S. intelligence services, flushed them away and it came off as being a puppet of Putin. . . . [P]eople are going to say there's the taint of treason around this White House."—CNN contributor Douglas Brinkley, 7/17/18

- "Well, if anybody is issuing demented words of violence and death, I would say it's the president of the United States. I mean it's quite a pass we've come to when the leadership of a country like Iran seems more stable and rational than the president of the United States."—CNN analyst Max Boot, 7/23/18

- "We got a guy [Trump] who gets up every morning and excretes the feces of his moral depravity into a nation he has turned into a psychic commode. That's what he's done. And he's a bigot-in-chief and a racist in residence. . . . Look at this mendacious, relentlessly lying, bigoted, ill-informed person that we have."—MSNBC political analyst Michael Eric Dyson, 6/4/18

- "I don't think he's [Trump] capable of the basic empathies that we feel as human beings, and that's what a sociopath is."—MSNBC guest Donny Deutsch, 3/12/18

- "This is not the party of Lincoln, the party of Nixon, or even the party of Reagan. This is the party of [*Birth of a Nation* film director] D. W. Griffith, this is the party of the KKK, and the party of Trump."—SiriusXM host Karen Hunter on MSNBC's *Deadline*, 2/26/18

- "Article III in Section Three of the Constitution says this: 'treason against the United States shall consist only in levying war against them or in adhering to their enemies, giving them aid and comfort.' So, no president has ever been charged with treason.

Douglas, do you believe the president's actions fall anywhere within that definition?"—CNN host Don Lemon, 7/17/18

- "That is just the emboldening of white bigotry by a white nationalist, white supremacist presidency, and his cronies . . . and all the other white nationalists that he has empowered. . . . The emboldening of sort of your random white bigots and then the loosening of the grips on white terrorism in this country has raised the stakes for all of us."—MSNBC guest Jason Johnson, 7/29/18

- "'What does Putin have on Trump? Has Trump been compromised?' All of those people, those experts, those reporters, they are looking at the fact pattern and seeing something strange, even sinister."—CNN host Brian Stelter, 7/22/18

- "[I]t is astonishing how he [Trump] has become such an effective and destructive virus created by Vladimir Putin."—Former *Time* editor Walter Isaacson, 7/23/18

- "He's inciting, through mass rallies and constantly lying, fervor in a political base. He scapegoats minority populations and affixes blame to them for every problem the country faces. He alleges conspiracies of nefarious forces. . . . [This] could be straight out of Munich circa 1928."—MSNBC contributor Steve Schmidt, 6/26/18

- Under Trump, "[c]hildren are being marched away to showers, just like the Nazis said they were taking people to the showers, and then they never came back."—MSNBC host Joe Scarborough, 6/15/18

- Trump's detention centers at the border: "I call this a concentration camp for kids because that's exactly what it's turning out to [be]."—MSNBC analyst Michael Steele, 6/15/18

- Trump "has very deliberately set up the press as the enemy of the people. . . . You know, this is something that we first heard from Joseph Stalin. This is very dangerous. It undercuts democracy."—NBC News correspondent Andrea Mitchell, 7/30/18

- Trumps' administration follows "the exact pattern that Hitler has—I hate to say it—with the propaganda, even down to the Red Cross went into Auschwitz. They cleaned it up for two days—it looked fine—they went back—they said everything seems fine there. . . . To quote that new book that just came out, he is evil. He is evil."—MSNBC producer Michele Reiner, 6/24/18

- Trump "is completely detached from reality. . . . [P]eople close to him say is mentally unfit, that people close to him during the campaign told me had early stages of dementia."—MSNBC host Joe Scarborough, 11/30/17

- "Donald Trump is a racist. He isn't just a white supremacist—he's a flat-out, full racist. . . ."—former *New York Times* reporter David Cay Johnston, 9/16/17

- "If you vote for Trump, then you, the voter, you, not Donald Trump, are standing at the border like Nazis going 'you here, you here.' . . . It's a given, the evilness of Donald Trump."—MSNBC guest Donny Deutsch, 6/18/18

- "This whole administration . . . These guys are terrorists, right? . . . [A] white nationalist government that will take children hostage to get what they want."—MSNBC guest Jason Johnson, 6/17/18

- "This is the time for the Democratic base to roar up and say no more of this crap! . . . This is time for vengeance for what happened two years ago."—MSNBC host Chris Matthews, 6/27/18

- "He will be forever remembered as the president who traumatized little children. That's his brand now. He's the president, who purposefully traumatized babies and children and he traumatized them for his political gain or to look like Kim Jong-un."—MSNBC host Mika Brzezinski, 6/18/18

- Under Trump, "[w]e can imagine a future of jackboots crashing through our doors at 2 a.m., trucks in the streets to take people to the internment camps, bright lights and barking dogs—and worse."—*Politico* chief political columnist, Roger Simon, 2/1/17

- "Do citizens in dictatorships recognize what's happening right here, right now? Are they looking at the first two days of the Trump administration and saying, 'Oh, that's what my leader does?'"—CNN host Brian Stelter, 1/22/17

- "Is it time for newsrooms to think of new ways to convey Trump's lack of credibility? . . . Because he says so many things that are bogus. . . . He tells us all these lies, he spreads all these falsehoods."—CNN host Brian Stelter, 8/26/18

- "Trump's attacks on the American press as 'enemies of the American people' are more treacherous than Richard Nixon's attacks on the press. . . . There's a history of what 'enemy of the people,' that phrase means as used by dictators and authoritarians including Stalin, including Hitler."—CNN commentator Carl Bernstein, 2/19/17

- Trump is "not only not fit to be president. In my book, his lack of empathy, his lack of leadership, his lack of courage, he's unfit to be human."—CNN commentator Ana Navarro, 8/14/17

- "We haven't had a president this psychologically troubled in this way since at least Richard Nixon."—former CBS News anchor Dan Rather, 6/1/17

- Trump is "the chief recruiter and Dear Leader of a gang of domestic terrorists. . . . The president is the most powerful hate-monger in America. He is the imperial wizard of the new white supremacy. . . . He is our first neo-Nazi president."—*New Republic* contributing editor Bob Moser, 8/14/17

- Trump is "a sort of junior player in a block of authoritarian countries. . . . He's part of the block that includes Vladimir Putin, Duterte, he's you know, he's kind of part of kind of an Axis Power. . . . He'd certainly like to" murder people without due process.—*American Prospect* senior correspondent Michelle Goldberg, 8/17/187

- "We have a dangerous individual in the Oval Office who is a national security threat, and he needs to be removed from office. . . . He's unfit, and he needs to be removed."—MSNBC contributor Ron Reagan Jr., 5/22/17

- "He's unhinged, it's embarrassing. . . ."—CNN host Don Lemon, 8/22/17

- "We live in the age of the active shooter and the president is goading them. He is inciting them. . . . The blood will be on his hands the moment some whack-job thinks that he's carrying out the instructions of a president and goes into a newsroom like the one behind us or the one in my news organization or yours and murdered people."—*New York Times* columnist Bret Stephens, 8/6/18

- "It's hard to fire your son-in-law . . . but Mussolini had a great solution to that. He had him executed. . . . So, if I were

Jared [Kushner], I'd be a little careful."—MSNBC host Chris
Matthews, 1/20/17

- "There are a variety of ways that Trump could kill us all."—MTV
correspondent Jamil Smith

- "The party of Lincoln has become the party of Charlottesville,
Arpaio, DACA repeal and the Muslim ban. Embodying the very
worst sentiments and driven by irrational anger, it deserves not
defense but extinction."—*Washington Post* columnist Jennifer
Rubin, 9/4/17

- "People are saying we have to talk about his health now before
it's too late. Eugene Robinson saying: 'How long are we going
to pretend that President Trump is fully rational? How long are
we going to ignore the signs he's dangerously out of control?' . . .
That's the question. I'm going to ask you, Jeff Greenfield. Is now
the time?"—CNN host Brian Stelter, 12/3/17

- "How Murderer Charles Manson and Donald Trump Used
Language to Gain Followers"—*Newsweek* headline, 11/20/17

- "This is not a political party [Republicans]—this is a domestic
terror group."—MSNBC guest Fernand Amandi, 11/26/17

- "How surprised should we be? This is at least the fourth
mass killing in America using an AR-15 since the Las Vegas
massacre. . . . At the center, an unapologetically incendiary
president untrammeled by traditional norms of civility."—ABC
This Week's host George Stephanopoulos, 10/28/18

- "And I think what he [Trump] has done over the course of the
last few years is help foment this" violence.—*New York Times*
columnist Maureen Dowd on ABC's *This Week*, 10/28/18

- "The president is obviously a racist, he's obviously a demagogue.
He obviously condones anti-Semitism, stokes up nationalist

hatred."—NBC and MSNBC national affairs analyst John Heilemann, 10/29/18

- "I can't even call him president, this demagogue, this nationalist."—MSNBC host Joe Scarborough, 10/29/18[19]

This media-pack malevolency toward President Trump and his party belies the press's self-serving claims of professionalism and high standards; rather, it is every bit as tawdry, or worse, then the party-press "journalism" of the early 1800s, which they claim to frown upon. Indeed, during the Trump presidency, the press has engaged in lies, distortions, sloppiness, and overall malpractice to an extent previously unseen in modern times. At one point, the *DailyWire* kept a weekly tab of false media stories;[20] *The Federalist* had its own list;[21] ex–CBS reporter Sharyl Attkisson maintains a running list of "media mistakes" during the Trump era;[22] the *Daily Caller* kept a compilation of media "screw-ups" involving the Trump-Russia story; etc.

A particularly notorious and pervasive illustration of press transgressions occurred on January 17, 2019, when *BuzzFeed* posted a headline screaming, "President Trump Directed His Attorney Michael Cohen to Lie to Congress About the Moscow Tower Project." The subheadline declared, "Trump received 10 personal updates from Michael Cohen and encouraged a planned meeting with Vladimir Putin." The crux of the story was that President Trump had directed Michael Cohen, his former lawyer and current felon, to lie to Congress about a real estate development in Moscow that, ultimately, never happened.

BuzzFeed reported that "President Donald Trump directed his longtime attorney Michael Cohen to lie to Congress about nego-

tiations to build a Trump Tower in Moscow, according to two federal law enforcement officials involved in an investigation of the
matter. Trump also supported a plan, set up by Cohen, to visit Russia during the presidential campaign, in order to personally meet
President Vladimir Putin and jump-start the tower negotiations.
'Make it happen,' the sources said Trump told Cohen. And even as
Trump told the public he had no business deals with Russia, the
sources said Trump and his children Ivanka and Donald Trump
Jr. received regular, detailed updates about the real estate development from Cohen, whom they put in charge of the project."[23]

"Now," *BuzzFeed* stated, "the two [anonymous law enforce-
ment] sources have told BuzzFeed News that Cohen also told the
special counsel that after the election, the president personally instructed him to lie—by claiming that negotiations ended months
earlier than they actually did—in order to obscure Trump's involvement. The special counsel's office learned about Trump's
directive for Cohen to lie to Congress through interviews with
multiple witnesses from the Trump Organization and internal
company emails, text messages, and a cache of other documents.
Cohen then acknowledged those instructions during his interviews with that office."[24]

For an entire day, news outlets and journalists breathlessly repeated the "breaking" *BuzzFeed* story. Some provided the occasional caveat "if the story is true," a throwaway line meaning that
while they could not or, more likely, would not bother to independently verify the accuracy of the story, they would repeat it
anyway. Indeed, the story was not merely blared to the public with
repeated headlines and extensive coverage, but the "news" story
was imbued with wild speculation about the implications for the

president. Again, a conga line of congressional Democrats, former federal prosecutors, and other "experts" were paraded through newsrooms and appeared on telecasts claiming this was the bombshell that would result in President Trump's impeachment, if not secret and sealed indictment, speculating the president had committed obstruction of justice, etc.[25]

The *Daily Caller* reviewed television clippings from the Grabien news service and reported that "personalities on CNN and MSNBC used the words 'impeach,' 'impeachment,' or 'impeachable' 179 times" in less than one day of broadcasts."[26] NewsBusters reported that "[d]espite the fact that the BuzzFeed News story was not confirmed by . . . any news outlet . . . , the [NBC, ABC, and CBS] broadcast networks devoted 27 minutes and 33 seconds on their Friday morning and evening newscasts (minus opening teases)" to the story. Of course, "[a]ll three networks pointed to the questionable veracity of the BuzzFeed piece . . . to some degree," but they repeated the story nonetheless.[27]

After several days of this, the special counsel's office finally issued a statement denying the story. "Buzzfeed's description of specific statements to the Special Counsel's Office, and characterization of documents and testimony obtained by this office, regarding Michael Cohen's Congressional testimony are not accurate."[28]

Perhaps as objectional, if not more so, is the drive to smear President Trump as mentally unfit and malignantly unbalanced to hold office, in which his political opponents, helped by a cabal of "mental health experts" and an eager news media, invoke the Twenty-Fifth Amendment to the Constitution as a legal basis and option for removing him from office. This is perhaps the most inflammatory, scurrilous, and pernicious allegation that can be made against a mentally healthy individual, but especially a president of the United States, as the purpose is to destroy his reputation with the public and foreign leaders and make governing as difficult as possible. Consequently, this, too, requires exploration.

For example, on July 3, 2017, NBC News posted uncritically this story: "House Democrats are on a mission to educate the American people about a little-known power of the 25th Amendment—the ousting of the president. . . . Led by freshman Rep. Jamie Raskin of Maryland, a group of growing Democratic co-signers has put forth a bill that could force President Donald Trump from office if he were found mentally or physically unfit." NBC continued: "Although it was introduced in April, the bill has gained steam in the past week as Trump's tweet storms have grown in ferocity. . . . 'Given Donald Trump's continued erratic and baffling behavior, is it any wonder why we need to pursue this legislation?'" asked Representative Darren Soto, Democrat of Florida, a cosigner. "The mental and physical health of the leader of the United States and the free world is a matter of great public concern."[29]

These Democratic politicians were partly influenced by twenty-seven psychiatrists, psychologists, and mental health practitioners who met in March 2017 at what they labeled the "Duty to Warn" conference at Yale University to assess President Trump's mental health. The meeting was led by Professor Bandy X. Lee, M.D. The "experts" considered two questions: "What's wrong with him?" and "Does professional responsibility include a duty to warn the public if they believe the president is dangerously unfit for office?"

On October 3, 2017, they released their conclusions in a book titled *The Dangerous Case of Donald Trump* and summarized their position as follows: "There are those who still hold out hope that this president can be prevailed upon to listen to reason and curb his erratic behavior. Our professional experience would suggest otherwise. . . . Collectively with our coauthors, we warn that anyone as mentally unstable as Mr. Trump simply should not be entrusted with the life-and-death powers of the presidency."[30]

It is revealing that in the book's prologue, Lee and Dr. Judith Lewis Herman disclose that "[s]oon after the presidential election of 2016, alarmed by the apparent mental instability of the president-elect, we both separately circulated letters among some of our professional colleagues, expressing our concern." Thus their quest to alert the world to Donald Trump's alleged mental instability began immediately after his successful election over Hillary Clinton.

The various essays in the book were written by different authors, each assigned a chapter with titles such as "Unbridled and Extreme Present Hedonism: How the Leader of the Free World Has Proven Time and Again He Is Unfit for Duty"; "Pathological Narcissism and Politics: A Lethal Mix"; "Sociopathy"; "Donald Trump is: (A) Bad, (B) Mad, (C) All of the Above"; "Cognitive Impairment, Dementia, and POTUS"; "A Clinical Case for the Dangerousness of Donald J. Trump"; "Trump Anxiety Disorder: The Trump Effect on the Mental Health of Half the Nation and Special Populations"; "In Relationship with an Abusive President"; "Trump's Daddy Issues: A Toxic Mix for America"; "Who Goes Trump? Tyranny as a Triumph of Narcissism"; "He's Got the World in His Hands and His Finger on the Trigger: The Twenty-Fifth Amendment Solution."[31]

On January 3, 2018, Lee and congressional Democrats (and one Republican senator) met in secret. *Politico* reported: "Lawmakers concerned about President Trump's mental state summoned Yale

University psychiatry professor Dr. Bandy X. Lee to Capitol Hill last month for two days of briefings about his recent behavior. In private meetings with more than a dozen members of Congress held on December 5 and 6, Lee briefed lawmakers. . . . Her professional warning to Capitol Hill: 'He's going to unravel, and we are seeing the signs.'"[32]

The Democratic party-press was more than happy to use this slander against the president. In addition to Lee sitting for a number of interviews, the "mental illness" mantra was further employed by the press. For example, on January 3, 2018, "NBC anchor Peter Alexander asked White House press secretary Sarah Huckabee Sanders if Americans should be 'concerned about the president's mental fitness' after he tweeted that he has a bigger nuclear 'button' than [North Korea's dictator] Kim has. . . . Anchors and pundits on CNN began questioning Trump's mental stability, with media reporter Brian Stelter questioning whether the president had descended into 'madness.'"[33]

Concocting charges of mental illness backed by a relative handful of psychiatrists, psychologists, and mental health practitioners would be an extremely dangerous precedent and abuse of the Constitution if used as a basis for invoking the Twenty-Fifth Amendment. Apart from the vile allegations of mental unfitness against President Trump, discussed for months in the press, few news outlets bothered to explain, adequately or otherwise, the purpose of the Twenty-Fifth Amendment, ratified in 1967, how it works, and how politically complicated and constitutionally impracticable such an endeavor would be even under the right circumstances. Section 4 of the Twenty-Fifth Amendment states: "Whenever the vice president and a majority of either the principal officers of the executive departments or of such other body as Congress may by law provide, transmit to the President pro tempore of the Senate and the Speaker of the House of Representatives their written declaration that the President is unable to discharge the powers and duties of his office, the Vice President shall immediately assume the powers and duties of the office as acting president." The president has the right to challenge these actions, which, in the end, requires a two-thirds vote of both houses of Congress to sustain.[34] That was never going to happen. Therefore, the real purpose in this case appears to be to personally humiliate and politically damage President Trump.

President Trump is not the first Republican to be targeted with politically charged claims of mental instability. In 1964, Senator Barry Goldwater was the Republican nominee for president, running against President Lyndon Johnson. Goldwater was also a conservative leader and, therefore, considered a political outsider.

In September–October 1964, *Fact* magazine ran an entire issue on Goldwater's alleged mental unfitness for the Oval Office. It started with the title, "1,189 Psychiatrists Say Goldwater Is Psychologically Unfit to Be President!—The Unconscious of a Conservative: A Special Issue on the Mind of Barry Goldwater."

The editor and publisher, Ralph Ginzburg, wrote, in part: "Mr. Goldwater's illness is not just an emotional maladjustment, or a mild neurosis, or a queerness. As emphatically stated by many of the leading psychiatrists in this country, the pattern of his behavior is ominous. From his sadistic childhood pranks to his cruel practical jokes today, from his nervous breakdowns under pressure in his twenties to his present-day withdrawals and escapes in time of crisis, from his obsessive pre-occupation with firearms in his youth to his present fantasies about brandishing nuclear weapons to scare his enemies, from his conviction that he is surrounded by deadly enemies at home—whether [labor leader Walter] Reuther, [Nelson] Rockefeller, the American Press, or Someone Who Is Out to Kill Him—to his belief that every Russian ballerina is a spy, he shows unmistakable symptoms of paranoia. . . . Clearly, paranoia is not just *any* mental disease. In a leader who commands the most powerful nation and the most destructive arsenal in history it constitutes nothing short of mortal danger to mankind. A little over 30 years ago a paranoiac with a charismatic effect on his audiences, supported by an extremist, highly patriotic group, was *democratically* elected to the highest executive position in the government of his country. His name was Adolph Hitler."[35]

The magazine explained that it sent a questionnaire to all of the nation's 12,356 psychiatrists asking, "Do you believe Barry Goldwater is psychologically fit to serve as President of the United States." "In all, 2,417 psychiatrists responded. Of these, 571 said they did not know enough about Goldwater to answer the question; 657 said they thought Goldwater was psychologically fit; and 1,189 said that he was not. . . ." *Fact* also solicited comments from psychiatrists and published a "sampling," which it claimed "constitute the most intensive character analysis ever made of a living human being."[36] Needless to say, the published comments were vicious.

As a result of the *Fact* article, in 1973 the American Psychiatric Association (APA) issued what became know as the "Goldwater Rule": "On occasion, psychiatrists are asked for an opinion about an individual who is in the light of public attention or who has disclosed information about himself/herself through public media. In such circumstances, a psychiatrist may share with the public his or her expertise about psychiatric issues in general. However, it is unethical for a psychiatrist to offer a professional opinion unless he or she has conducted an examination and has been granted proper authorization for such a statement."[37]

Nonetheless, the Goldwater Rule did not stop the psychobabble and public maligning of President Trump by the psychiatrists and others who had gathered at Yale and penned their book. Nor did it deter the Democratic party-press from fully and excitedly exploiting it. In fact, the media have gone even further. Donald Trump's supporters are even targeted for mental evaluation.

On September 23, 2016, Bobby Azarian, Ph.D., "a cognitive neuroscientist affiliated with George Mason University and a freelance journalist whose work has appeared in *The Atlantic, The New York Times, BBC Future, Scientific American, Slate, The Huffington Post, Quartz,* and others," wrote in *Psychology Today* that "[t]he only thing that might be more perplexing than the psychology of Donald Trump is the psychology of his supporters. In their eyes, The Donald can do no wrong. Even Trump himself seems to be astonished by this phenomenon. . . ." Azarian, therefore, will undertake the superhuman task of psychoanalyzing tens of millions of the president's supporters from his lofty media perch at *Psychology Today.* "So how exactly are Trump loyalists psychologically or neurologically different from everyone else? What is going on in their brains that makes them so blindly devoted?"[38]

Azarian argues there are four possibilities:

"1. **The Dunning-Kruger Effect:** Some believe that many of those who support Donald Trump do so because of ignorance— basically they are underinformed or misinformed about the issues at hand. . . .

2. **Hypersensitivity to Threat:** Science has unequivocally shown that the conservative brain has an exaggerated fear response when faced with stimuli that may be perceived as threatening. . . . These brain responses are automatic, and not influenced by logic or reason. . . . Fear keeps [Trump's] followers energized and focused on safety.

3. **Terror Management Theory:** [W]hen people are reminded of their own mortality, which happens with fear mongering, they will more strongly defend those who share their worldviews and national or ethnic identity, and act out more aggressively towards those who do not. . . . By constantly emphasizing existential threat, Trump creates a psychological condition that makes the brain respond positively rather than negatively to bigoted statements and divisive rhetoric.

4. **High Attention Engagement:** . . . Essentially, the loyalty of Trump supporters may in part be explained by America's addiction with entertainment and reality TV. . . . He keeps us on the edge of our seat, and for that reason, some Trump supporters will forgive anything he says. They are happy as long as they are kept entertained.[39]"

Azarian assures us that "these explanations do not apply to all Trump supporters. In fact, some are likely intelligent people who know better, but are supporting Trump to be rebellious or to introduce chaos into the system. They may have such distaste for the establishment and Hillary Clinton that their vote for Trump is a symbolic middle finger directed at Washington."[40]

Azarian's disdainful attitude about Trump and his supporters is typical and widespread throughout newsrooms. The Democratic party-press is incurious about and even blind to objective truth and the reality that surrounds them.

On November 11, 2016, shortly after Donald Trump's election, Will Rahn, CBS News digital political correspondent and the network's managing director of politics, wrote an extraordinary opinion-piece, "The Unbearable Smugness of the Press," in which he excoriated the Democratic party-press and fellow journalists. Here is part of what he said:

> The mood in the Washington press corps is bleak, and deservedly so. It shouldn't come as a surprise to anyone that, with a few exceptions, we were all tacitly or explicitly #WithHer, which has led to a certain anguish in the face of Donald Trump's victory. More than that and more importantly, we also missed the story, after having spent months mocking the people who had a better sense of what was going on. This is all symptomatic of modern journalism's great moral and intellectual failing: its unbearable smugness. . . . Trump knew what he was doing when he invited his crowds to jeer and hiss the reporters covering him. They hate us, and have for some time. And can you blame them? Journalists love mocking Trump supporters. . . .
>
> We diagnose them as racists in the way Dark Age clerics confused medical problems with demonic possession. Journalists, at our worst, see ourselves as a priestly caste. We believe we not only have access to the indisputable facts, but also a greater truth, a system of beliefs divined from an advanced understanding of justice. This is all a "whitelash," you see. Trump voters are racist and sexist, so there must be more racists and sexists than we realized. . . .

Journalists increasingly don't even believe in the possibility
of reasoned disagreement, and as such ascribe cynical motives
to those who think about things a different way. . . .

As a direct result, we get it wrong with greater frequency.
Out on the road, we forget to ask the right questions. We can't
even imagine the right question. We go into assignments too
certain that what we find will serve to justify our biases. . . .[41]

Unfortunately, Rahn's wise counsel to his media colleagues has
fallen on deaf ears. Indeed, despite Rahn's warnings to his media
colleagues, since the election the Democratic party-press has unleashed a relentless and hellish campaign of insult and condemnation against President Trump, whom they seek to drive from
office, and his supporters, for whom they have open disdain. Aside
from certain news media platforms, a few cable programs, newspapers, and conservative talk radio, there is little current ability to
counter or balance the large, old-media platforms of the Democratic party-press.

Furthermore, the kinship between journalists and the Democratic Party and progressive ideology debases professional journalistic standards, in which advocacy is treated and presented as news.
One striking historical illustration of such behavior is portrayed in
the 2012 book *Yours in Truth: A Personal Portrait of Ben Bradlee,
Legendary Editor of the* Washington Post—authored by journalist
Jeff Himmelman.[42] Of course, the *Washington Post* is among the
most influential news outlets in the country. It was instrumental
in President Richard Nixon's downfall, with the assistance of leaks
from the FBI, among others.

Himmelman was a *Washington Post* journalist who had at one
point reported directly to Bob Woodward. In writing his biogra-

phy of Ben Bradlee, who had been the executive editor of the *Post* from 1968 to 1991, he was given full access to Bradlee, with whom he had worked and studied for four years, as well as Bradlee's personal papers. Bradlee, of course, had been treated as a press icon, most famously for his overseeing the publishing of the Pentagon Papers and the reporting on Watergate. Upon his death on October 21, 2014, Bradlee received lavish praise from the media class and many politicians, including President Barack Obama, for his courage and exceptionalism as a journalist and press executive. Obama issued a statement in which he said that "[t]he standard [Bradlee] set—a standard for honest, objective, meticulous reporting—encouraged so many others to enter the profession."[43]

When Himmelman's book was published, he was roundly criticized by Woodward and others in the press world because he dared to call into question Bradlee's exceptionally close friendship with President John Kennedy and certain of Bradlee's unethical journalistic practices when he was a correspondent for *Newsweek* covering Kennedy. From the time Kennedy was a senator, during his presidential campaign, and throughout his short presidency, Bradlee and his wife, with the exception of a few-month period, were close friends. They were neighbors before Kennedy moved into the White House. They had frequent private dinners, went to the movies, attended dances, etc. "The uniform perception is that most editors today would never allow a friend to cover a friend the way Ben covered Kennedy," Himmelman writes.[44] Let us hope not. But the converse should be true as well—that is, if a journalist has deep-seated antipathy for a public figure, such as CNN's Jim Acosta or a host of other reporters for President Trump, they should never be allowed to cover that person, either.

Clearly, however, there is no such concern among editors today.

In the case of Kennedy and Bradlee, Himmelman recounts that "[i]n May of 1959, before Kennedy had officially announced his candidacy [for president], Ben covered a speech of Lyndon Johnson's in Harrisburg, Pennsylvania, for *Newsweek*. At the time, Johnson was widely perceived to be one of Kennedy's potential rivals for the Democratic nomination. Ben filed for *Newsweek*, but he also wrote a private, critical assessment of the speech in a 'Memorandum for Sen. John F. Kennedy' that definitely crosses the line between what a reporter should and shouldn't do for a friend. (He never mentioned having written this memo in any of his books or interviews; I found it at the Kennedy Library.)"[45]

Himmelman continued: "After calling the speech 'a masterpiece of corn,' Ben deconstructs Johnson's entire presentation: 'My own response to Johnson is that, almost all other considerations aside, he could never make it. The image is poor. The accent hurts. . . . [H]e really does not have the requisite dignity. I watched closely. His personal mannerisms are destructive of the dignified image. He's somebody's gabby Texas cousin from Fort Worth.'"[46]

As an aside, one can imagine that this kind of attitude pervades and reflects present-day newsrooms respecting President Trump and his supporters. The evidence can be regularly seen and heard in daily news programs and commentaries, as described earlier.

Bradlee further advised Kennedy that "[f]or safety's sake, I think your present assumption, that he is a candidate has to be the one. . . . The danger is, of course, not that he makes it or that he can hand his strength intact to anybody else. What is to be feared is that he will come to Los Angeles with a block of 300 or more delegates and hold them off the market for three or four ballots. . . . Not only do you have to advance steadily, but you have to do it in pretty big leaps. . . . This is the peril of Johnson. Every piece written that touts him as a candidate should, it seems to me, be read in this light rather than on its apparent face value. . . . He's to be feared not as a potential winner but as a game-player who might try to maneuver you right out of the contest in Los Angeles."[47]

Himmelman reassures the reader that "[f]or the most part, Ben stuck to being a reporter. Kennedy never gave Ben big scoops, particularly during the campaign, but he handed out tidbits."[48] But the fact is they were very close friends, as were their wives, as Himmelman explains throughout his book. And this undoubtedly affected Bradlee's reporting and *Newsweek*'s coverage.

Indeed, Himmelman reports on "one of the sketchier episodes in their relationship," when "[r]umors had been circulating for a while that Kennedy had been married once, before Jackie, and that he had gotten a quickie divorce. Untrue, evidently, but lingering— probably because of some of the widespread extra-curricular skinny-dipping that Kennedy was engaged in. Pierre Salinger, Kennedy's press secretary, negotiated to have Ben come up to Newport, Rhode Island (where Jackie's family had an enormous waterfront estate, Hammersmith Farm), to review FBI files that would prove that organizations spreading the rumors about Kennedy were shady themselves. This would discredit the opposition and advance a story line that the administration wanted to advance."[49]

Kennedy shared FBI files with Bradlee about shady organizations he wanted to discredit. And there was more to Himmelman's telling. "On top of that, the president demanded approval over anything that ran in *Newsweek*." Bradlee and *Newsweek* complied. "'This is a right all presidents covet,' Ben wrote later, 'but which they should normally not be given. This one time, the book seemed worth the candle, however, and we decided to strike the deal.'"[50]

In essence, Kennedy had editing control over the Bradlee-*Newsweek* story, which was intended to help Kennedy and involved Kennedy's sharing of FBI information with them.

All of this was done in the shadows. And Bradlee was compliant.

At least the party-press of old was honest enough to identify themselves as partisans. And, for the most part, the public knew which newspaper stood with which party or candidate. Here, and throughout the modern media, the bias may usually be determined by the news-consuming public from the content put out by the newsroom. Of course, there are also those who, when watching "the news" or reading "the news," take it at face value. And there are times when you simply cannot discern truth from fiction. But the newsrooms themselves do not transparently label or self-identify their partisanship or bias, enabling the public to weigh and filter what is being presented to it.

In fact, they protest when called out and claim that they are protecting freedom of the press against their critics. But are they? Or does the threat to press freedom lie with them?

FOUR

THE REAL THREAT TO PRESS FREEDOM

WHEN THINKING OF threats to freedom of the press, the usual scenario is of the government taking actions to intimidate or silence media organizations, journalists, etc. Today the American media insist they are under an unprecedented barrage of rhetorical criticism from President Donald Trump, and that his calling media factions "the enemy of the people" or "fake news" and using press events and political rallies to call out for criticism individual news organizations and individual reporters is a menace to freedom of the press. It is said that like no president before him, President Trump is using the language of a dictator and undermining the public's respect for the press. Therefore, pushback by the media is not only warranted but essential, as they are defending the First Amendment and freedom of the press, whereas President Trump is endangering them.

So traumatized are the media by President Trump's verbal bouts with them that, led by the *Boston Globe*, they organized a coordinated editorial response. "We are not the enemy of the people," said Marjorie Pritchard, deputy managing editor for the *Globe*'s editorial page and a leader of the media campaign. "I hope it would educate readers to realize that an attack on the First Amendment is unacceptable. We are a free and independent press, it is one of the most sacred principles enshrined in the Constitution."[1]

On August 15, 2018, "[m]ore than 300 newspapers around the nation joined together to each publish editorials that explained the role of journalists and amplified the positive role journalism plays in society."[2] The editorial in the *Boston Globe* is illustrative. Titled "Journalists Are Not the Enemy," it states, in part: "Replacing a free media with a state-run media has always been a first order of business for any corrupt regime taking over a country. Today in the United States we have a president who has created a mantra that members of the media who do not blatantly support the policies of the current U.S. administration are the 'enemy of the people.' This is one of the many lies that have been thrown out by this president, much like an old-time charlatan threw out 'magic' dust or water on a hopeful crowd."[3]

Has President Trump advocated for "state-run media"? Ironically, the closest the United States comes to such official media are the Public Broadcasting System and National Public Radio, but any effort to eliminate taxpayer subsidies for these broadcast outlets is strongly opposed by, among others, other media outlets. But President Trump has never endorsed state-run journalism.

Does the president demand that the media "blatantly support [his] policies"? This is an inaccurate characterization of his beef with the press. President Trump denounces what are often media-driven stories about such things as collusion with Russia, speculation about his mental health, gossip about his family members, predictions about indictments, demands for his impeachment, claims that he is a racist or white supremacist, charges of immigration internment camps, etc.

Indeed, on December 6, 2018, RealClearPolitics did an analysis of the media's Trump coverage and concluded it was "obsessive." "Since he rode down the Trump Tower escalator in June 2015, Donald Trump has loomed large over the media landscape. From the mail bomber to the Khashoggi slaying to Bush 41's death, news outlets have organized their stories to emphasize Trump, while often undermining his legitimacy. In doing so, the press has devoted so much attention to him that he has in some ways helped revive American journalism. It turns out the media's obsession with the president is greater than one might imagine."[4]

For example, focusing on cable channels CNN, MSNBC, and Fox News, RealClearPolitics found that "[w]hile Obama typically hovered around 3 percent to 5 percent airtime over most of his presidency, Trump's steady state appears to be around 13 percent to 17 percent. In total from June 2009 to January 20, 2017, Obama averaged around 4.9 percent of the combined daily airtime of CNN, MSNBC, and Fox News. From June 16, 2015 to present, Trump has averaged 15 percent, three times as much."[5]

Moreover, as reported by the Shorenstein Center on May 18, 2017, and referenced earlier, the center's study found that "Trump's attacks on the press have been aimed at what he calls the 'mainstream media.' Six of the seven U.S. outlets in our study—CBS, CNN, NBC, *The New York Times*, *The Wall Street Journal*, and *The Washington Post*—are among those he's attacked by name. All six portrayed Trump's first 100 days in highly unfavorable terms." Again, "Trump's coverage during his first 100 days was not merely negative in overall terms. It was unfavorable on every dimension. There was not a single major topic where Trump's coverage was more positive than negative."[6]

President Trump is not demanding slavish media support for his policies. He is rightly acknowledging the overwhelmingly negative coverage he receives from an extremely hostile media. And much of that is due to the progressive ideological mindset of America's newsrooms and their outrage over his electoral victory.

The *Globe* editorial further laments that "[t]here was once broad, bipartisan, intergenerational agreement in the United States that the press played this important role. Yet that view is no longer shared by many Americans. 'The news media is the enemy of the American people,' is a sentiment endorsed by 48 percent of Republicans surveyed this month by Ipsos polling firm. That poll is not an outlier. One published this week found 51 percent of Republicans considered the press 'the enemy of the people rather than an important part of democracy.'"[7]

The *Globe* appears to conflate support for freedom of the press, which is a nonpartisan issue and undoubtedly embraced widely among Americans of all political stripes—especially Republican originalists and constitutionalists—with opposition by Republicans to the manner in which present-day journalists are almost single-mindedly and compulsively pursuing President Trump, his family, and his administration. More broadly, Republican objections relate to the modern view of news reporting—that is, the progressive ideological and partisan nature of reporting, rather than the principle of freedom of the press. Of course, the *Globe* editorial skirts this issue altogether, as it would require some level of self-evaluation and circumspection.

On September 5, 2018, the Reporters Committee for Freedom of the Press released a survey that found, among other things, that "95 percent of voters agree on the importance of having a free press."[8] "According to the survey, 56 percent of voters say they value the national news media most for its role in keeping citizens informed." However, "[p]erceived bias in reporting is a top concern, with 55 percent of both Republicans and Independents citing journalists 'filtering all the news with their own political opinions' as one of their biggest doubts about the national news media. Democrats are more concerned about sensationalizing news stories, with 52 percent citing it as their largest doubt."[9]

Unlike the *Globe* and the more than three hundred other newspaper editorials, the survey also found that "[a] majority of voters, 52 percent, said they did not see press freedom as under threat—a lack of perceived risk that was even higher among some when viewed through a partisan lens: 66 percent of Republicans and 56 percent of Independents said they perceived little or no threat to the press, while just 38 percent of Democrats gave the same response."[10]

Could it be that the public is right and the media are wrong? Is President Trump's criticism of press coverage an existential threat to freedom of the press? Of course not. However, there are numerous examples of past presidents taking governmental actions that did, in fact, suppress press freedom. The *Globe* editorial ignored these past presidential acts, for to acknowledge them would provide context for the reader and undermine the newspaper's entire proposition and anti-Trump campaign.

Interestingly, the *Globe* editorial highlights a quote from founder John Adams: "The liberty of the press is essential to the security of freedom."[11] Yet, incongruously and intentionally, it expurgates by omission President Adams's grievous attack on press freedom.

Not long after the nation's founding, President Adams and his Federalist Party instituted the Sedition Act of 1798. As Richard Buel Jr. of Wesleyan University explained: "Men in the thick of a revolution may well be forgiven if they sacrifice principles to the needs of a desperate moment. But the events of the late 1790s cannot be so explained. Less than ten years after framing the First Amendment, Congress passed [and President Adams signed] the sedition law. . . ."[12] It made illegal the following: "To write, print, utter or publish, or cause it to be done, or assist in it, any false, scandalous, and malicious writing against the government of the United States, or either House of Congress, or the President, with intent to defame, or bring either into contempt or disrepute, or to excite against either the hatred of the people of the United States, or to stir up sedition, or to excite unlawful combinations against the government, or to resist it, or to aid or encourage hostile designs of foreign nations."[13]

"Armed with this statute," Buel writes, "the secretary of state, Timothy Pickering, proceeded to launch a systematic attack on the major opposition presses, clearly with the design of silencing them during the election of 1800. In addition, several Republican printers in the states with Federalist-controlled judicial systems were prosecuted under the common law. No one could seriously have doubted that these prosecutions represented a deliberate attempt to muzzle the Republican presses. Nevertheless, Federalists maintained that nothing, either in the sedition law or its administration, was inconsistent with the First Amendment, and that the law actually expanded the freedom of publishers by liberalizing the common law of libels. The Revolutionaries had an explanation for the apparent conflict between their words and deeds. None had ever denied that the press could abuse its privileges and that such abuse should be restrained."[14]

The Adams administration actually prosecuted more than two dozen individuals, including journalists Thomas Cooper, editor of the *North Cumberland Gazette* in Pennsylvania; James Callender, a writer with the *Richmond Examiner* in Virginia; and Charles Holt, editor of the *New London Bee* in Connecticut—all of whom were fined and served prison sentences, and all of whom were more sympathetic to the Jeffersonian-Republican cause.[15]

Among other things, Adams and his party, witnesses to the bloody French Revolution and the ensuing decade-long upheaval of that society, claimed the sedition law would not prevent legitimate criticism of the government and the exercise of press freedom, but would restrain lies from various factions and groups aimed at delegitimizing democratic rule. The Jeffersonian Republicans countered that "political criticism necessarily contained opinion as well as fact, and that no jury could determine the truth or falsehood of an opinion. . . ." Moreover, various state laws provided recourse for seditious libel.[16]

With Thomas Jefferson's victory in 1800, and his more libertarian beliefs, as well as the Republican takeover of Congress, the Sedition Act would die and freedom of the press would be honored. "Despite extraordinary provocations, the Republicans never responded as the Federalists had in the analogous circumstances of the late 1790s."[17]

Decades later, during the Civil War, Abraham Lincoln and the Republicans were dealing with the gravest threat to the republic since its founding—a war over secession and slavery that engulfed the country, eventually resulting in more than 700,000 casualties.

Historian Harold Holzer noted that "[f]ollowing the [first] Bull Run [disaster], the administration turned its attention not only to forging weaponry and raising more troops, but also to quelling home-front newspaper criticism that the president, his cabinet advisors, and, more surprisingly, many Northern newspaper editors believed was morphing from tolerable dissent into nation-threatening treason." The Lincoln administration believed that in the case of "an unprecedented rebellion, and under the powers the president had claimed in order to crush it, military necessity superseded constitutional protection. . . . Based on this argument, the administration began conducting—or, when it occurred spontaneously, tolerating—repressive actions against opposition newspapers."[18]

As time went on, "the military and the government began punishing editorial opposition to the war itself. Authorities banned pro-peace newspapers from the U.S. mails, shut down newspaper offices, and confiscated printing materials. They intimidated, and sometimes imprisoned, reporters, editors, and publishers who sympathized with the South or objected to armed struggle to restore the Union. For the first year of the war, Lincoln left no trail of documents attesting to any personal conviction that dissenting newspapers ought to be muzzled. But neither did he say anything to control or contradict such efforts when they were undertaken . . . by his cabinet officers or military commanders. Lincoln did not initiate press suppression, and remained ambivalent about its execution, but seldom intervened to prevent it."[19]

Saint Michael's College professor David T. Z. Mindich adds that "[i]n 1862, after . . . Lincoln appointed him secretary of war, Edwin M. Stanton penned a letter to the president requesting sweeping powers, which would include total control of the telegraph lines. By rerouting those lines through his office, Stanton would keep tabs on vast amounts of communication, journalistic, governmental and personal. On the back of Stanton's letter Lincoln scribbled his approval: 'The Secretary of War has my authority to exercise his discretion in the matter within mentioned.' . . . Having the telegraph lines running through Stanton's office made his department the nexus of war information; Lincoln visited regularly to get the latest on the war. Stanton collected news from generals, telegraph operators, and reporters. He had a journalist's love of breaking the story and an autocrat's obsession with information control. He used his power over the telegraphs to influence what journalists did or didn't publish. In 1862, the House Judiciary Committee took up the question of 'telegraphic censorship' and called for restraint on the part of the administration's censors."[20]

On May 18, 1864, the Associated Press distributed what turned out to be a forged copy of a presidential proclamation. Its inauthenticity was unknown to the publishers and editors of the pro-Democrat, antiwar *New York World* and *New York Journal of Commerce* newspapers, who fell for the ruse and printed it. The document "urged a national day of 'fasting, humiliation and

prayers,' hinted darkly about 'the general state of the country,' and
called for a breathtaking 400,000 new volunteers. With Ulysses S.
Grant enduring a bloodbath of casualties in a struggle to subdue
Robert E. Lee in Virginia, the proclamation seemed a cry of desperation—an admission that to prevail, the Union required both
divine intervention and a huge infusion of fresh troops. It was
major news."[21]

An outraged Lincoln took direct action, believing these papers
were damaging the Union effort, and issued an executive order
stating:

> Whereas there has been wickedly and traitorously printed and
> published this morning in the New York World and New York
> Journal of Commerce, newspapers printed and published in the
> city of New York, a false and spurious proclamation purporting
> to be signed by the President and to be countersigned by the
> Secretary of State, which publication is of a treasonable nature,
> designed to give aid and comfort to the enemies of the United
> States and to the rebels now at war against the Government and
> their aiders and abettors, you are therefore hereby commanded
> forthwith to arrest and imprison in any fort or military prison
> in your command the editors, proprietors, and publishers of
> the aforesaid newspapers, and all such persons as, after pub-
> lic notice has been given of the falsehood of said publication,
> print and publish the same with intent to give aid and com-
> fort to the enemy; and you will hold the persons so arrested in
> close custody until they can be brought to trial before a military
> commission for their offense. You will also take possession by
> military force of the printing establishments of the New York

World and Journal of Commerce, and hold the same until further orders, and prohibit any further publication therefrom.[22]

Major General John Adams Dix was ordered to execute the presidential directive, which he did reluctantly. The two papers were shut down and the two editors detained at army headquarters. Dix soon uncovered the perpetrator of the hoax, a onetime *New York Times* correspondent, Joseph Howard Jr., On May 21, 1864, both editors were permitted to reopen their newspapers. However, Lincoln's angry reaction to the two newspapers apparently was less about a hoax and more about the fact that the night before the publication of the forged presidential proclamation, "the president had been working on an authentic proclamation that indeed called for more troops—300,000 more . . .—by either enlistment or conscription." The published forgery "unleashed panic within the White House and cabinet . . . that someone may have leaked a genuine proclamation" and potentially harmed the war effort.[23]

During the course of another war, this time World War I, President Woodrow Wilson, who had been a leading progressive intellectual for decades, supported a series of congressional amendments that Congress added to the Espionage Act, which collectively became known as the Sedition Act of May 16, 1918. The act stated, in part:

[W]hoever, when the United States is at war, shall willfully utter, print, write or publish any disloyal, profane, scurrilous, or abusive language about the form of government of the United States or the Constitution of the United States, or

the military or naval forces of the United States, or the flag
of the United States, or the uniform of the Army or Navy of
the United States into contempt, scorn, contumely, or disrepute, . . . shall be punished by a fine of not more than $10,000
or the imprisonment for not more than twenty years, or both:
Provided, That any employee or official of the United States
Government who commits any disloyal act or utters any unpa-
triotic or disloyal language, or who, in an abusive and violent
manner criticizes the Army or Navy or the flag of the United
States shall be at once dismissed from the service. . . .[24]

Numerous opponents of Wilson's war policies were charged
and imprisoned.[25] Indeed, Wilson had already instituted extensive measures to curtail press freedom. Christopher B. Daly, professor at Boston University, has written that during the lead-up
to America's entrance into World War I, "the Wilson administration took immediate steps at home to curtail one of the pillars of
democracy—press freedom—by implementing a plan to control,
manipulate and censor all news coverage, on a scale never seen
in U.S. history. Following the lead of the Germans and British,
Wilson elevated propaganda and censorship to strategic elements
of all-out war. Even before the U.S. entered the war, Wilson had
expressed the expectation that his fellow Americans would show
what he considered 'loyalty.' . . . Wilson started one of the earliest
uses of government propaganda. He waged a campaign of intimidation and outright suppression against those ethnic and socialist
papers that continued to oppose the war. Taken together, these
wartime measures added up to an unprecedented assault on press
freedom."[26]

Wilson also created an elaborate domestic spy network "to watch German immigrants and American radicals. Federal agents arrested hundreds for making anti-war speeches, and sometimes for informal and private remarks. Eugene Debs, four-time presidential candidate for the Socialist Party, was arrested in June 1918 for suggesting during a speech that young American men were 'fit for something better than slavery and cannon fodder.' Sentenced to ten years in prison, he defiantly ran for president in 1920 from his jail cell in Atlanta, and received almost a million votes. During the war, more than 2,000 men and women were arrested for 'disloyal' speech, and over 1,200 went to jail."[27]

Furthermore, Wilson issued an executive order on April 13, 1917, establishing the Committee on Public Information (CPI), a massive propaganda machine "that would put the government in the business of actively shaping press coverage" about the war. Wilson appointed a former journalist and loyal political supporter, George Creel, to lead the operation. "[T]he CPI was 'a veritable magnet' for political progressives of all stripes—intellectuals, muckrakers, even some socialists—all sharing a sense of the threat to democracy posed by German militarism." The Wilson administration planted official "news" stories with media outlets, published an "official" government newspaper that was widely distributed, and secured free advertising in press publications. The CPI had a film division, foreign-language newspaper division, advertising division, and speakers' division. At the same time, the government severely limited press access to people and operations related to the war effort.[28]

The CPI was pervasive. "The CPI mobilized 150,000 American word-maestros to pitch America's involvement in the war as necessary and noble. . . . Commandeering the four minutes projectionists needed to change movie reels, Creel and his people trained 75,000 citizens to deliver seemingly impromptu, carefully coached, perfectly timed four-minute pro-war harangues. . . . Creel would estimate his speakers delivered 755,190 talks . . . [and papered] the country with 1,438 different posters."[29]

David T. Beito, professor at the University of Alabama, has written of President Franklin Roosevelt's "war against the press" during the New Deal and later World War II. For example, "[a]t its inception in 1934, the Federal Communications Commission (FCC) reduced the license renewal period for stations from three years to only six months."[30] This would allow Roosevelt maximum authority over the life and death of radio stations. "Meanwhile, Roosevelt tapped Herbert L. Pettey as secretary of the FCC (and its predecessor, the Federal Radio Commission). Pettey had overseen radio for Roosevelt in the 1932 campaign. After his appointment, he worked in tandem with the Democratic National Committee to handle 'radio matters' with both the networks and local stations. It did not take long for broadcasters to get the message. NBC . . . announced that it was limiting broadcasts 'contrary to the policies of the United States government.' CBS Vice President Henry A. Bellows said that 'no broadcast would be permitted over the Columbia Broadcasting System that in any way was critical of any policy of the Administration.' He elaborated 'that the Columbia system was at the disposal of President Roosevelt and his administration and they would permit no broadcast that did not have his approval.' Local station owners and network executives alike took it for granted, as *Editor and Publisher* observed, that each station had 'to dance to Government tunes because it is under Government license.'"[31]

But Roosevelt's manipulation and reach went well beyond the nascent broadcast media. Beito explained that "Roosevelt's intimidation efforts reached their apogee in the hands of the Special Senate Committee on Lobbying. The president indirectly recruited Sen. Hugo L. Black (D-Ala.), a zealous and effective New Deal loyalist, as chair." The Black Committee undertook a wide-ranging investigation into anti–New Deal critics, including journalists.[32]

Black was granted "access to tax returns dating back to 1925 of such critics as David Lawrence of the *United States News.*" He then demanded that his targets turn over their private telegrams and the "telegraph companies let the committee search copies of all incoming and outgoing telegrams for the first nine months of 1935. When Western Union refused on privacy grounds, the FCC, at Black's urging, ordered it to comply."[33]

The extent of the government's intrusion into private telegram communications was shocking. "Over a nearly three-month period at the end of 1935," writes Beito, "FCC and Black Committee staffers searched great stacks of telegrams in Western Union's D.C. office. Operating with virtually no restriction, they read the communications of sundry lobbyists, newspaper publishers, and conservative political activists as well as every member of Congress. Writing to Black, one investigator stated that they had gone through '35,000 to 50,000 [telegrams] per day.' Various newspapers and members of Congress later estimated that staffers had examined some five million telegrams over the course of the investigation.... The committee used the information it found as a basis for more than 1,000 new subpoenas. One of these was for all incoming and outgoing telegrams, not just those sent through Washington, D.C., of W. H. Cowles' anti–New Deal newspaper chain in the Northwest."[34]

Hugo Black would become Roosevelt's first appointment to the U.S. Supreme Court. Early in his career he had been a member of the Ku Klux Klan.

In another example, Beito writes that "[d]uring the 1930s, [newspaper publisher] Edward Rumely formed an alliance with other New Deal critics, including newspaper publisher Frank Gannett and the well-known conservationist and civil libertarian Amos Pinchot. On the same day that Franklin Roosevelt announced his court-packing plan in 1937, the trio organized the Committee for Constitutional Government (CCG). Gannett wrote the checks, and Rumely ran day-to-day operations. CCG led perhaps the first successful offensive against the New Deal, pioneering the use of direct mail and helping to defeat the court-packing plan."[35]

For this, Rumely was singled out by Roosevelt's congressional loyalists. "It didn't take long for Democrats to strike back. In 1938, Senator Sherman Minton of Indiana announced a sweeping investigation of lobbies, targeting forces opposed to 'the objectives of the administration.' Minton-committee staff arrived en masse at CCG's office, where they began copying files. After watching this for several hours, Rumely ordered them out, charging them with an illegal 'fishing expedition.' Minton's undoing, however, was his proposal to make it a felony 'to publish as a fact anything known to be false.' The resulting public backlash over a perceived threat to free speech led to the collapse of the investigation. Over the next decade, CCG distributed over 82 million pieces of literature criticizing such policies as expanded government medical insurance, public housing, and labor legislation."[36]

Roosevelt was also a huge admirer of George Creel, Woodrow Wilson's top propagandist. In his book, *FDR and the Press*, Graham

J. White explained: "Unbeknown, apparently, to the Washington press, Roosevelt repeatedly used Creel's articles to outline his plans and purposes and to test public reaction to them.... Often Roosevelt actually dictated whole paragraphs to Creel for opinion-pieces Roosevelt would write and speeches he would deliver."[37]

Roosevelt was known to give a tongue-lashing to the media during contentious periods of his presidency, as have other presidents. But he sought to separate media owners, publishers, and columnists from the so-called working press, and in this he had great success. While many who have written on this subject credit Roosevelt's adeptness at press relations, what they do not admit is the provable fondness for Roosevelt's progressive domestic agenda by the working press. It is also a principal reason they tolerated Roosevelt's (and Wilson's) violations of press freedom and championed many of his New Deal programs.

James E. Pollard, who in 1947 wrote about the relationship between presidents and the press, said of Roosevelt, in part, that his administration "[p]eriodically...sounded the alarm about the U.S. press; it was false to its trust, it failed to give the public the whole story, it played down anything favorable to the administration and exaggerated what was bad, it manufactured anti-Roosevelt stuff out of whole cloth, it was owned and controlled by men of predatory wealth. By the same token, writers, editors, and publishers [not so much the working press] were forever reading danger to the freedom of the press in the acts and attitudes of the administration. They saw it in Presidential actions and utterances. They sensed it in New Deal legislation. They scented it in the actions of subordinates or of the New Deal agencies."[38]

In fact, some prominent individuals feared that Roosevelt was intent on suppressing media owners and publishers. Pollard explained: "Each saw only the worst in the other. To borrow the Roosevelt expression, both were seeing things under the bed. Yet the columnist Gen. Hugh Johnson, at one time in the confidence of the President, asserted that the administration attacks on the press had 'appeared over long enough periods of time and with enough consistency to indicate a policy or at least a conviction.' He feared that they were 'opening steps in a furtive purpose to suppress or soften criticism of governmental action by legislation, intimidation or whatever it takes.'"[39]

However, as Pollard wrote: "The Roosevelt strength in dealing with the working press lay in the fact that he found common ground with the correspondents. He understood their needs and their problems. He faced them as man to man, usually with no holds barred. He matched wits with them, he fenced with them, he was quite frank with them in most matters. His achievements in these respects far outran those of any of his predecessors. He was a master of the art of applied psychology in the field of broad public relations."[40]

Therefore, other than all the press manipulation, threats, and suppression, "the working press of the United States is forever in [Roosevelt's] debt for meeting it on common ground over so many critical years."[41]

The same can be said of President Barack Obama, of course, and his relationship not just with the "working press" but with media owners, publishers, and commentators. Like Roosevelt, Obama acted against the media in a variety of significant ways. A retired *Washington Post* executive editor, writing on the opinion page, explained that "[t]he Justice Department secretly subpoenaed and seized from telephone companies two months of records for 20 AP phone lines and switchboards used by more than 100 reporters in four of its news bureaus." "[T]he Obama administration . . . subpoenaed and seized records of telephone calls and e-mails between several *New York Times* reporters and government officials, between a Fox News reporter and a State Department contract analyst, and between two journalists and a former CIA officer."[42]

Specifically, in 2010, the FBI spied on James Rosen, a then Fox News reporter, collecting his cell phone records, seizing two days of his personal emails, and using his State Department security badge to track his movements in and out of the department. The FBI also accused him of violating the Espionage Act of 1917, "at the very least, either as an aider, abettor and/or co-conspirator" with one of his government sources.[43]

James Risen, a reporter for the *New York Times*, was also treated as a coconspirator with a government source who was indicted by the Obama administration under the Espionage Act of 1917. Risen was subpoenaed; the government sought access to his phone and computer records, tried to compel him to testify against one of his sources, and for several years threatened him with imprisonment. Risen would later describe the Obama administration as "the greatest enemy of press freedom in a generation."[44]

The Associated Press found that "[t]he Obama administration used the 1917 Espionage Act with unprecedented vigor, prosecuting more people under that law for leaking sensitive information to the public than all previous modern administrations combined. Obama's Justice Department dug into confidential communications between news organizations and their sources as part of that effort."[45]

In response to the Obama administration's surveillance of the Associated Press, its CEO, Gary Pruitt, asserted that "[t]hese records potentially reveal communications with confidential sources across all of the newsgathering activities undertaken by the AP during a two-month period, provide a road map to AP's newsgathering operations and disclose information about AP's activities and operations that the government has no conceivable right to know."[46]

The Obama administration also briefly entertained the idea of overseeing the content of radio programming because of the "structural imbalance" of such content. The draft proposal from the Federal Communications Commission's legal department included a program that would place government monitors in newsrooms "to determine how stories were selected, whether there was bias in reporting," and whether "critical information needs" were being met. If the program had been instituted, the "monitors would have been placed not only in broadcast newsrooms, but also print media outlets that the FCC had no regulatory authority over."[47]

Even the Freedom of Information Act (FOIA) was intentionally abused to deny the press and other groups and individuals access to public information in executive branch departments and agencies, making the functioning of the vast bureaucracy transparent to the public. *Politico*'s Jack Shafer observed, among other things, that "[u]nder [the Obama] administration, the U.S. government has set a new record for withholding Freedom of Information Act requests, according to a recent Associated Press investigation. FOIA gives the public and press an irreplaceable view into the workings of the executive branch. Without timely release of government documents and data, vital questions can't be answered and stories can't be written."[48]

No matter. For the vast majority of journalists, Obama's transformative progressive agenda was paramount. And the Democratic party-press was mainly there to help him. Shafer wrote that at an awards ceremony for excellence in political reporting, Obama was the keynote speaker and praised journalists. Shafer noted that "[t]he last person in the world who should be lecturing journalists on how to do journalism is President Barack Obama. Yet there Obama was . . . at a journalism award ceremony, yodeling banalities about the role of a press in a free society, moaning over the dangers posed by 'he said/she said' reporting, and—to the delight of the assembled audience—attacking Donald Trump in every way but by name. The press-heavy crowd . . . clapped at Obama's 30-minute address, encouraging his best Trump-baiting lines about 'free media' and the dangers of 'false equivalence.' What they should have done is bombard Obama with rotten fruit or ripped him with raspberries for his hypocrisy."[49]

But they did not. Why?

Shafer, who dislikes Trump, stumbles around the point—that is, the journalists agreed with Obama's politics and policies, just as earlier "working reporters" agreed with Roosevelt's. Shafer writes: "Obama didn't invent the White House's in-house media shop, which produces videos and other media to disseminate approved 'news' to the public and the press. As long ago as the early 1930s, H. L. Mencken was complaining about how the Roosevelt administration's press agents choked the information pipeline with mimeographed handouts that lazy reporters would then repurpose as news. But Obama's White House has perfected the practice, with a 14-member operation called the White House Office of Digital Strategy that bypasses the press corps with tweets, YouTube videos, Facebook postings and more."[50]

President Trump does not pose a threat to freedom of press, as did certain of his predecessors.

Newsrooms and journalists are not imperiled by the current president.

There are no known sedition-act efforts attacking speech and press freedom; no executive orders imprisoning reporters and shuttering newspapers; no FCC actions against broadcast stations; no unprecedented criminal charges against media organizations or reporters; no omnipresent propaganda operations; etc.

Nonetheless, the constant media refrain, whether from journalists or editorialists, trying to convince the American people of a demonstrably false narrative—that President Trump has launched an unprecedented battering on freedom of the press, thereby undermining the credibility of the institution of a free press and the First Amendment with the public—is media propaganda *and* a media-concocted pseudo-event. Unfortunately, too much of what the public reads, hears, and sees from the Democratic party-press fits this description.

FIVE

NEWS, PROPAGANDA, AND PSEUDO-EVENTS

GIVEN THE PROGRESSIVE ideology and Democratic Party attachment of most of the modern media and journalists, their commitment to "community" journalism and social activism, and with the integration of opinion and news making objective truth increasingly difficult to discern, is the public actually receiving predominantly news or propaganda or pseudo-information?

One of the keys to answering this question points to Edward Bernays. "Bernays," one of his publishers tells us, "pioneered the scientific technique of shaping and manipulating public opinion, which he called 'engineering consent.'"[1] George Creel enlisted him into President Woodrow Wilson's propaganda operation. Bernays was a nephew of Sigmund Freud and according to Christopher B. Daly was "a pioneer in theorizing about human thoughts and emotions. Bernays volunteered for the Committee on Public Information and threw himself into the work. His outlook—a mixture of idealism about the cause of spreading democracy and cynicism about the methods involved—was typical of many at the agency."[2]

Bernays is considered in some quarters the founder of the contemporary public relations profession. He believed in the power of propaganda, and the manipulation and brainwashing of "the masses." "The minority [that is, masterminds or elites] has discovered a powerful help in influencing majorities. It has been found possible so to mold the mind of the masses that they will throw their newly gained strength in the desired direction. In the present structure of society, this practice is inevitable. Whatever of social importance is done today, whether in politics, finance, manufacture, agriculture, charity, education, or other fields, must be done with the help of propaganda. Propaganda is the executive arm of the invisible government."[3]

First and foremost, this means using the media, or the media exercising its own ideologically driven will, as a propaganda enterprise. "The extent to which propaganda shapes the progress of affairs about us," wrote Bernays, "may surprise even well-informed persons. Nevertheless, it is only necessary to look under the surface of the newspaper for a hint as to propaganda's authority over public opinion. Page one of the *New York Times* on the day these paragraphs are written contains eight important news stories. Four of them, or one-half, are propaganda. The casual reader accepts them as accounts of spontaneous happenings. But are they? Here are the headlines which announce them: 'TWELVE NATIONS WARN CHINA REAL REFORM MUST COME BEFORE THEY GIVE RELIEF,' 'PRITCHETT REPORTS ZIONISM WILL FAIL,' 'REALTY

MEN DEMAND A TRANSIT INQUIRY,' and 'OUR LIVING STAN-
DARD HIGHEST IN HISTORY, SAYS HOOVER REPORT.'"[4]

How are they propaganda? Bernays writes:

Take them in order: the article on China explains the joint
report of the Commission on Extraterritoriality in China,
presenting an exposition of the Powers' stand in the Chinese
muddle. What it says is less important than what it is. It was
"made public by the State Department today" with the purpose of presenting to the American public a picture of the
State Department's position. Its source gives it authority, and
the American public tends to accept and support the State
Department view. The report of Dr. Pritchett, a trustee of the
Carnegie Foundation for International Peace, is an attempt to
find the facts about this Jewish colony in the midst of a restless
Arab world. When Dr. Pritchett's survey convinced him that in
the long run Zionism would "bring more bitterness and more
unhappiness both for the Jew and for the Arab," this point
of view was broadcast with all the authority of the Carnegie
Foundation, so that the public would hear and believe. The
statement by the president of the Real Estate Board of New
York, and Secretary Hoover's report, are similar attempts to
influence the public toward an opinion.[5]

For Bernays, propaganda was not troubling but in fact inevitable and useful. The public was not capable of enlightened thinking and decisions in a republic; therefore, they need to be led by
those who supposedly are, or at least by those who self-servingly
claim to be. He explained that "[t]hese examples are not given to

create the impression that there is anything sinister about propaganda. They are set down rather to illustrate how conscious direction is given to events, and how the men behind these events influence public opinion. As such they are examples of modern propaganda."[6]

Bernays argues that "[m]odern propaganda is a consistent, enduring effort to create or shape events to influence the relations of the public to an enterprise, idea or group. This practice of creating circumstances and of creating pictures in the minds of millions of persons is very common. Virtually no important undertaking is now carried on without it. . . ."[7] According to Bernays, there is a new propaganda, which "takes account not merely of the individual, nor even of the mass mind alone, but also and especially of the anatomy of society, with its interlocking group formations and loyalties. It sees the individual not only as a cell in the social organism but as a cell organized into the social unit. Touch a nerve at a sensitive spot and you get an automatic response from certain specific members of the organism."[8]

There is a despotic odor to Bernays's elevation of propaganda as a righteous yet routine undertaking exercised for virtuous purposes by a supposedly intellectually astute and superior minority. The masses must be shepherded and managed, for their own good and the betterment of society. "The new propaganda," Bernays explains, "having regard to the constitution of society as a whole, not infrequently serves to focus and realize the desires of the masses. . . . [C]learly it is the intelligent minorities which need to make use of propaganda continuously and systematically. In the active proselytizing minorities in whom selfish interests and public interests coincide lie the progress and development of America. Only through the active energy of the intelligent few can the public at large become aware of and act upon new ideas...."[9]

A modern illustration of Bernays's new propaganda in action was the selling of the Obama administration's Iran nuclear deal. On May 5, 2016, in a long profile piece in the *New York Times* Sunday magazine, President Barack Obama's deputy national security adviser, Ben Rhodes, bragged about his ability and success in deceiving the American people with a complicit press. The article was titled "The Aspiring Novelist Who Became Obama's Foreign-Policy Guru: How Ben Rhodes Rewrote the Rules of Diplomacy for the Digital Age" and was written by David Samuels, who was seemingly both amused by and approving of Rhodes's propaganda techniques.

Samuels wrote, in part, that "Rhodes's innovative campaign to sell the Iran deal is likely to be a model for how future administrations explain foreign policy to Congress and the public. The way in which most Americans have heard the story of the Iran deal presented—that the Obama administration began seriously engaging with Iranian officials in 2013 in order to take advantage of a new political reality in Iran, which came about because of elections that brought moderates to power in that country—was largely manufactured for the purpose of selling the deal."[10]

A main argument for negotiating with the Iran regime was "actively misleading" and regurgitated by journalists who wanted to support Obama's policy. As Samuels reported: "In the narrative that Rhodes shaped, the 'story' of the Iran deal began in 2013, when a 'moderate' faction inside the Iranian regime led by Hassan Rouhani beat regime 'hard-liners' in an election and then began

to pursue a policy of 'openness,' which included a newfound willingness to negotiate the dismantling of its illicit nuclear-weapons
program. The president set out the timeline himself in his speech
announcing the nuclear deal on July 14, 2015: 'Today, after two
years of negotiations, the United States, together with our international partners, has achieved something that decades of animosity has not.' While the president's statement was technically
accurate—there had in fact been two years of formal negotiations
leading up to the signing of the J.C.P.O.A.—it was also actively
misleading, because the most meaningful part of the negotiations
with Iran had begun in mid-2012, many months before Rouhani
and the 'moderate' camp were chosen in an election among candidates handpicked by Iran's supreme leader, the Ayatollah Ali
Khamenei. The idea that there was a new reality in Iran was politically useful to the Obama administration."[11]

No doubt Bernays would be impressed with the effectiveness
of this propaganda.

Indeed, Samuels seemed to find virtue in the Obama administration's successful propaganda campaign. "By obtaining broad
public currency for the thought that there was a significant split
in the regime, and that the administration was reaching out to
moderate-minded Iranians who wanted peaceful relations with
their neighbors and with America, Obama was able to evade what
might have otherwise been a divisive but clarifying debate over the
actual policy choices that his administration was making. . . ."[12]

Then came the conga line of experts, whose appearances
were orchestrated and statements were scripted by Rhodes, who
bragged about the ruse. "'We created an echo chamber,' Rhodes
admitted, when I asked him to explain the onslaught of freshly

minted experts cheerleading for the deal. 'They were saying things that validated what we had given them to say.'"[13]

Rhodes would also plant the administration's talking points with journalists, some of whom would repeat them verbatim. "In this environment," wrote Samuels, "Rhodes has become adept at ventriloquizing many people at once. Ned Price, Rhodes's assistant, gave me a primer on how it's done. The easiest way for the White House to shape the news, he explained, is from the briefing podiums, each of which has its own dedicated press corps. 'But then there are sort of these force multipliers,' he said, adding, 'We have our compadres, I will reach out to a couple people, and you know I wouldn't want to name them—'"[14] Media "compadres," also known as journalists who were ideological soul mates and willing to report the administration's message as news.

Samuels and Price are insiders who know how the propaganda game is played. Samuels replied to Price: "'I can name them [the reporters],' I said, ticking off a few names of prominent Washington reporters and columnists who often tweet in sync with White House messaging.' Price laughed. 'I'll say, Hey, look, some people are spinning this narrative that this is a sign of American weakness,' he continued, 'but—'"[15]

Samuels, entertained by it all, interrupted: "'In fact it's a sign of strength!' I said, chuckling." Price continued, "'And I'll give them some color and the next thing I know, lots of these guys are in the dot-com publishing space, and have huge Twitter followings, and they'll be putting this message out on their own.'"[16]

Bernays's description of the new propaganda is also on display throughout the 24/7 news cycle. Another particularly barefaced example occurred on Sunday, December 30, 2018, when Chuck

Todd, host of NBC's *Meet the Press* and NBC's political director, issued an on-air proclamation to the nation, followed by a full hour of one-sided propaganda, in which Todd asserted that man-made climate change is a scientific fact, and he would not allow the voices of "climate-deniers" (an offensive term to many, as it is coined after the reference to Holocaust deniers) to be heard now or in the future. He stated:

> This morning, we're going to do something that we don't often get to do, dive in on one topic. It's obviously extraordinarily difficult to do this, as the end of this year has proven, in the era of Trump. But we're going to take an in-depth look, regardless of that, at a literally Earth-changing subject that doesn't get talked about this thoroughly on television news, at least, climate change. But just as important as what we are going to do this hour is what we're not going to do. We're not going to debate climate change, the existence of it. The Earth is getting hotter. And human activity is a major cause, period. We're not going to give time to climate deniers. The science is settled, even if political opinion is not. And we're not going to confuse weather with climate. A heat wave is not more evidence that climate change exists than a blizzard means that it doesn't, unless the blizzard hits Miami. We do have a panel of experts with us today to help us understand the science and consequences of climate change and, yes, ideas to break the political paralysis over it.[17]

Todd and his NBC producers and researchers know, as a matter of fact, that there are many legitimate, credentialed, and scrious scientists and climate experts who are either skeptical of or outright reject the claims of man-made climate change. Several are academicians, work at think-tanks, have produced statistical studies, written significant books, etc. Some question the accuracy of certain research; or the sources of global warming; or whether global warming is occurring; or the role of mankind in global warming; or whether any of this actually matters; or whether a slight increase in warming is actually beneficial to the planet (as it increases plant growth, etc.).[18]

For example, as the National Association of Scholars writes: "S. Fred Singer, a leading scientific skeptic of anthropocentric global warming (AGW), is an atmospheric physicist, and founder of the Science and Environmental Policy Project (SEPP), an organization that began challenging the published findings of the United Nations Intergovernmental Panel on Climate Change (IPCC) in the 1990s. SEPP established the Leipzig Declaration, a statement of dissent from the 1997 Kyoto Protocol that has been signed by over one hundred scientists and meteorologists."[19]

Singer established the Nongovernmental International Panel on Climate Change, which "in 2009 published *Climate Change Reconsidered*, an 880-page report on scientific research that contradicts the models of man-made global warming. Singer believes that global warming exists but that human contributions to it are minimal. In the interview Singer said he believed his efforts in the last twenty years had been successful in disproving the notion that 'the science is settled.'"[20] Chuck Todd dismisses all such experts as deniers and therefore cuts off all intellectual inquiry and discussion about man-made climate change by those who have something worthwhile to contribute to the debate.

Patrick Michaels, formerly professor at the University of Virginia and currently director of the Center for the Study of Science at the Cato Institute, as well as a senior fellow in research and economic development at George Mason University, explains "that climate models have done remarkably *poorly* in replicating the evolution of global temperature during the past several decades, and that high-end climate horror stories emanating from these lousy models are largely unsupported by observations. Further, they managed to ignore a spate of published science demonstrating that the sensitivity of temperature to carbon dioxide changes was substantially overestimated in those models. . . ."[21]

Richard S. Lindzen is a distinguished senior fellow at Cato's Center for the Study of Science, emeritus professor of meteorology at the Massachusetts Institute of Technology, and previously professor of dynamic meteorology at Harvard University. Lindzen is a member of the National Academy of Sciences and fellow of both the American Meteorological Society and the American Association for the Advancement of Science. He received the Jule G. Charney Award for "highly significant research" in the atmospheric sciences from the American Meteorological Society and the Distinguished Engineering Achievement Award from the Engineer's Council in 2009. "Lindzen's pioneering research in atmospheric dynamics has led to his conclusion that the sensitivity of surface temperature to increases in atmospheric carbon dioxide is considerably below that necessary to generate disastrous climate change."[22]

Patrick Moore, Greenpeace cofounder and Canadian ecologist, testified before the United States Senate that "there is 'little correlation' to support a 'direct causal relationship' between CO_2

emissions and rising global temperatures. 'There is no scientific proof that human emissions of carbon dioxide are the dominant cause of the minor warming of the Earth's atmosphere over the past 100 years. If there were such a proof, it would be written down for all to see. No actual proof, as it is understood in science, exists.'" Moore "also criticized the UN's Intergovernmental Panel on Climate Change (IPCC) for claiming 'it is extremely likely' that human activity is the 'dominant cause' for global warming, noting that 'extremely likely' is not a scientific term. Moore warned the statistics presented by the IPCC are not the result of mathematical calculations or statistical analysis, and may have been 'invented' to support the IPCC's 'expert judgement.'"[23]

Roy W. Spencer "received his Ph.D. in meteorology at the University of Wisconsin–Madison in 1981. Before becoming a Principal Research Scientist at the University of Alabama in Huntsville in 2001, he was a Senior Scientist for Climate Studies at NASA's Marshall Space Flight Center, where he and Dr. John Christy received NASA's Exceptional Scientific Achievement Medal for their global temperature monitoring work with satellites. Dr. Spencer's work with NASA continues as the U.S. Science Team leader for the Advanced Microwave Scanning Radiometer flying on NASA's Aqua satellite."[24]

During a presentation at the Heartland Institute's Ninth International Conference on Climate Change in Las Vegas, Spencer explained that "[t]oo many people think that all areas of science are created equal and that scientists objectively look for the answers, but no, there's two kinds of scientists, male and female. Other than that they're the same as everybody else, and in many instances [in the climate sciences] more biased than your average person. . . . Spencer went on to criticize the temperature data of the National Oceanic and Atmospheric Administration (NOAA) because it has never taken into account the phenomenon of urban heat island effect."[25]

Indeed, Spencer pointed to the thermometer-related algorithms as one of the problems in measuring heat. "A lot of us still think that a lot of the warming we are seeing in the thermometer record is just urban heat island effect. In fact, Las Vegas, here, even though it's built in the desert basically . . . in the last forty years or so, nighttime temperatures here have risen by ten degrees Fahrenheit because of urbanization. This is an effect that they can't take out of the thermometer record. Their algorithms can't take it out because you can't separate it from global warming. If you've got a long-term warming trend because of urbanization there's no way NOAA can take out that effect because it's indistinguishable from other temperature readings."[26]

In the end, Spencer argues, very little is really known about global warming, also known as climate change. "After working on global warming for the last 20 plus years, what do we know about it now? The longer you go [into the research] you get more questions than you get answers. So, what do we really know about it? Almost nothing."[27]

There are many more highly educated and experienced experts who raise a variety of substantive issues and questions about man-made climate change. And henceforth, none of them are welcome on NBC's *Meet the Press*. Moreover, like NBC, they are not likely to be taken seriously in most newsrooms or by most journalists because they dare to challenge the orthodoxy of the Democratic party-press and the progressive agenda—in which "solutions" to climate change involve new ways of expanding the government's regulatory and taxing role in society via the "urgency" of climate change, and surrendering national sovereignty to international organizations through multigovernment agreements. Thus one-sided opinion is treated as objective truth; reputable and legitimate individuals who could provide contrary factual information to the public are dismissed as science deniers and climate impostors; and the government and public are urged to engage in immediate political and social activism and demand far-reaching national solutions, such as the "Green New Deal." NBC and Chuck Todd, among other media outlets and journalists, have "interpreted" and "analyzed" the relevant facts through their progressive approach and their conclusion is final. "Period."

No doubt Bernays would be proud of Todd, too, for his outstanding effort at manipulating the public and the use of propaganda in the pursuit of his progressive ideological agenda. Indeed, Todd even cited the "Trump government's" climate report as incontrovertible evidence of global warming, thereby giving the impression of universal validity to Todd's edict. Todd declared that "[t]his year, a series of climate reports, including one produced by thirteen agencies in Mr. Trump's government, issued dire warnings of economic catastrophe, if there is not immediate action to reduce greenhouse gas emissions. But the federal response to the climate crisis has been [met with] political paralysis and denial."[28]

Of course, Todd did not mention that the report was produced by holdovers from the Obama administration. Furthermore, the Heartland Institute's H. Sterling Burnett explains in an audit report titled "Executive Branch Websites Promoting Global Warming Alarmism and Propaganda," that "the websites of NASA, the

National Oceanic and Atmospheric Administration, National Institutes of Health, U.S. Global Change Research Program, and the Departments of Agriculture, Defense, and Energy . . . are continuing to push false claims about climate and environmental issues, including that humans are verifiably causing dangerous climate change. Not only are these agencies failing to accurately describe the active debate concerning the causes and consequences of climate change, they are making normative claims about the past that reflect progressive and liberal value judgments concerning America's development, rather than objective scientific facts about various technological innovations and the contributions they have made toward extending human life and economic development."[29]

Given the abundance of experts and research challenging the man-made-climate-change narrative, who is Todd to throw down the gauntlet and declare the debate over? He does not have any of the background or expertise of the true professionals he dismisses as deniers. He attended college, majored in political science, and did not graduate. While in college he worked in the presidential campaign of Democratic senator Tom Harkin. He is forty-seven years old, with no credentials whatsoever in any of the climate-related sciences. Of course, Todd is not alone among journalists with thin academic records and limited experiential backgrounds. Then again, propagandizing does not require exceptional knowledge or talent.

When looking at media propaganda, it is also necessary to examine its equally deceitful and destructive close companion: "pseudo-events," or what President Trump has termed "fake news." Among the most prominent to identify and explicate this modus operandi more than half a century ago was Daniel Boorstin, a widely esteemed historian at the University of Chicago and the twelfth librarian of the United States Congress.

Writing in 1961, Boorstin observed in his book, *The Image: A Guide to Pseudo-Events in America,* "We need not be theologians to see that we have shifted responsibility for making the world interesting from God to the newspaperman. We used to believe there were only so many 'events' in the world. If there were not many intriguing or startling consequences, it was not the fault of the reporter. He could not be expected to report what did not exist. Within the last hundred years, however, and especially in the twentieth century, all this has changed. We expect the papers to be full of news. If there is no news visible to the naked eye, or to the average citizen, we still expect it to be there for the enterprising newsman. The successful reporter is one who can find a story, even if there is no earthquake or assassination or civil war. If he cannot find a story, then he must make one—by the questions he asks of public figures, by the surprising human interest he unfolds from some commonplace event, or by 'the news behind the news.' If all this fails, then he must give us a 'think piece'—an embroidering of well-known facts, or a speculation about startling things to come. . . ." This, explained Boorstin, is a new kind of "synthetic novelty which has flooded our experience"—that being "pseudo-events." "The common prefix 'pseudo' comes from the Greek word meaning false, or intended to deceive. . . ."[30]

Boorstin explained that with the advent of round-the-clock media, "[t]he news gap soon became so narrow that in order to have additional 'news' for each new edition or each new broadcast it was necessary to plan in advance the stages by which any available news would be unveiled. . . . With more space to fill, [the newsman] had to fill it ever more quickly. . . . News gathering turned into news making."[31]

Moreover, "[p]seudo-events spawn other pseudo-events in geometric progression," writes Boorstin. "This is partly because every kind of pseudo-event (being planned) tends to become ritualized, with a protocol and a rigidity all its own. As each type of pseudo-event acquires this rigidity, pressures arise to produce other, derivative forms of pseudo-events which are more fluid, more tantalizing, and more interestingly ambiguous. . . . Nowadays the test of a Washington reporter is seldom his skill at precise dramatic reporting, but more often his adeptness at dark intimation. If he wishes to keep his news channels open, he must accumulate a vocabulary and develop a style to conceal his sources and obscure the relation of a supposed event or statement to the underlying facts of life, at the same time seeming to offer hard facts. Much of his stock in trade is his own and other people's speculation about the reality of what he reports. He helps create that very obscurity without which the supposed illumination of his reports would be unnecessary. . . ."[32]

A perfect example of this process involves the so-called Russian collusion allegation—which, to summarize, started as a political accusation leveled against candidate Donald Trump by Hillary Clinton and her campaign; followed by political demands by Democratic members of the Senate and House for the appointment of a special counsel, despite the lack of any criminal prerequisite; the chorus of Democratic party-press outlets and their reporters encouraging such an appointment by promoting the demands; the actual appointment of Robert Mueller as special counsel; the countless leaks and speculation about the investigation; the indictments, plea deals, and convictions of individuals unrelated to the original allegation of "Russian collusion" and President Trump; the various investigative tributaries flowing from the Mueller investigation, including the subsequent investigation by the United States Attorney's Office for the Southern District of New York, leading to the Michael Cohen plea deal and claims of campaign violations, and now the multiple congressional investigations.

This was followed by news reports speculating about President Trump's legal peril, and implications that he would be indicted, that he was already secretly indicted, that his son Donald Jr. would be indicted, that his son-in-law Jared Kushner would be indicted, etc. The point is reached where pseudo-events, and the pseudo-news, drive the Democratic party-press and the progressive agenda, which certainly includes the removal of President Trump from office as a top priority.

In the end, the collusion story turned out to be the biggest pseudo-event and news scam perpetuated against the American people by the Democratic party-press in modern times. The special counsel's report concluded that "the investigation did not establish that members of the Trump Campaign conspired or coordinated with the Russian government in its election interference activities." Notice that the special counsel did not say that prosecutors lacked probable cause to bring charges, or that prosecutors did not believe they could secure a conviction, given the beyond-a-reasonable-doubt legal standard. The report stated emphatically that collusion could not be established. The special counsel would know. According to Attorney General William Barr, "the Special Counsel . . . employed 19 lawyers who were assisted by a team of approximately 40 FBI agents, intelligence analysts, forensic accountants, and other professional staff . . . [He] issued more than 2,800 subpoenas, executed nearly 500 search warrants, obtained more than 230 orders for communication records, issued almost 50 orders authorizing use of pen registers, made 13 request to foreign governments for evidence, and interviewed approximately 500 witnesses."[33]

Consequently, the Democratic party-press narrative that the Trump campaign colluded with the Russian government during the 2016 presidential election was a complete fabrication that consumed two and a half years of broadcast, print, and internet "reporting," twenty-four hours a day, and involved an untold number of media-inspired and media-promoted conspiracies, plots, allegations, inferences, suppositions, and conclusions.

On March 25, 2019, Newsbuster's Rich Noyes confirmed the extent of the media's saturation bombing of the public with false information about this pseudo-event with these incredible statistics: "From January 20, 2017 (Inauguration Day) through March 21, 2019 (the last night before special counsel Robert Mueller sent his report to the Attorney General), the ABC, CBS and NBC evening newscasts produced a combined 2,284 minutes of 'collusion' coverage, most of it (1,909 minutes) following Mueller's appointment on May 17, 2017. That's an average of roughly three minutes a night, every night, for an astonishing 791 days. . . . From January 1 through March 21 of this year, the spin of Trump coverage on the evening newscast has been 92% negative vs. just eight percent positive. . . ."[34]

Among the news organizations with some of the most spectacularly irresponsible reporting were the *New York Times* and the

Washington Post, both of which won a Pulitzer Prize "for scoops on links between Donald Trump's presidential campaign and Russia, the focus of an ongoing special counsel investigation into the 2016 election."[35]

New York Times executive editor Dean P. Baquet was proud of his newspaper's journalism, even after the special counsel concluded that there was no collusion. "We wrote a lot about Russia, and I have no regrets. It's not our job to determine whether or not there was illegality."[36] However, the issue is not about illegality, but the obsessive promotion and perpetuation of a pseudo-event as real news.

CNN was among the most rabid collusion hunters in the news industry. On March 26, 2019, Breitbart's Joshua Caplan reported: "Last December, CNN congressional correspondent Manu Raju reported that Wikileaks emailed Donald Trump Jr. access to information nearly two weeks prior to their public release. However, the network failed to verify the email's date—September 14, 2016—by which time the emails had already been released. In June, CNN reported that White House communications director Anthony Scaramucci was being investigated for meeting with a Russian banker ahead of President Trump's inauguration. Scaramucci denied the claim, and CNN eventually apologized for its inaccurate report. CNN executive editor Lex Harris, editor Eric Lichtblau, and journalist Thomas Frank resigned in shame over the story. Further, CNN claimed in July that Michael Cohen, President Trump's personal lawyer, was prepared to tell special counsel investigators that the president possessed advanced knowledge of the Trump Tower meeting between his son Donald Trump Jr. and a Russian lawyer, and others. Cohen's lawyer, Lanny Davis, later said CNN had 'mixed up' its facts and denied claims that Cohen had any such knowledge about the meeting."[37]

Nonetheless, CNN's President, Jeffrey Zucker, self-righteously declared: "We are not investigators. We are journalists, and our role is to report the facts as we know them, which is exactly what we did. A sitting president's own Justice Department investigated his campaign for collusion with a hostile nation. That's not enormous because the media says so. That's enormous because it's unprecedented."[38] But CNN repeatedly reported not facts but fiction.

Indeed, the media wagons began to circle, again, as a growing number of media executives, journalists, and commentators shamelessly pushed back against their critics. For example, on March 25, 2019, while appearing on the *View*, ABC News chief White House correspondent John Karl asserted that ". . . I think there are some questions that need to be asked. I think there were significant mistakes in some of the reporting. But I also think this is a huge story. This is the most significant investigation of a president since Watergate. The allegations couldn't have been more high-stakes, the idea of a foreign power potentially colluding with a presidential candidate. Now, it turned out that was not the case, but there were significant steps along the way. There was a major criminal investigation here. How could reporters not cover that and cover it aggressively and consistently?"[39]

Perhaps the best answer was provided by Fox News senior political analyst and former ABC News chief White House correspondent Brit Hume. On March 25, 2019, during an appearance on Fox, Hume declared: "If you think about it . . . this investigation actually goes back to about the middle of 2016, so it's been going on for quite a long time and this endless speculation about it and indeed the accusations about it that came out of many mouths on cable television and in the public prints, the list of people who got it wrong is really quite extensive. And, you know, to include many news organizations that got the prospect of Donald Trump being elected in the first place badly wrong and seemed not to learn very much from that. One hopes, and expects, perhaps, that after this debacle, and that's exactly what it is, in the worst journalistic de-bacle of my lifetime, that there'll be some serious soul searching. Unfortunately . . . I'm not seeing a lot of it. I noticed that a couple of our cable news competitors have moved on, kind of, seamlessly on to speculation about obstruction of justice now, following as they so often seem to do, the Democratic party script."[40]

Having learned nothing, and not interested in changing course, the Democratic party-press looks for new opportunities to cre-ate pseudo-events, as one event spawns another event. Again, as Boorstin stated, these events become "ritualized, with a protocol and rigidity all [their] own."[41] Indeed, the media turned to ques-tioning Attorney General Barr's motives, running stories based on anonymous sources about dissension on the special counsel's staff, treating a PR stunt—a legally baseless subpoena issued by House Democrats for an unredacted copy of the Mueller report—as breaking news, etc.

More broadly, the media inundate the public with "news" stories based on claims, speculation, and spin from "anonymous sources," or "unattributed sources," or "leaks" that typically sup-port and promote their narrative. Nearly entire books critical of the president and his management style, including by investiga-tive journalist Bob Woodward, rely heavily on anonymous sources. Frequently the books and their authors are themselves treated as newsworthy and receive considerable subsequent "news" coverage. Meanwhile, the public is unable to rationally judge the authenticity of these reports and books because they are unable to take the measure of those who are supposedly providing the information to the journalists and authors, and whether they are reliable, disgruntled, have an ax to grind, etc.

In fact, on September 5, 2018, the *New York Times* published an opinion-piece authored by "Anonymous" titled, "I Am Part of the Resistance Inside the Trump Administration—I work for the president but like-minded colleagues and I have vowed to thwart part of his agenda and his worst inclinations." The *Times* explained its extraordinary decision, stating: "The Times is taking the rare step of publishing an anonymous Op-Ed essay. We have done so at the request of the author, a senior official in the Trump administration whose identity is known to us and whose job would be jeopardized by its disclosure. We believe publishing this essay anonymously is the only way to deliver an important perspective to our readers."[42]

Here is a sample of the anonymous author's assertions:

- The dilemma—which [the president] does not fully grasp—is that many of the senior officials in his own administration are working diligently from within to frustrate parts of his agenda and his worst inclinations.
- But we believe our first duty is to this country, and the president continues to act in a manner that is detrimental to the health of our republic.
- The root of the problem is the president's amorality. Anyone who works with him knows he is not moored to any discernible first principles that guide his decision making.

- Given the instability many witnessed, there were early whispers within the cabinet of invoking the 25th Amendment, which would start a complex process for removing the president. But no one wanted to precipitate a constitutional crisis. So we will do what we can to steer the administration in the right direction until—one way or another—it's over.

- The bigger concern is not what Mr. Trump has done to the presidency but rather what we as a nation have allowed him to do to us. We have sunk low with him and allowed our discourse to be stripped of civility.[43]

From the moment the *Times* published the op-ed and for weeks thereafter, this single individual's unsigned opinion-essay, disputed on the substance and on the record by several current and former Trump White House officials, was the subject of extravagant, baying "news" coverage. This is exactly what the *Times* editors had hoped for, and the rest of the Democratic party-press was more than happy to oblige.

A pseudo-event gone wild.

Boorstin described another pseudo-event spectacle—the making of the newsman's public persona. "At first it may seem strange that the rise of pseudo-events has coincided with the growth of the professional ethic which obliges newsmen to omit editorializing and personal judgments from their news accounts. But now it is in the making of pseudo-events that newsmen find ample scope for their individuality and creative imagination."[44]

CNN's chief White House correspondent, Jim Acosta, fits this characterization well. On November 7, 2018, the nation witnessed Acosta's attempt to hijack the presidential press conference and use his position in the press to argue with President Trump about the thousands of illegal aliens headed in an organized march to the southern U.S. border. Acosta did not ask actual questions. He made assertions in the form of questions, and he did so repeatedly, refusing to give up the microphone. He was rude to the president and his press colleagues. Moreover, when arguing with the president, he was wrong on essential facts.

At the outset, Acosta provocatively confronted the president:

"I wanted to challenge you on one of the statements that you made in the tail end of the campaign in the midterms that . . ."

President Barack Obama was never addressed this way by the Democratic party-press at any of his presidential press conferences. In fact, there is no reason for any journalist to behave this way with a president during a press conference. Just ask the question respectfully.

Acosta then essentially accused the president of lying and race-baiting:

ACOSTA: . . . that this caravan was an invasion. As you know, Mr. President . . .

TRUMP: I consider it to be an invasion.

ACOSTA: As you know, Mr. President, the caravan was not an invasion. It's a group of migrants moving up from Central America towards the border with the U.S. And . . .

TRUMP: Thank you for telling me that. I appreciate it.

ACOSTA: . . . why did you characterize it as such?

TRUMP: Because I consider it an invasion. You and I have a difference of opinion.

ACOSTA: But do you think that you demonized immigrants in this election to try to keep . . .[45]

At the time, Acosta had not covered, in person, the illegal-alien march to the border; their arrival later in Tijuana and the turmoil that transpired there;[46] nor did he investigate the organizations and funding sources for the march.[47] Acosta knew no more than the public and less than those who had actually done real reporting. Nor did Acosta have the information provided to the presidents on a daily basis by the Department of Homeland Security.

By his insolent and theatrical conduct at this presidential press conference, which is consistent with his conduct at most press conferences, he created a pseudo-event starring himself, which neither informed nor benefited the public, but resulted in subsequent pseudo-events when his press pass was pulled by the White House and CNN went to court to retrieve it with the support of most of the other media. Moreover, recent events on the border, with unprecedented numbers of migrants pouring into the United States, overwhelming law enforcement, administrative courts, and detention centers, underscores just how wrong Acosta was.

Acosta's antics have also made him a favorite on the late-night show circuit, where he is treated like a Hollywood celebrity.

Acosta then secured a book deal with HarperCollins Publishers. He was paid to dish on the president and his staff, collecting information and writing notes for his book while reporting on the White House for CNN. Is there any doubt that Acosta's confrontations and tone with the president and his staff were, at least in part, premeditated, for the purpose of providing fodder for his book?

Is that how news reporting is supposed to work?

How does this benefit or serve the American people?

The Acosta book's title is *The Enemy of the People: A Dangerous Time to Tell the Truth in America*. According to the publisher's press release, it provides "never before revealed stories of his

White House's rejection of truth, while laying out the stakes for how Trump's hostility toward facts poses an unprecedented threat to our democracy."[48]

In further hype for Acosta's book, the press release exclaimed: "The president and his team, not to mention some of his supporters, have attempted to silence the press in ways we have never seen before. As just about everybody has seen, I witnessed this first-hand. As difficult as that challenge may be for the free press in America, we must continue to do our jobs and report the news. The truth is worth the fight."[49]

Acosta is illustrative of a media mentality, filled with self-promotion and near-hysterical claims and spin, intended to draw attention to one's self, to highlight a particular event or agenda, and to make news. Even the press release is laced with propaganda and preposterous allegations, including Acosta's self-aggrandizing assertion that there have been "unprecedented" attempts by the Trump administration to silence the press. [See chapter 4, which addresses such propaganda.]

What, therefore, have the modern media and present-day journalists created? Boorstin argued that having discarded the journalism of objective truth, "[i]n a democratic society like ours—and more especially in a highly literate, wealthy, competitive, and technologically advanced society—the people can be flooded by pseudo-events. For us, freedom of speech and of the press and of broadcasting includes freedom to create pseudo-events. Competing politicians, competing newsmen, and competing news media contend in this creation. They vie with one another in offering attractive, 'informative' accounts and images of the world. They are free to speculate on facts, to bring new facts into being, to demand answers to their own contrived questions. Our 'free market place of ideas' is a place where people are confronted by competing pseudo-events and are allowed to judge among them. When we speak of 'informing' the people this is what we really mean."[50]

Consequently, Boorstin maintained, we spend much of our waking hours living in a world of unreality fashioned by, among others, the press: "The American citizen thus lives in a world where fantasy is more real than reality, where the image has more dignity than its original. We hardly dare face our bewilderment because our ambiguous experience is so pleasantly iridescent, and the solace of belief in contrived reality is so thoroughly real. We have become eager accessories to the great hoaxes of the age. These are the hoaxes we play on ourselves."[51]

Boorstin astutely advised: "What ails us most is not what we have done with America, but what we have substituted for America. We suffer primarily not from our vices or weaknesses, but from our illusions. We are haunted, not by reality, but by those images we have put in place of reality. To discover our illusion will not solve the problems of our world. But if we do not discover them, we will never discover our real problems. To dispel the ghosts which populate the world of our making will not give us the power to conquer the real enemies of the real world or to remake the real world. But it may help us discover that we cannot make the world in our image. It will liberate us and sharpen our vision. It will clear away the fog so we can face the world we share with all mankind."[52]

Good advice, but is there any indication that the Democratic party-press will accept it? Not yet. They continue on a destructive course.

Indeed, when their reporting is challenged, these same media groups and reporters respond to criticism by insisting it is *they* who are the guardians of freedom of the press. "That was once an institution preserved in the interest of the community," wrote Boorstin. "Now it is often a euphemism for the prerogative of reporters to produce their synthetic commodity."[53]

In addition to the routine use of propaganda and the dissemination of pseudo-events, the media also engage in another form of manipulation: self-censorship and outright suppression of information or events to advance a narrative or kill actual news. Two particularly hideous examples of this dishonest practice involved the real-time evidence in the 1930s and 1940s of the Nazis' liquidation of Europe's Jews and in the early 1930s of the Stalin regime's starvation of the Ukrainians.

As hard as it may be to believe, most of the American press, led by the *New York Times*, consciously downplayed or ignored the Holocaust and the Holodomor. Therefore, for some time most Americans were oblivious to what was taking place.

===

SIX

THE *NEW YORK TIMES*
BETRAYS MILLIONS

BRITISH JOURNALIST CLAUD Cockburn once wrote: "All stories are written backwards—they are supposed to begin with the facts and develop from there, but in reality, they begin with a journalist's point of view, a conception, and it is the point of view from which the facts are subsequently organized...."[1]

And so it was when it came to reporting about the Holocaust, where, among other things, journalistic groupthink and other professional malpractices—suppression and outright self-censorship—came together to create a monumental betrayal of millions of European Jews and the American public, and in what was the greatest example of American media recklessness and deceit ever perpetrated by the press.

In 1984, Dr. David S. Wyman, in his book *The Abandonment*

of the Jews, explained that "[o]ne reason ordinary Americans were not more responsive to the plight of European Jews [during the Holocaust] was that very many (probably a majority) were unaware of Hitler's extermination program until well into 1944 or later. The information was not readily available to the public, because the mass media treated the systematic murder of millions of Jews as though it were minor news."[2]

Yet, on November 24, 1942, unambiguous evidence of the Nazis' ongoing extermination of European Jews was made publicly available, but was largely ignored by the media. "Lack of solid press coverage in the weeks immediately following [November 24] . . . muffled the historic news at the outset."[3]

In fact, newly released documents prove that the Allied powers knew firsthand of the mass murder of Jews by December 1942. As first reported on April 18, 2017, by the *Independent,* a British newspaper: "Newly accessed material from the United Nations—not seen for around 70 years—shows that as early as December 1942, the US, UK and Soviet governments were aware that at least two million Jews had been murdered and a further five million were at risk of being killed, and were preparing charges. Despite this, the Allied Powers did very little to try and rescue or provide sanctuary to those in mortal danger. . . . In late December 1942 . . . UK Foreign Secretary Anthony Eden told the British parliament: 'The German authorities, not content with denying to persons of Jewish race in all the territories over which their barbarous rule extends, the most elementary human rights, are now carrying into effect Hitler's oft-repeated intention to exterminate the Jewish people.'"[4]

In the United States, Wyman asserted, "two or three clear statements from Franklin Roosevelt would have moved this news into public view and kept it there for some time. But the president was not so inclined, nor did Washington reporters press him. In retrospect, it seems almost unbelievable that in Roosevelt's press conferences (normally held twice a week) not one word was spoken about the mass killing of European Jews until almost a year later. The President had nothing to say to reporters on the matter, and no correspondent asked him about it."[5]

Roosevelt and his State Department—which was populated with several individuals who were, at a minimum, "indifferent" to the fate of the European Jews and others who were flat-out anti-Semites—did not want to draw attention to the Holocaust. Roosevelt was assisted in this policy by the American press. For most of the war, news outlets and journalists censored information about the ongoing extermination of Jews or hid the information in infrequent and sporadic reports among voluminous other news stories. "Most newspapers printed very little about the Holocaust," wrote Wyman, "even though extensive information on it [eventually] reached their desks from news services (AP, UP, and others) and from their own correspondents. . . ."[6]

Surely the *New York Times*, with its wide reach, resources, access to foreign sources of information, reputation as the foremost newspaper in the country, large Jewish readership, and its Jewish ownership, would do everything possible to investigate and disclose the horrors of Jewish genocide. But the opposite was true. Wyman explained that "[t]he *Times*, Jewish-owned but anxious not to be seen as Jewish-oriented, was the premier American newspaper of the era. It printed a substantial amount of information on Holocaust-related events but almost always buried it on the inner pages. . . ." And the *Washington Post*? "The Jewish-owned

Washington Post printed a few editorials advocating rescue, but only infrequently carried news reports on the European Jewish situation. The other Washington newspapers provided similarly limited information on the mass murder of European Jewry."[7] And most of the other press? "Outside New York and Washington, press coverage was even thinner. All major newspapers carried some Holocaust-related news, but it appeared infrequently and almost always in small items located on inside pages. . . . American mass-circulation magazines all but ignored the Holocaust. . . . Radio coverage of Holocaust news was sparse."[8]

Emory University professor Deborah E. Lipstadt, in her book *Beyond Belief*, saw the media's self-censorship during the Holocaust as a broadly institutional problem. She wrote that "the press bears a great measure of responsibility for the public's skepticism and ignorance of the scope of the wartime tragedy [the Nazi mass murder of Jews]. The public's doubts were strengthened and possibly even created by the manner in which the media told the story. If the press did not help plant the seeds of doubt in readers' minds, it did little to eradicate them. During the war journalists frequently said that the news of deportations and executions did not come from eyewitnesses who could personally confirm what had happened and they, as journalists, were obliged to treat it skeptically. This explanation is faulty because much of the information came from German statements, broadcasts, and newspapers. If anything, these sources would have been inclined to deny, not verify, the news. Neutral sources also affirmed the reliability of reports. Moreover, even when the press did encounter witnesses, it often dismissed what they had to say because there were not considered 'reliable' or 'impartial.'"[9]

Certainly by 1943 (and we now know by 1942), wrote Lipstadt, "the Nazi threat to 'exterminate' the Jews should have been understood as a literal one. There was little reason, in light of the abundance of evidence, to deny that multitudes were being murdered as part of a planned program of annihilation. But despite all the details there was a feeling among some correspondents, *New York Times* reporter Bill Lawrence most prominent among them, that the reports that Hitler and his followers had conducted a systematic extermination campaign were untrue. Lawrence did not doubt that Hitler had 'treated the Jews badly, forcing many of them to flee to the sanctuaries of the West'; but even in October 1943—ten months after the Allied declaration confirming the Nazi policy of exterminating the Jews . . .—he could not believe that the Nazis had murdered 'millions of Jews, Slavs, gypsies. . . . And those who might be mentally retarded.'"[10]

Lipstadt's research also found that for much of the war, the Roosevelt administration whitewashed or deemphasized the Nazi eradication of Jews, and the mass media were compliant, regurgitating the government's propaganda or suppressing the evidence. Lipstadt explained that "[t]he Office of War Information, working in tandem with the [Roosevelt] Administration, tried to severely limit any public attention paid to [the mass murder of the Jews]. Despite the fact that the Final Solution was the prime illustration of the enemy's 'strategy and principles,' the Office of War Information wanted it to be avoided by news agencies and not mentioned in war propaganda. . . . The press mirrored the official policy of omitting mention of Jews or incorporating them into the general suffering faced by many other national groups. . . ."[11]

When Winston Churchill, Franklin Roosevelt, and Joseph Stalin issued a formal declaration condemning Nazi atrocities, they were calculatedly silent about the active eradication of the Jews. Lipstadt emphasized: "Probably the most outrageous example of this explicit policy of ignoring the Jewish aspect of the tragedy occurred in Moscow in the fall of 1943. There, Churchill, Roosevelt, and Stalin met and affixed their signature to what is known as the Moscow Declaration,"[12] which warned:

> Germans who take part in the wholesale shooting of Italian officers or in the execution of French, Dutch, Belgian or Norwegian hostages or of the Cretan peasants, or who have shared in slaughters inflicted on the people of Poland or in the territories of the Soviet Union . . . will be brought back to the scene of their crimes and judged on the spot by the peoples whom they have outraged.[13]

"Nowhere in the declaration were the Jews even obliquely mentioned," Lipstadt noted, "a phenomenon the press simply ignored."[14]

Shockingly, the media's cover-up continued nearly up to the war's conclusion. Lipstadt wrote that "[e]ven when the war had virtually ended and the [death] camps were being liberated, reporters continued to incorporate the fate of the Jews into that of all other national groups that had been incarcerated and murdered at the camps" for the purpose of minimizing the targeted atrocities against the Jews and Hitler's Final Solution.[15]

Taking direct aim at the *New York Times*, Professor Laurel Leff of Northeastern University, formerly a journalist, meticulously scrutinized not only the role of the media generally during the

Holocaust, but the *Times* in particular. She has written extensively about "how the *New York Times* failed in its coverage of the fate of European Jews from 1939 to 1945."[16] In her book *Buried by the* Times, she asks: "What was it about prevailing press standards and the policies and personalities at the *Times* that led the nation's most important newspaper to discount one of the century's most important news stories? . . . The *Times* was unique . . . in the comprehensiveness of its coverage and the extent of its influence among American opinion makers. . . . Because of its long-time commitment to international affairs, and its willingness to sacrifice advertising rather than articles in the face of a newsprint crunch, and its substantial Jewish readership, the *Times* was able to obtain and publish more news than other mainstream newspapers. The way the *Times* published that news also had a disproportionate impact on both policy makers and fellow journalists who considered it the newspaper of record. That the *Times* was owned by Jews of German ancestry, who would seemingly be more sensitive to the plight of their European brethren, further magnified the *Times*' critical role in shaping contemporaneous coverage of the Holocaust."[17]

Leff then makes this damning disclosure: "The *Times*' judgment that the murder of millions of Jews was a relatively unimportant story reverberated among other journalists trying to assess the news, among Jewish groups trying to arouse public opinion, and among government leaders trying to decide on an American response."[18]

The *Times*' publisher, Arthur Hays Sulzberger, intentionally and repeatedly buried news about the Holocaust deep within his paper, or ignored it altogether. Leff writes, "Although the war was the dominant news, it need not have been, and was not, the only front-page news. The *New York Times* printed between 12 and 15 front-page stories every day. Fewer than half of these typically concerned the war. . . . The *Times*' first story on the Nazi extermination campaign, which described it as 'the greatest mass slaughter in history,' appeared on page five, tacked onto the bottom of a column of stories. Yet, the deaths of other civilians, often fewer than 100, regularly appeared on the front page."[19]

Sulzberger's personal philosophical views of Judaism also played a major part in his callous disengagement from the plight of the European Jews. "In the case of . . . Sulzberger," writes Leff, "concerns about special pleading and dual loyalties were not purely a pragmatic calculation. They also reflected a deeply felt religious and philosophical belief that made Sulzberger resistant to changing his views in the light of changing circumstances. Being Jewish was solely a religious, not a racial or ethnic orientation, he maintained, that carried with it no special obligation to help fellow Jews. As anti-Semitism intensified in Germany, and to a lesser extent in America, he protested—a bit too vigorously perhaps— that Jews were just like any other citizen. They should not be persecuted as Jews, but they should not be rescued as Jews either. In fact, American Jews who helped other Jews because they were Jews threatened to undercut their position as Americans, Sulzberger believed. The *Times* publisher thus was philosophically opposed to emphasizing the unique plight of the Jews in occupied Europe, a conviction that at least partially explains the *Times*' tendency to place stories about Jews inside the paper, and to universalize their plight [that is, not identifying them specifically] in editorials and front page stories."[20]

Incredibly, Sulzberger's personal dislike of certain Jewish leaders and opposition to their efforts to establish a Jewish state in the original Jewish homeland further soured him and, hence, the *Times'* coverage of the Holocaust. Leff wrote that "Sulzberger's involvement with the American Jewish community also led him to be less inclined to emphasize the Jews' fate. His antipathy for Jewish leaders in the United States and Palestine tempered somewhat his sympathy for persecuted Jews in Europe."[21] Sulzberger's opposition to a Jewish state in Palestine "drew the publisher into fierce, public fights with American Jewry's top leaders that colored his views not only of their activities on behalf of a Jewish state, but also of other efforts on behalf of European Jews. . . ."[22]

Indeed, Leff's research, like that of Wyman and Lipstadt, found that the *Times* and the media overall withheld or buried much of what they knew about the Holocaust from the American public. "The way the press in general and the *Times* in particular presented the facts played an important role in creating the gap between information and action. . . . The way the *Times* and the rest of the mass media told the story of the Holocaust engendered no chance of arousing public opinion. . . . [T]he *Times* never treated the news of the Holocaust as important—or at least as important as, say, informing motorists to visit the Office of Price Administration if they did not have their automobile registration number and state written on their gasoline ration coupons. A story about that possible bureaucratic snafu appears on the front page on March 2, 1944, the same day that the 'last voice from the abyss' was relegated to page four."[23]

Moreover, it deserves emphasizing that the Roosevelt administration, and its determination to censor news directly related to the plight of the Jews, was a key factor in influencing how the press behaved. "[T]he government did not have to give publishers' and editors' special instructions. The government influenced the coverage by directing the flow of information, issuing statements about certain subjects, keeping quiet about others, playing up parts of the war, and downplaying others. A press corps that tended to define news as government actions would have gone along. The government's message that nothing special should be done to save the Jews also found a receptive journalistic audience."[24] At the *Times*, "[t]he second most influential *Times*man on political issues went a step further; Washington Bureau Chief and columnist Arthur Krock allied himself with the forces in the State Department working hardest to stifle any rescue efforts. . . ."[25]

On November 14, 2001, before the release of Leff's book, but several years after the publication of Wyman's and Lipstadt's books, Max Frankel, who had worked for the *New York Times* for fifty years and served as executive editor from 1986 to 1994, penned an opinion piece in the *Times* titled "150th Anniversary: 1851–2001; Turning Away from the Holocaust." It appears to be the first attempted thoroughgoing engagement by the *Times* of its "staggering, staining failure . . . to depict Hitler's methodical extermination of the Jews of Europe as a horror beyond all other horrors in World War II—a Nazi war within the war crying out for illumination."[26]

Frankel asked: "Why, then, were the terrifying tales almost hidden in the back pages? Like most—though not all—American media, and most of official Washington, the *Times* drowned its reports about the fate of the Jews in the flood of wartime news. . . . Only six times in nearly six years did the *Times*'s front page mention Jews as Hitler's unique target for total annihilation. Only once was their fate the subject of a lead editorial. Only twice did their rescue inspire passionate cries in the Sunday magazine."[27]

Obviously, Frankel had read the scholarly research presented by, among others, Wyman and Lipstadt (he acknowledged the latter), stating that "[t]his reticence has been a subject of extensive scholarly inquiry and also much speculation and condemnation." He goes on: critics have blamed "'self-hating Jews' and 'anti-Zionists' among the paper's owners and staff. Defenders have cited the sketchiness of much information about the death camps in Eastern Europe and also the inability of prewar generations to fully comprehend the industrial gassing of millions of innocents by those chilling mounds of Jews' bones, hair, shoes, rings."[28]

Frankel goes through most of the various scenarios already presented by the earlier authors, noting that "[n]o single explanation seems to suffice for what was surely the century's biggest journalistic failure." But he also draws attention to some of the articles the *Times* did run "[o]n its dense inside pages." Nonetheless, Frankel points out, "No article about the Jews' plight ever qualified as the *Times'* leading story of the day, or as a major event of a week or year. The ordinary reader of its pages could hardly be blamed for failing to comprehend the enormity of the Nazis' crime."[29]

Frankel concluded his piece by assuring readers that the Sulzberger family and the *News York Times* corporation had learned their lessons: "After the Nazis' slaughter of the Jews was fully exposed at war's end, Iphigene Ochs Sulzberger, the influential daughter, wife and mother of *Times* publishers, changed her mind about the need for a Jewish state and helped her husband, Arthur Hays Sulzberger, accept the idea of Israel and befriended its leaders. Later, led by their son, Arthur Ochs Sulzberger, and their grandson, Arthur Sulzberger, Jr., the *Times* shed its insensitivity about its Jewish roots, allowed Jews to ascend to the editor's chair and warmly supported Israel in many editorials."[30]

But the Sulzbergers knew far more than Frankel suggests in this vague and self-serving declaration. He failed to mention a rather pertinent fact raised in a paper published by the Shorenstein Center: "[W]hile downplaying in the *Times* to a ludicrous degree the Jewish identity of the victims of some Nazi horrors (an editorial about the Warsaw Ghetto uprising somehow managed to omit that it was a ghetto of Jews), Arthur and Iphigene worked diligently to help distant relatives still in Germany emigrate to the United States. They surely understood these people were in danger from Hitler because of something more than their 'choice' to subscribe to the Jewish, rather than say, the Lutheran, religion." Therefore, the *Times* publisher and his wife knew well of the dire plight of the European Jews from their own personal information and personal actions and still downplayed the Holocaust in real time and opposed efforts to establish a Jewish state.[31]

Indeed, the Zionist movement had been under way since at least the late nineteenth century. The *Times* published throughout this period. At the end of World War II and after the death of Roosevelt, in 1945 the United States endorsed the establishment of a Jewish state; after decades of war, the state of Israel was founded by the Jewish people on May 14, 1948. All of this came together no thanks to the reporting of the *Times* and the directives of the Sulzberger family but in spite of them.

Frankel ended his piece with an assurance to the readers: "And to this day the failure of America's media to fasten upon Hitler's mad atrocities stirs the conscience of succeeding generations of

reporters and editors. It has made them acutely alert to ethnic bar-
barities in far-off places like Uganda, Rwanda, Bosnia and Kosovo.
It leaves them obviously resolved that in the face of genocide, journalism shall not have failed in vain."[32]

In significant ways, however, the attitudes and even antipathy
prevalent at the *Times*, in many newsrooms, and among many
journalists and commentators during that period do not appear
to have substantially receded. In fact, since the Israelis won the
Six-Day War in 1967, demonstrating that they can and will successfully fight for their survival, Israel has been their regular target.

For example, on June 1, 2006, former New York City mayor Ed
Koch wrote an opinion piece in the *Times* titled "The New York
Times' Anti-Israel Bias," asserting that "[t]he British Broadcasting
Corporation and *The New York Times* consistently carry news stories and editorials that are slanted against Israel and sympathetic to
the Palestinian Authority and Hamas." Koch eviscerated the *Times*:
"What idiocy on the part of the *Times*. Of course, the Palestinian
people should be punished for their election decision [the election
of the terrorist group Hamas as the governing authority in Gaza].
That same view—not to criticize or take action—was in vogue in
1932 and thereafter following Hitler's democratic victory in Germany when he became the lawful Chancellor of the German government and began his war against the Jews and later the nations
of Europe. Had the German nation been criticized and punished
for electing Hitler in 1932, the world may have been spared the
slaughter by the Nazis of 50 million people including six million
Jews. All of this historical background was ignored by the *Times*
and it was ignored by the BBC anchor in his commentary when
he simply stated, 'Israel has not recognized the new Hamas gov-

ernment and Hamas does not recognize the existence of Israel.'"
Koch finished his piece with this: "In the 1930s and '40s, the critical failure of *The Times*, reported on and acknowledged by *The
Times* after World War II, was its omission to adequately report on
the murderous war against the Jews undertaken by Hitler and his
Nazi government." "In my opinion, *The Times*, editorially, is back
to where it was in the '30s and '40s—unconcerned with Hamas'
stated goal of destroying the Jewish nation."[33]

Matti Friedman, a former Associated Press correspondent who
covered Israel for a time, explained the modus operandi of most
of her former journalist colleagues when reporting about Israel.
On November 30, 2014, she wrote an article in the *Atlantic* titled
"What the Media Gets Wrong About Israel—The news tells us less
about Israel than about the people writing the news, a former AP
reporter says." Friedman wrote: "Journalistic decisions are made
by people who exist in a particular social milieu, one which, like
most social groups, involves a certain uniformity of attitude, behavior, and even dress (the fashion these days, for those interested,
is less vests with unnecessary pockets than shirts with unnecessary
buttons). These people know each other, meet regularly, exchange
information, and closely watch one another's work. This helps explain why a reader looking at articles written by the half-dozen
biggest news providers in the region on a particular day will find
that though the pieces are composed and edited by completely different people and organizations, they tend to tell the same story."[34]

Sound familiar? So does this: "In these circles, in my experience," writes Friedman, "a distaste for Israel has come to be something between an acceptable prejudice and a prerequisite for entry.
I don't mean a critical approach to Israeli policies or to the ham-

fisted government currently in charge in this country, but a belief that to some extent the Jews of Israel are a symbol of the world's ills, particularly those connected to nationalism, militarism, colonialism, and racism—an idea quickly becoming one of the central elements of the 'progressive' Western *zeitgeist*, spreading from the European left to American college campuses and intellectuals, including journalists. In this social group, this sentiment is translated into editorial decisions made by individual reporters and editors covering Israel, and this, in turn, gives such thinking the means of mass self-replication."[35]

Have you ever wondered how the terrorist group Hamas receives so much favorable coverage in the American and international press? Friedman explains: "Most consumers of the Israel story don't understand how the story is manufactured. But Hamas does. Since assuming power in Gaza in 2007, the Islamic Resistance Movement has come to understand that many reporters are committed to a narrative wherein Israelis are oppressors and Palestinians passive victims with reasonable goals, and are uninterested in contradictory information. Recognizing this, certain Hamas spokesmen have taken to confiding to Western journalists, including some I know personally, that the group is in fact a secretly pragmatic outfit with bellicose rhetoric, and journalists—eager to believe the confession, and sometimes unwilling to credit locals with the smarts necessary to deceive them—have taken it as a scoop instead of as spin."[36]

Once again, the media are complicit in suppressing news and promoting propaganda, as Koch had complained. "In Gaza, this goes from being a curious detail of press psychology to a major deficiency," writes Friedman. "Hamas's strategy is to provoke a response from Israel by attacking from behind the cover of Palestinian civilians, thus drawing Israeli strikes that kill those civilians, and then to have the casualties filmed by one of the world's largest press contingents, with the understanding that the resulting outrage abroad will blunt Israel's response. This is a ruthless strategy, and an effective one. It is predicated on the cooperation of journalists. One of the reasons it works is because of the reflex I mentioned. If you report that Hamas has a strategy based on co-opting the media, this raises several difficult questions, like, What exactly is the relationship between the media and Hamas? And has this relationship corrupted the media?"[37]

As recently as May 2018, the media reporting on Hamas's aggressions against Israel was so distorted that America's ambassador to Israel, David Friedman, felt compelled to publicly author an opinion piece condemning the press. He wrote, in part, that "[f]or weeks, Hamas had been pursuing a direct and unambiguous operation against Israel: On Fridays, after stirring up emotions at weekly prayers, it incited waves of Gaza residents to violently storm the border with Israel, hoping to break through and kill Israeli citizens and kidnap Israeli soldiers. In addition, given the likelihood that these malign efforts would fail, Hamas also created 'kite bombs' painted with swastikas that it launched in Israel's direction when the winds were favorable. Some 60 Gazans, the overwhelming majority of whom were known Hamas terrorists, lost their lives because Hamas turned them into a collective suicide bomb. They were neither heroes nor the peaceful protesters they were advertised to be. At least not before the liberal media entered the scene."[38]

Ambassador Friedman was so disgusted with the newsroom antics and dishonesty, he blew the whistle on them. "Desperate for a narrative to discredit the president's decision to move our embassy to Jerusalem, they broadcast the opening ceremony on a split screen simultaneously displaying the Gaza riots, and condemned the insensitivity of the ceremony's participants to the carnage that seemed next door on TV *but which in actuality was occurring 60 miles away*! The next day, the liberal media vilified everyone associated with the embassy move and glorified the poor Hamas terrorists. Failed diplomats who never brought peace or stability to the region were pulled out of mothballs to regurgitate their calcified thinking. And the most deranged even accused the administration of having blood on its hands. Tellingly, not a single pundit offered a less-lethal alternative to protecting Israel from being overrun by killers or its soldiers from being within range of pistols, IEDs or Molotov cocktails."[39]

On Christmas Eve in 2018, the *Times* published as news an event by the Lebanon-based Iranian-backed terrorist group Hezbollah, intended to portray the killers in a "Kumbaya" moment. It was a perfect piece of propaganda. The *Times* "news" story set the stage this way:

> The Iranian cultural attaché stepped up to the microphone on a stage flanked by banners bearing the faces of Iran's two foremost religious authorities: Ayatollah Khomeini, founder of the Islamic Republic, and Ayatollah Khamenei, the current supreme leader.
>
> To the left of Ayatollah Khomeini stood a twinkling Christmas tree, a gold star gilding its tip. Angel ornaments and miniature Santa hats nestled among its branches. Fake snow dusted fake pine needles.

"Today, we're celebrating the birth of Christ," the cultural attaché, Mohamed Mehdi Shari'tamdar, announced into the microphone, "and also the 40th anniversary of the Islamic Revolution."

"Hallelujah!" boomed another speaker, Elias Hachem, reciting a poem he had written for the event. "Jesus the savior is born. The king of peace, the son of Mary. He frees the slaves. He heals. The angels protect him. The Bible and the Quran embrace."

"We're celebrating a rebel," proclaimed a third speaker, the new mufti of the Shiite Muslims of Lebanon, the rebel in question being Jesus.

The mufti, Ahmed Kabalan, went on to engage in some novel religious and political thinking: Christians and Muslims, he said, "are one family, against corruption, with social justice, against authority, against Israel, with the Lebanese Army and with the resistance."[40]

Thus Hezbollah compares its wanton terrorist bloodlust against the Jews with the life of Jesus and the birth of Christianity. And the mufti's "novel religious and political thinking" is not novel at all. It is a purposeful act of propaganda aimed at the *Times* and its ilk, and it works. The *Times* editorialized favorably within its news column.

Later, the *Times* took a slap at the U.S. government's designating Hezbollah as a terrorist organization, and wrote of Hezbollah's earlier acts of religious tolerance toward Christians. "Even Hezbollah, the Shiite political movement and militia that the United States has branded a terrorist organization, has helped ring in the season. In previous years, it imported a Santa to Beirut's southern suburbs to distribute gifts. On Saturday, Hezbollah representatives were on hand for the Iranian Christmas concert, an event that also featured handicrafts by Iranian artists, but the organization skipped Santa this year because of financial constraints."[41] Then, in a preposterous explanation, the *Times* declared, with the help of "analysts," that Hezbollah is preaching unity and is a legitimate political entity. "These demonstrations of Christmas spirit seem intended, analysts said, to demonstrate Hezbollah's inclusivity as a major political and military force in Lebanese society and to highlight its political alliances with Christian parties."[42]

But Hezbollah is none of these things. As the Counter Extremism Project has stated: "Like Iran, Hezbollah considers the United States and Israel to be its chief enemies, which has led to a global terrorist campaign against the two nations. Until September 11, 2001, Hezbollah was responsible for killing more Americans than any other terrorist organization. Among other deadly attacks, Hezbollah has been linked to the 1983 attack on U.S. Marine barracks in Lebanon; the 1992 suicide bombing at the Israeli embassy in Buenos Aires, Argentina; the 1994 suicide bombing of the Argentine Jewish Mutual Association in Buenos Aires; and, the 2012 bombing of an Israeli tourist bus in Bulgaria. Hezbollah is also suspected of involvement in the February 2005 Beirut suicide bombing that killed 23 people, including former Lebanese Prime Minister Rafik Hariri."[43]

The examples of the *Times'* and mass media's hostility toward the Jewish state is not even a matter of indifference, as it was during the plight of European Jews in the 1930s and 1940s, which was horrifying. Instead there is frequently open and affirmative hostility toward the Jewish state, despite the fact that the small country, a democracy and ally, faces daily threats of extermination from terrorist groups and surrounding terrorist states, including if not especially nuclear-weapons-obsessed Iran. After examining more than a year's worth of recent coverage by the *Times*, Gilead Ini of the Committee for Accuracy in Middle East Reporting in America (CAMERA) concluded that the *Times* "consistently flouts the rules of ethical journalism. And it does so as part of a campaign to protect anti-Israel activists and steer public opinion against the Jewish state."[44]

However, unbelievably, for the *New York Times* and other newsrooms the effective cover-up of the Holocaust was not the first time they knowingly censored the horrors of genocide while it was occurring. From approximately 1932 to 1933, Soviet dictator Joseph Stalin starved the people of Ukraine, resulting in the mass genocide of millions of Ukrainians. Bruce Bartlett, writing in *Human Events*, explained that the Holodomor—or Great Famine—"of 1932–33 was the culmination of a long struggle between the Soviet state, non-Russian nationalities like the Ukrainians and historically independent-minded farmers who had been forced onto collective farms. It also resulted from Stalin's need for foreign exchange to buy Western machinery to aid industrialization."[45]

"In late 1932," wrote Bartlett, "Stalin decreed that all grain should be confiscated and anyone interfering with this action should be considered an enemy of the state. More than 5,000 people received the death penalty as a result. Throughout the countryside in Ukraine and other grain-growing areas, starvation set in. Stalin sent troops to prevent farmers from leaving the land, where increasingly there was nothing to eat. In response to pleas for food aid, Stalin called the famine 'one of the minor inconveniences of our system.'"[46]

A *Manchester Guardian* reporter, Malcolm Muggeridge, traveled to Ukraine to see for himself what was taking place there. In her book *Stalin's Apologist,* Sally J. Taylor recounts that "[i]n a series of articles published in the *Guardian* at the end of March 1933, [Muggeridge] confirmed the existence of widespread famine in his eyewitness account. The peasant population, he wrote, was starving: 'I mean starving in its absolute sense; not undernourished . . . but having for weeks next to nothing to eat. . . .'" "'It was true,' Muggeridge wrote. 'The famine is an organized occupation; worse, active war. . . .'"[47]

Thus even from other news sources, such as the *Manchester Guardian*, the *New York Times* had to know the truth about the famine that was taking place in Ukraine. Even more, as Hoover Institution historian and scholar Robert Conquest wrote in his book *The Harvest of Sorrow,* "let us . . . insist on the fact that the truth was indeed widely available in the West. In spite of everything, full or adequate reports appeared in the *Manchester Guardian* and the *Daily Telegraph; Le Matin* and *Le Figaro;* the *Neue Zürcher Zeitung* and the *Gazette de Lausanne; La Stampa* in Italy, the *Reichpost* in Austria, and scores of other Western papers. In the United States, wide-circulation newspapers printed very full first-hand accounts by Ukrainian-American and other visitors (though these were mostly discounted as, often, appearing in 'Right Wing' journals); and the *Christian Science Monitor,* the *New York Herald Tribune* and the New York Jewish *Forwaerts,* gave broad coverage. . . ."[48]

However, the *Times's* long-time man in Moscow, Walter Duranty, a propagandist and apologist for the 1917 communist revolution in Russia and later Stalin and his murderous regime, reported otherwise. Indeed, the *Times* was proud of their man in Moscow. In 1932, Duranty was awarded a Pulitzer Prize for a series of articles in the *Times* that covered up Stalinism's atrocities. And from 1932 to 1933, Duranty wrote news columns for the *Times* not only denying the fact of the catastrophic famine taking place in Ukraine, but censoring Stalin's role in the genocide of multiple millions of Ukrainians.

Another *Guardian* reporter, Gareth Jones, also filed news stories about the famine in Ukraine. Like Muggeridge, Jones had gone to the areas where widespread starvation was occurring, traveling some forty miles into the midst of it, and was also horrified by what he witnessed and was told—which he reported in detail. But Duranty then took aim at Jones's credibility and used his powerful perch at the *Times* to publicly demean him and the accuracy of his reporting in the news pages of the *Times*.

On March 30, 1932, Duranty wrote a piece in the *Times* titled "Russians Hungry, but Not Starving," in which he, among other things, dismissed Jones's firsthand accounts and countered him with disinformation. "Since I talked to Mr. Jones, I have made exhaustive inquiries about this alleged famine situation. I have inquired in Soviet commissariats and in foreign embassies with their network of consuls, and I have tabulated information from Britons working as specialists and from my personal connections, Russian and foreign. All of this seems to me to be more trustworthy information than I could get by a brief trip through any one area. The Soviet Union is too big to permit a hasty study, and it is the foreign correspondent's job to present a whole picture, not a part of it."[49]

Duranty then exclaimed, "[a]nd here are the facts: There is a serious food shortage throughout the country, with occasional cases of well-managed State or collective farms. The big cities and the army are adequately supplied with food. There is no actual starvation or deaths from starvation, but there is widespread mortality from diseases due to malnutrition. In short, conditions are definitely bad in certain sections—the Ukraine, North Caucasus and Lower Volga. The rest of the country is on short rations but nothing worse. These conditions are bad, but there is no famine."[50]

Of course, this was a flat-out lie.

The famine peaked in the summer of 1933. Unbelievably, on September 17, 1933, Duranty was at it again. In another report from Russia, Duranty assured the *Times*'s readers that all was well in Ukraine and that suggestions to the contrary were nonsense. "The writer has just completed a 200-mile auto trip through the heart of the Ukraine and can say positively that the harvest is splendid and all talk of famine now is ridiculous. Everywhere one goes and with everyone with whom one talks—from Communists and officials to local peasants—it is the same story: 'Now we will be all right, now we are assured for the winter, now we have more grain that can easily be harvested.'"[51]

But Duranty knew the ugly truth. As Professor Lubomyr Luciuk of the Royal Military College of Canada has written: "On September 26, 1933, at the British Embassy in Moscow, Duranty privately confided to William Strang that as many as 10 million people had died directly or indirectly of famine conditions in the USSR during the past year. Meanwhile, publicly, Duranty orchestrated a vicious ostracizing of those journalists who risked much by reporting on the brutalities of forced collectivization and the ensuing demographic catastrophe, Muggeridge among them. Even as the fertile Ukraine, once the breadbasket of Europe, became a modern-day Golgotha, a place of skulls, Duranty plowed the truth under. Occasionally pressed on the human costs of the Soviet experiment he did, however, evolve a dismissive dodge, canting 'you can't make an omelet without breaking eggs.'"[52]

Indeed, wrote Conquest, "Duranty had personally told Eugene Lyons [United Press's Moscow correspondent] and others that he estimated the famine victims at around seven million. . . . What the American public got was not the straight stuff, but the false reporting. Its influence was enormous and long-lasting."[53]

But what did the management at the *New York Times* know about the unreliability of and outright lies involving Duranty's reporting? Top executives had every reason to be suspicious and, in fact, they were. For one, they could read what the other newspapers had written at the time of the famine. But the *Times* kept publishing Duranty's stories anyway. Journalist and scholar Arnold Beichman explained that "the *Times's* top brass suspected that Duranty was writing Stalinist propaganda, but did nothing. . . . [In her book] Taylor makes it clear that Carr Van Anda, the managing editor, Frederick T. Birchall, an assistant managing editor, and Edwin L. James, the later managing editor, were troubled with Duranty's Moscow reporting but did nothing about it. Birchall recommended that Duranty be replaced but, says Taylor, 'the recommendation fell by the wayside.'"[54]

Even so, in furtherance of its deception, in the November–December 2003 issue of the *Columbia Journalism Review*, Douglas McCollam critically observed that "[w]hen Walter Duranty left the *Times* and Russia in 1934, the paper said his twelve-year stint in

Moscow had 'perhaps been the most important assignment ever entrusted by a newspaper to a single correspondent over a considerable period of time.'" In other words, *Times* executives could not have been happier with his "journalistic" record. "By that time," writes McCollam, "Duranty was a journalistic celebrity—an absentia member of the Algonquin Roundtable, a confidant of Isadora Duncan, George Bernard Shaw, and Sinclair Lewis. He was held in such esteem that the presidential candidate Franklin Roosevelt brought him in for consultations on whether the Soviet Union should be officially recognized. When recognition was granted [to the Soviet Union by the United States] in 1934, Duranty traveled with the Soviet foreign minister, Maxim Litvinov, to the signing ceremony and spoke privately with FDR. At a banquet at the Waldorf-Astoria in New York held to celebrate the event, Duranty was introduced as 'one of the great foreign correspondents of modern times,' and 1,500 dignitaries gave him a standing ovation."[55] Duranty was an admired journalist among his colleagues.

The *Times*' longtime Russia correspondent was unquestionably a longtime favorite mouthpiece for the brutal Soviet regime, about which he wrote in the pages of the *Times* for a dozen years, and for which he was rewarded by Stalin. McCollam notes that "[i]n Moscow, Duranty was known as 'the dean of foreign correspondents,' and was renowned for his lavish hospitality. In an austere city, he enjoyed generous living quarters and food rations, as well as the use of assistants, a chauffeur, and a cook/secretary/mistress named Katya, who bore him a son named Michael. Duranty, who had a wooden left leg caused by a train accident, was driven through the streets in a giant Buick outfitted with the Klaxon horn used by the Soviet secret police. His competitors gossiped that these perks were allowed because of his cozy relationship with the Soviet government. Eugene Lyons, a United Press correspondent, even suspected that Duranty might be on the Soviet payroll, but no evidence of that seems to exist. Still, many then and later wondered if the status Duranty enjoyed in Moscow led him to curtail his coverage of the Soviets. Malcolm Muggeridge . . . would later call Duranty 'the greatest liar of any journalist I have met in fifty years of journalism.' Joseph Alsop would tab him a 'fashionable prostitute,' in the service of Communists. . . ."[56]

More than a decade ago there came a growing movement to strip the deceased Duranty of his Pulitzer Prize. On October 23, 2003, the *Times*, writing about itself, reported that "[a] Columbia University history professor [was] hired by *The New York Times* to make an independent assessment of the coverage of one of its correspondents in the Soviet Union during the 1930's . . ." And what were the findings? "In his report to *The Times*, Professor Mark von Hagen described the coverage for which Mr. Duranty won the Pulitzer—his writing in 1931, a year before the onset of the famine—as a 'dull and largely uncritical recitation of Soviet sources.' That lack of balance and uncritical acceptance of the Soviet self-justification for its cruel and wasteful regime was a disservice to the American readers of *The New York Times* and the liberal values they subscribe to and to the historical experience of the peoples of the Russian and Soviet empires and their struggle for a better life."[57]

In a subsequent interview, von Hagen said, "[The Pulitzer Board] should take [the award] away for the greater honor and glory of *The New York Times*," he said. "He really was kind of a disgrace in the history of *The New York Times*."

Arthur Sulzberger Jr., the publisher of the *Times*, was opposed to having the Pulitzer withdrawn. "First, he wrote, such an action might evoke the 'Stalinist practice to airbrush purged figures out of official records and histories.' He also wrote of his fear that 'the board would be setting a precedent for revisiting its judgments over many decades.'"[58]

Despite such preposterous objections, Duranty's Pulitzer was not withdrawn.

But what of the rest of the press? How did they report about Stalin's purposeful famine and the resulting genocide? In his book *Angels in Stalin's Paradise*, James William Crowl writes that "[t]he information about the famine seems to have been commonplace within the Moscow press corps. Western travelers returned to Moscow with reports of what they had found, and correspondents discovered that they could verify such accounts by checking the suburbs and railroad stations of the major cities. Peasants seemed to flock to such locations despite the efforts of the authorities. Still more important, several reporters learned that they could slip onto trains and spend days or weeks in stricken areas despite the travel ban. During the early months of 1933, Ralph Barned of the *New York Herald Tribune* made such a trip, as . . . Jones and . . . Muggeridge of the *Manchester Guardian*. This information about the famine seems to have been plentiful among the correspondents in Moscow, and it seems unlikely that any reporter could have been unaware of its existence. According to Eugene Lyons [the Moscow correspondent for United Press from 1928 to 1934], 'the famine was accepted as a matter of course in our casual conversation at the hotels and in our homes.' William Henry Chamberlin [the Moscow correspondent for the *Christian Science Monitor*] has gone even further stating 'to anyone who lived in Russia in 1933 and who kept his eyes and ears open the historicity of the famine is simply not open to question.' . . . Most of the reporters took shelter behind the [Soviet regime's] censorship and kept quiet about the famine. . . ."[59]

Yale professor Timothy Snyder also notes in his book *Bloodlands—Europe Between Hitler and Stalin* that most of the journalists in Moscow knew of the mass starvation that was taking place. "The basic facts of mass hunger and death, although sometimes reported in the European and American press, never took on the clarity of an undisputed event. Almost no one claimed that Stalin meant to starve Ukrainians to death. . . . Though the journalists knew less than the diplomats, most of them understood that millions were dying from hunger."[60]

How is it possible that such colossal media failures of integrity, morality, and professional canons in the face of the mass extermination of Jews and Ukrainians do not permanently cripple the reputation and standing of the *New York Times* and the other press organizations, or at least force serious circumspection within and reformation of the media industry? And what of the weak excuses and feeble explanations offered decades later, as if they are atonement enough for the abhorrent consequences of the media's role in the cover-up of the genocidal murder of millions?

Is there another industry of any sort that can so blithely if not arrogantly and self-righteously carry on as if none of this happened? Surely, if the dead could speak, they would declare the *Times* and the other press outlets "the enemy of the people" for their wanton inhumanity in the face of genocide.

SEVEN

THE TRUTH ABOUT COLLUSION, ABUSE OF POWER, AND CHARACTER

SO MANY OF THE media allegations against President Trump and his administration are overwrought and, in many respects, utterly dishonest. To read their daily blitzkrieg of outrages against Trump and his administration, you would think that the president has corruptly used the instrumentalities of his office and executive authority in ways unimagined by past presidents and administrations.

In truth, he has done no such thing.

You would believe that he is some kind of flack or even mole for Vladimir Putin and the Russians. And you would conclude that he has damaged the office of the presidency with prurient personal behavior.

But this Democratic party-press narrative began even before Trump entered the presidency, starting with his candidacy. And given its constant drumbeat in the press, it requires a brief unraveling, the purpose of which is to further demonstrate the overall unobjective and propagandistic nature of today's newsrooms and journalists.

Let us look at the three areas of accusations against the president.

COLLUSION

For all the years Donald Trump has been president, the mass media have been fixated on a story line that had no basis in fact—that Donald Trump colluded with "the Russians" during the 2016 presidential race to defeat Hillary Clinton. To this day, and after all this time—despite congressional, criminal, and media investigations—there is nothing but Democratic party-press innuendo, supposition, and dissembling.

In addition to Special Counsel Robert Mueller's declaration of no collusion between the Trump campaign and Russia, on February 7, 2019, Senator Richard Burr, chairman of the Senate Intelligence Committee, told CBS News that "[i]f we write a report based upon the facts that we have, then we don't have anything that would suggest there was collusion by the Trump campaign and Russia."[1] A few days later, Burr reiterated his conclusion to NBC News: "There is no factual evidence of collusion between the Trump campaign and Russia."[2]

It merits emphasizing that the supposed plot was in fact launched by the Hillary Clinton campaign and the Democratic National Committee, with assistance from the Obama FBI and Department of Justice. In short, as *The Federalist* explained: "Perkins Coie, an international law firm, was directed by both the Democratic National Committee and Hillary Clinton's campaign to retain Fusion GPS in April of 2016 to dig up dirt on then-candidate Donald Trump. Fusion GPS then hired Christopher Steele, a former British spy, to compile a dossier of allegations that Trump and his campaign actively colluded with the Russian government during the 2016 election. Though many of the claims in the dossier have been directly refuted, none of the dossier's allegations of collusion have been independently verified. Lawyers for Steele admitted in court filings last April that his work was not verified and was never meant to be made public."[3]

The *Hill*'s John Solomon discovered that the dossier was provided to the FBI by at least six different people with connections to the Hillary Clinton campaign.[4] And information from the dossier, along with a news story planted by Steele with Yahoo reporter Michael Isikoff, was used by the FBI and the Department of Justice to expand a counterintelligence investigation aimed at the Trump campaign and businesses and to secure successive surveillance warrants from the Foreign Intelligence Surveillance Act (FISA) court. The FISA court was never appropriately alerted to the funding source or purpose of the dossier; however, several senior FBI officials involved in using the dossier were warned about its political nature.[5] Ultimately, this and other events led to the appointment of Special Counsel Robert Mueller and the initiation of a criminal investigation (despite the fact that there was no criminal basis justifying his appointment), which found no collusion after nearly two years of investigation.

Incredibly, in a December 2018 podcast interview, Isikoff, the

Yahoo reporter who "broke" the September 23, 2016, Steele dossier story (with left-wing coauthor David Corn of *Mother Jones*, who fed a copy of the dossier to the FBI), said when "you actually get into the details of the Steele dossier, the specific allegations, we have not seen the evidence to support them, and, in fact, there's good grounds to think that some of the more sensational allegations will never be proven and are likely false." "It's a mixed record at best," he said. "Things could change. Mueller may yet produce evidence that changes this calculation but based on the public record at this point, I'd have to say that most of the specific allegations have not been borne out."[6]

However, so committed to this plot have been the media that they actually played an active role in the investigations and were relied on by unethical FBI officials and others to do their bidding. On September 5, 2018, Solomon detailed a number of examples of media-government collusion. "From the beginning of this investigation, key figures involved in it have had extensive contacts with or connections to media."[7]

Among them, writes Solomon:

- Fired FBI official Peter Strzok and his alleged paramour, former FBI lawyer Lisa Page, texted frequently about leaks in the media affecting their cases, and even suggested the FBI was behind some of those.[8]
- FBI Deputy Director Andrew McCabe was fired for lying about one media leak he authorized.[9]
- The FBI secured a FISA warrant against Trump campaign adviser Carter Page in part by citing a Yahoo News article by Michael Isikoff that, it turns out, was based on a leak from the FBI's

own informant in the case, former British intelligence operative Christopher Steele, whose dirt on Trump was bought and paid for by the Clinton campaign and the Democratic National Committee.[10]

- The court that approved the surveillance warrant apparently was never told that the article was not independent corroboration but, rather, circular intelligence from the poisoned Steele tree.[11]

- DOJ notes recently provided to Congress show one of the media leaks with which Steele was involved was considered by his boss, Fusion GPS founder Glenn Simpson, to be a "hail Mary attempt" to swing the election, rather than to inform the FBI and courts. That's the sort of biased evidence the FBI should eschew, not embrace, of course.[12]

- And Strzok's own FBI communications show the FBI—after firing Steele—continued to receive versions of his now-infamous but still-unverified dossier on alleged Trump collusion with Russia. One of those was delivered to the bureau by *Mother Jones* magazine writer David Corn, who openly has opposed Trump's presidency.[13]

Moreover, former FBI general counsel James Baker is under a criminal leak investigation.[14]

The media have crossed the line between reporting and activism, where they have, in fact, participated in the promotion of events about which they then report. This is precisely the concern raised by those who questioned the wisdom of "public" journalism or social-activism journalism, described in chapter 1. Moreover, their progressive ideology and Democratic Party bias are in full bloom, as evidenced by their frenzied obsession with "getting"

President Trump and, conversely, their disinterest and laxity respecting the roles of the Clinton campaign and the DNC, as well as the part played by the Obama FBI, Department of Justice, and intelligence agencies to thwart the Trump campaign and presidency.

This has also led to newsrooms and journalists repeatedly spoon-feeding stories to the public that are erroneous or outright fabrications. Virtually every major news outlet is guilty, including the Associated Press,[15] CNN,[16] *New York Times*,[17] *Washington Post*,[18] McClatchy,[19] NPR,[20] etc.

Moreover, the media are left with desperate efforts to invent even tenuous links to third parties as supposed evidence of Trump-Russia collusion and the latest "shoe to drop," or they hype as evidence of Trump-related criminality or corruption guilty pleas and convictions having nothing to do with collusion and President Trump.

Indeed, faced with actual firsthand evidence, even a confession, of what is arguably the greatest act of political subversion perhaps in American history, by a cabal of federal bureaucrats seeking the removal of a recently elected sitting president whose campaign they sought to earlier sabotage, the media mostly celebrated the event and one of its primary architects rather than deplore the conspiracy—as the target was President Trump. Here is a brief exchange between CBS *60 Minutes* correspondent Scott Pelley and disgraced former FBI deputy director Andrew McCabe on February 17, 2019:

Referring to the firing of former FBI deputy director, James Comey, Pelley asked McCabe: "How long was it after that, that you decided to start the obstruction of justice and counterintelligence investigations involving the president?"

McCABE: "I think the next day I met with the team investigating the Russia cases, and I asked the team to go back and conduct an assessment to determine where are we with these efforts and what steps do we need to take going forward. I was very concerned that I was able to put the Russia case on absolutely solid ground in an indelible fashion that were I removed quickly or reassigned or fired, that the case could not be closed or vanish in the night without a trace. I wanted to make sure that our case was on solid ground and if somebody came in behind me and closed it and tried to walk away from it, they would not be able to do that without creating a record of why they'd made that decision.

PELLEY: You wanted a documentary record—that those investigations had begun, because you feared that they would be made to go away?

McCABE: That's exactly right.[21]

Later McCabe explained: "I can't describe to you accurately enough the pressure and the chaos that [Deputy Attorney General] Rod [Rosenstein] and I were trying to operate under at that time. It was incredibly turbulent, incredibly stressful. And it was clear to me that that stress was . . . was impacting the deputy attorney general. We talked about why the president had insisted on firing the director and whether or not he was thinking about the Russia investigation, and did that impact his decision. And in the context of that conversation, the deputy attorney general offered to wear a wire into the White House. He said, 'I never get searched when I go into the White House. I could easily wear a recording device. They wouldn't know it was there.' Now, he was not joking.

He was absolutely serious. And, in fact, he brought it up in the next meeting we had. I never actually considered taking him up on the offer. I did discuss it with my general counsel and my leadership team back at the F.B.I. after he brought it up the first time."[22]

PELLEY: Rosenstein was actually openly talking about whether there was a majority of the cabinet who would vote to remove the president.

McCABE: That's correct. Counting votes or possible votes.[23]

Much of the rest of the media's response was consistent with the next-day comments by CNN's legal analyst, Jeffrey Toobin, who reacted to President Trump's tweet accusing McCabe of treason thus:

I think the correct term is not treasonous, but patriotic. I mean, they are thinking about the national security of the United States. These are all career officials. These are not Democratic political appointees. These are people whose job it is to care about the national security of the United States. And remember, all this evidence has only gotten stronger over the past two years. You know, [Congressman] Adam Schiff is now conducting an investigation to determine, in effect, if the President is a Russian asset. This remains a serious concern and there is much more evidence to support this idea. They didn't even know at the time about all the business deals that were going on between Russia and Trump during 2016, all those discussions about Trump Tower in Moscow. I mean, the idea that they were treasonous is 180 degrees wrong.[24]

While the case for collusion was manufactured in large part by the Democratic party-press, and the abhorrent acts of senior FBI and Department of Justice officials in attempting to destroy a presidency, among others, it is worth a brief journey into history to recall some actual occasions when presidents or near presidents colluded or committed other acts of treachery, thereby providing a measure of sober perspective to the specious allegations of abuse of power directed at President Trump.

For starters, the media and others who share the progressive outlook are infatuated with their new favorite founding father, Alexander Hamilton, who was directly involved in colluding with a foreign power and undermining President George Washington's neutral foreign policy, leading to the much-condemned (rightly or wrongly) Jay Treaty.

For example, Ben Brantley, a *New York Times* journalist and chief theater critic, fawns over *Hamilton* the musical, which is a progressive twist on Hamilton's life, through which many progressives find validation for their own political agenda and "resistance" mindset. Brantley wrote: "During the past several months, while it was being pumped up and trimmed down for its move from the East Village to Broadway, Lin-Manuel Miranda's rap-driven portrait of the rise and fall of Alexander Hamilton (this country's first secretary of the Treasury) has been the stuff of encomiums in both fashion magazines and op-ed columns.... Even I, one of the many critics who enthused about 'Hamilton' in February like a born-again convert in a revival tent, was beginning to think, 'Enough already.' Then I saw the show at the Richard Rodgers."[25]

"I am loath to tell people to mortgage their houses and lease their children to acquire tickets to a hit Broadway show," writes Brantley. "But 'Hamilton' . . . might just about be worth it—at least to anyone who wants proof that the American musical is not only surviving but also evolving in ways that should allow it to thrive and transmogrify in years to come."[26]

The same Democratic party-press that seeks President Trump's indictment, impeachment, and tar and feathering for his noninvolvement in a supposed Russian collusion scheme celebrate their remake of Hamilton despite Hamilton's collusion with the British during the Washington presidency.

Do they even know of Hamilton's collusion with Britain?

As the late historian and Pulitzer Prize winner Lance Banning explained: "Near the end of March 1793, news arrived that the revolutionary French Republic had declared war on Great Britain. . . . [President George Washington] was determined to maintain the strictest neutrality. . . . Locked in a struggle for survival, both France and Britain interfered with American neutral trade. Moreover, few Americans could be impartial about the war. The two political parties were involved in a struggle between liberty and order at home, and both saw a similar struggle in the conflict abroad. Republicans were certain that domestic conspirators desired a connection with Great Britain in order to advance their plot and to bring the United States into the war against liberty in Europe. Similarly, Federalists suspected a connection between the Republicans and the French which might involve America in the war and bring about a second and more violent revolution in the United States. 'French' and 'British' factions, and political division assumed a ferocity seldom equaled. Washington found it impossible to maintain the national harmony he desired and increasingly difficult to stay above the fray."[27]

"Each political party became more and more convinced that its opponents were unduly influenced by affection for a foreign power if not by foreign money," writes Banning. "Accusations of foreign bribery have never been substantiated, at least as to high executive officers; and although historians would later turn up evidence of questionable conduct on the part of Jefferson and more especially Hamilton, none of this evidence was known in the 1790s. . . . Hamilton was more or less constantly involved in confidential, even clandestine, communications with British agents or ministers from 1789. Jefferson came to suspect that Hamilton was secretly sabotaging his negotiations with foreign powers, particularly Britain, and this contributed to the frustrations that led him to resign his post at the end of 1793. Most historians have found Hamilton's actions improper, perhaps even damaging to the country's foreign relations, but have acquitted him of culpable misconduct. . . ."[28]

Now that Hamilton's collusion with Britain has been made broadly known, will progressives care? Of course not.

What of the late Democratic senator Edward Kennedy, also known as "the Lion of the Senate," who was a onetime candidate for the Democratic Party nomination for president in 1980 and was contemplating another run in 1988? He sought the assistance of the Soviet Union in the midst of the Cold War to help defeat President Ronald Reagan's reelection effort.

As Peter Robinson explained in *Forbes*: "Picking his way through the Soviet archives that Boris Yeltsin had just thrown open, in 1991 Tim Sebastian, a reporter for the *London Times*, came across an arresting memorandum. Composed in 1983 by Victor Chebrikov, the top man at the KGB, the memorandum was addressed to Yuri Andropov, the top man in the entire USSR. The subject: Sen. Edward Kennedy."[29]

In 1992, Sebastian published a story about the memorandum in the London *Times*. Here in the United States, Sebastian's story received no attention. In his 2006 book, *The Crusader: Ronald Reagan and the Fall of Communism*, historian Paul Kengor reprinted the memorandum in full. "The media," Kengor says, "ignored the revelation."

Grove City College professor Kengor is a Cold War expert who has written extensively of Kennedy's collusion with the Soviets. For example, on April 12, 2018, writing in *The American Spectator*, Kengor discusses "a highly classified May 14, 1983, memo from the head of the KGB, Victor Chebrikov, to his boss, the head of the USSR, Yuri Andropov," which was discovered in the former Soviet Union's archives, about which Kengor has written in earlier books. Kengor explains that "[t]he lead words atop the document stated in caps: 'SPECIAL IMPORTANCE.' The next words: 'Committee on State Security of the USSR.' That's the KGB. Under that followed this stunning header: 'Regarding Senator Kennedy's request to the General Secretary of the Communist Party Y. V. Andropov.' Kennedy's request was delivered directly to Moscow by his law school roommate, John Tunney, a former Democratic senator from California."[30]

Digging further into the memo, Kengor observes that "Kennedy was described by Chebrikov as 'very troubled' by U.S.-Soviet relations, which Kennedy attributed not to the odious dictator spearheading the USSR but to President Ronald Reagan. The problem was Reagan's 'belligerence,' compounded by his alleged stubbornness. 'According to Kennedy,' reported Chebrikov, 'the current threat is due to the President's refusal to engage any modification to his politics.' This was made worse, said the memo, because the 1984 presidential campaign was just around the corner, and Reagan was looking easily re-electable."[31]

Kennedy provided advice to the Soviets on what he believed to be President Reagan's electoral weaknesses. "The KGB memo speculated—compliments of Kennedy's appraisal—that the chink in Reagan's political armor was matters of war and peace. Thus, said the head of the KGB: 'Kennedy believes that, given the state of current affairs, and in the interest of peace, it would be prudent and timely to undertake the following steps to counter the militaristic politics of Reagan.'"[32]

Next, Kennedy offered potential action items to the Kremlin. Kengor writes: "In the memo, Chebrikov then delineated for Andropov a series of specific steps proposed by Kennedy to help the Soviets 'influence Americans.' This included Kennedy arranging for Kremlin officials to meet with certain American media. Which media? The memo went so far as to directly name Walter Cronkite and Barbara Walters. Kennedy offered to help bring Soviet political and military officials to New York and Washington to connect them with friends in the press. And further, the memo included an offer from Kennedy himself to personally fly to the Kremlin to meet with Andropov."[33]

The memo makes explicit Kennedy's ultimate interest: "Tunney remarked that the senator wants to run for president in 1988. Kennedy does not discount that during the 1984 campaign, the Democratic Party may officially turn to him to lead the fight against the Republicans and elect their candidate president."[34]

This would seem to be the collusion of all collusions. Yet, despite the explosive bombshells about Kennedy's betrayal published in the London *Times* in 1992, and Kengor's revelations in his 2006 book, *The Crusader—Ronald Reagan and the Fall of Communism*[35]—not a single major news outlet was interested in interviewing Kengor or seriously covering Kennedy's actions during his lifetime (he would pass away in 2009, after these revelations were made public). Kengor observed that "[t]he press response was the exact opposite of today's maniacal digging on Donald Trump. Sources like CNN, which have now launched into 24/7 'breaking news' mode on Trump and the Russians, didn't do a single news story on Kennedy and the Russians. I can tell you unequivocally that I was never contacted once by CNN, MSNBC, the *New York Times*, the *Washington Post*, and on and on. And my 2006 book was published by HarperCollins, one of the top publishing houses. My publisher couldn't be dismissed as the 'right-wing press.'"[36]

Furthermore, there were no congressional inquiries or hearings, no ethics investigations, no Logan Act–related probe[37] (of the sort that was used as a pretext to investigate retired lieutenant general Michael Flynn), no special counsel criminal investigation—nothing.

And the Democratic party-press was utterly uninterested.

The following decade, there was another attempt to influence America's presidential election. This time it involved the reelection of Bill Clinton for president and Communist China. As Byron York wrote in the *Washington Examiner* on September 9, 2018, "[i]n the 1990s, a hostile foreign power meddled in our presidential election. There were serious questions about whether one party's candidate—the beneficiary—was complicit in the meddling, or at least looked the other way while it was going on. The candidate fiercely resisted the appointment of a special prosecutor, then known as an independent counsel, to investigate. Finally, amid only moderate media interest and public concern, it all faded away."[38]

The *Los Angeles Times*, which did take an investigative interest in the story, reported: "The chief of China's military intelligence secretly directed funds from Beijing to help re-elect President Clinton in 1996, former Democratic fund-raiser Johnny Chung has told federal investigators. Chung says he met three times with the intelligence official, Gen. Ji Shengde, who ordered $300,000 deposited into the Torrance businessman's bank account to subsidize campaign donations intended for Clinton, according to sources familiar with Chung's sealed statements to federal prosecutors."[39]

Chung provided damning testimony before a federal grand jury that the Chinese government wanted Clinton reelected. "During their initial meeting on Aug. 11, 1996, in Hong Kong, Ji conveyed to Chung the Chinese government's specific interest in supporting Clinton: 'We like your president,' Ji said, according to sources familiar with Chung's grand jury testimony. Chung testified that he was introduced to the intelligence chief by the daughter of China's retired senior military officer."[40]

Chung spread around a great deal of foreign money on Democratic candidates and organizations and bought himself repeated access to the White House. He "contributed more than $400,000 to various Democratic campaigns and causes, visited the White House no fewer than 50 times and brought numerous Chinese associates to events with the president and First Lady Hillary

Rodham Clinton. He pleaded guilty last year to election law violations and became the first major figure to cooperate with a Justice
Department investigation of campaign finance abuses, including a
probe into improper foreign donations. A number of contributors
have been indicted in the scandal."[41]

So concerned were the Chinese government and others about
Chung's knowledge and testimony that "[t]he FBI feared for
Chung's safety after he received veiled threats and bribe offers
from individuals pressing him to keep silent about his China deal-
ings. Those concerns grew after the FBI received information from
overseas indicating that Chung could be in danger." Consequently,
on numerous occasions the FBI placed Chung and his family in
protective custody.[42] He was eventually sentenced to probation.

Moreover, writes York, Charlie Trie, a longtime friend of President Clinton, "raised $1.2 million in foreign dollars for the Clinton
legal defense fund and the DNC. In March 1996, Trie dropped off
a donation of $460,000 at the Washington offices of the defense
fund, with some of the money in sequentially-numbered money
orders made out in the same handwriting. He visited the White
House 22 times. He pleaded guilty to violating federal election
laws and was sentenced to probation."[43]

In addition, reported the *Los Angeles Times*, James T. Riady, another "longtime friend of President Clinton" and "who heads the
worldwide Lippo banking group, pleaded guilty . . . to conspiracy
related to illegal campaign contributions in the 1996 Democratic
fund-raising scandal and during the previous eight years." Riady,
who had extensive ties to China, "and his banking group acknowledged in court papers that they made millions of dollars in illegal
campaign donations to Democratic presidential and congressional

candidates dating to 1988, including hundreds of thousands of dollars to Clinton's first campaign for the White House in 1992." Riady was also sentenced to probation.[44] The *Times* added, "There was no indication that any candidates knew the contributions were tainted foreign funds."[45]

The *Times* also noted that "[f]ormer Democratic fund-raiser John Huang . . . [a] onetime official of Lippo California, pleaded guilty in the scandal two years ago and cooperated in the case against Riady, who he said directed all political giving."[46] York noted that Huang "raised more than $1.5 million from illegal foreign sources" and "visited the White House 78 times."[47]

Then–attorney general Janet Reno had refused to seek the appointment of an independent counsel (the independent counsel statute has since lapsed) to investigate the Chinese–Democratic Party–Clinton collusion scandal. There would be no formal questioning of the Clintons under penalty of perjury. There would be no prosecutorial report. Bill Clinton had already been reelected to his second presidential term. The scandal died, never to be raised again despite Hillary Clinton's race in the Democratic Party presidential primary in 2008 and her subsequent presidential run in 2016 as the Democratic Party nominee. The Democratic party-press had no interest.

There are numerous other occasions in which elected Democrats sought to undermine Republican presidents and their foreign policy by colluding with foreign governments. For example, Democratic House Speaker Nancy Pelosi, who has been among the leading voices promoting the Russia-collusion narrative, was herself openly defiant of President George W. Bush's efforts to isolate Syria's genocidal dictator, Bashar al-Assad. She led other congressional members—"the Gang of Eight"—on an unauthorized diplomatic mission to Syria.

In April 2007, the Associated Press reported, "U.S. House Speaker Nancy Pelosi met Syrian President Bashar al-Assad on Wednesday for talks criticized by the White House as undermining American efforts to isolate the hard-line Arab country. Pelosi and accompanying members of Congress began their day by holding separate talks with Foreign Minister Walid al-Moallem and Vice President Farouk al-Sharaa and then met Assad, who hosted them for lunch after their talks. Pelosi's visit to Syria was the latest challenge to the White House by congressional Democrats, who are taking a more assertive role in influencing policy in the Middle East and the Iraq war."[48]

President Bush was none too happy. "Bush has said Pelosi's trip signals that the Assad government is part of the international mainstream when it is not. The United States says Syria allows Iraqi Sunni insurgents to operate from its territory, backs the Hezbollah and Hamas militant groups and is trying to destabilize the Lebanese government. Syria denies the allegations."[49]

The Associated Press understated Syria's brutal offenses. As columnist Tom Rogan wrote in *National Review*, "between 2005 and 2008, foreign jihadists flooded along the arterial highways that connect eastern Syria and western Iraq. Once in Iraq, they joined up with facilitators from the Islamic State's precursor, al-Qaeda in Iraq (AQI). The zealots were then assigned to murder American soldiers and Marines. And AQI was responsible for particularly gruesome crimes. . . . But it wasn't just AQI that received Assad's support. A long-term ally of Iranian intelligence and the Lebanese Hezbollah, Assad's regime harbored those waging Explosively Formed Penetrator (EFP) terrorism against U.S. military patrols in Iraq (and power-drill wars against the heads of innocent Sunnis). Again, the facts are clear. When the CIA finally caught up with Imad Mughniyah (a key organizer of these attacks) in February 2008, he was in Damascus. Think on that. Nearly a year after Pelosi's 'peace' visit, Assad was still protecting this murderer as he lived openly."[50] As Speaker, Pelosi would have known this and much more.

But Pelosi was not the first Democratic House speaker to try to subvert a Republican president's foreign policy this way. The late Jim Wright had taken it upon himself to lead negotiations among the various factions in Nicaragua, including the communist regime led by strongman Daniel Ortega, in contravention of President Ronald Reagan's policy. On November 17, 1987, the *Los Angeles Times* reported that "President Reagan . . . personally admonished House Speaker Jim Wright . . . for talking with Nicaraguan leaders, but Wright left the meeting unapologetic for the unorthodox role that he is playing in the Central America peace negotiations."[51]

The *Times* added: "The stand-off between Reagan and Wright is certain to complicate the task of State Department officials assigned to carry out U.S. policy in Central America. Wright's continued participation also will serve to bring additional pressure on the Administration to talk with the Sandinista government in a bilateral setting."[52]

In a meeting at the White House with President Reagan and his top foreign policy team, "[Reagan] spokesman Marlin Fitzwater said that the President told Wright he disapproves of the meetings between the Speaker and Sandinista leader Daniel Ortega late last week at a time when Administration officials are refusing to talk to Ortega. Fitzwater said that Reagan, who has long supported the Contras' effort to overthrow the Sandinistas, told the Speaker that by injecting himself into the middle of the Nicaraguan peace talks, he is 'getting involved in what should be essentially a matter between the Sandinista government and the Nicaraguan Resistance.' Indeed, after the meeting Wright insisted that 'he still intends to continue meeting with Central American leaders and will make a trip to Costa Rica on Dec. 1.'"53

Again, there was not much uproar in the Democratic party-press about this or other instances of collusion and open interference by Democrats with the foreign policies of past Republican administrations. Certainly the mass media did not prod for or demand criminal investigations or a political reckoning against any of these Democratic Party actors. Compare these multiple events, all involving Democratic officials, with the press treatment of President Trump.

ABUSE OF POWER

Newsrooms and editorial pages insist that President Trump is frequently and relentlessly "abusing power" in more ways than one can count or categorize. By way of "news reports," "news analysis," "news interpretation," "news roundtables," "expert commentary," and clear-cut propaganda, the public is served by the Democratic party-press a daily dose of President Trump's alleged criminal violations, legal violations, ethics violations, norm violations, unprecedented actions, bullying, threatening, etc., suggesting or asserting that Trump is a tyrant or would-be tyrant.

A typical example: *Huffington Post* contributor Philip Rotner proclaimed on July 27, 2017, only six months into the Trump presidency, that "Donald Trump is using the bully pulpit of the presidency (emphasis on 'bully') to politicize the criminal justice system, punish politicians who won't toe his line, and humiliate private citizens who dare to speak out against him. Whether Trump's abuse of power is criminal, or only dangerously unethical, probably depends on whether he has crossed the line into criminal obstruction of justice. That judgment will be made by Special Counsel Robert Mueller, assuming that Mueller will be allowed to complete his investigation. . . ."[54]

Of course, Mueller did finish his investigation, and there was no criminal obstruction of justice. Rotner later declared that "neither criminal accountability nor the prospect of impeachment takes the full measure of Trump's abuse of power. More important is the damage Trump is inflicting upon the rule of law, separation of powers, and the checks and balances that protect our democracy."[55]

Rotner's wildly absurd and hysterical assertions are not uncommon among those who work in America's newsrooms. The mass media's coverage of Donald Trump treats as a given that he is a power-hungry law breaker. But to what end is he supposedly so inclined? He has not financially enriched himself as president. On the contrary, he left a lucrative business career to run and then serve in public office, and donates his presidential salary to the government and charities. He is not an ideologue who seeks to fundamentally transform America into something it is not, and against the public's will, as Barack Obama openly proclaimed, or like Senator Bernie Sanders and other Democratic candidates seeking the presidency have declared. Indeed, his policy initiatives range from mainstream conservative to even center-left in some cases, such as so-called prison reform, trade tariffs imposed on allies, price controls on domestically produced drugs, paid family leave, etc. He has not assumed or exercised presidential powers in some extraordinary way despite, for example, efforts to falsely characterize his use of the National Emergencies Act of 1976 and the funding of physical barriers on the southern border as such. (The president has both legal and budgetary *congressional authorization* to act.)

An examination of news reporting and media commentary over a score of months demonstrates that many of the president's statements, decisions, and actions are met with a predictable and knee-jerk chorus of media excoriations and allegations. However, it seemed at one point that President Trump's firing of former FBI director James Comey, whose resignation or removal Democratic officials and the Democratic party-press had earlier demanded, turned out to be an especially traumatizing event for the mass media or, more accurately, an opportunity for them to crystallize their loathing for the president around a set of accusations—such as "constitutional crisis," "obstruction of justice" and "cover-up"—which, they hoped, would lead to his political and legal undoing.

The *Washington Free Beacon* observed that "Comey's dismissal drew accusations that Trump was trying to cover up the federal investigation into alleged collusion between his presidential campaign and the Russians in 2016. CNN legal analyst Jeffrey Toobin said the firing was a 'grotesque abuse of power' by Trump and was the sort of thing that happens in 'non-democracies.' Fellow CNN analyst David Gregory said Trump's actions and the subsequent White House spin demonstrated 'disdain for the presidency.'"[56]

The *Free Beacon* also reported that "MSNBC host Chris Matthews called it the 'Tuesday Night Massacre,' a reference to the 'Saturday Night Massacre' when Richard Nixon ordered the firing of Watergate special prosecutor Archibald Cox in 1973. He later added Trump's actions had the 'whiff of fascism' to them. One of the reporters who broke the Watergate scandal, Carl Bernstein, said on CNN that the dismissal marked a 'terribly dangerous moment in American history.'"[57] Moreover, "ABC's Cokie Roberts said the Watergate comparisons were 'understandable,' and MSNBC host Joe Scarborough said . . . that the 'echoes of Watergate' were filling Washington, D.C. 'The question this morning is whether the centuries-old system of checks and balances will swing into action,' he said."[58]

What was missing from most of these "reports" was accuracy and context.

There were many good and legitimate reasons for Comey's firing. And many Democrats had been on record denouncing him. For example, on November 2, 2016, Bloomberg News reported: "Sen. Charles Schumer . . . is joining a growing chorus of criticism over FBI Director James Comey's decision to alert lawmakers to new emails potentially linked to the bureau's investigation into Hillary Clinton's private server. 'I do not have confidence in him any longer,' Schumer told Bloomberg [News]."[59] On January 13, 2017, in a story headlined "Tensions Boil Up Between Democrats and FBI Director," CBS News reported that "Democrats stormed out of a briefing on Russian hacking—furious with one of the briefers, Comey. 'The FBI director has no credibility,' said Rep. Maxine Waters of California. 'My confidence in the FBI director's ability to lead this agency has been shaken,' said Rep. Hank Johnson of Georgia."[60]

Furthermore, on May 9, 2017, then–deputy attorney general

Rod Rosenstein set forth in a detailed memorandum titled "Restoring Public Confidence in the FBI" the reasons he and the Department of Justice had lost faith in Comey and the basis for his firing. Among other things, Rosenstein wrote: "Although the President has the power to remove the FBI director, the decision should not be taken lightly. I agree with the nearly unanimous opinions of former Department officials. The way the Director handled the conclusion of the [Hillary Clinton] email investigation was wrong. As a result, the FBI is unlikely to gain public and congressional trust until it has a Director who understands the gravity of the mistakes and pledges never to repeat them. Having refused to admit his errors, the Director cannot be expected to implement the necessary corrective actions."[61]

In fact, shortly after his firing, Comey stated in a letter "to all" that "I have long believed that a President can fire an FBI Director for any reason, or no reason at all. I am not going to spend time on the decision or the way it was executed. . . ."[62] Of course, a disgruntled Comey has never stopped criticizing the president for his removal, but at the time he understood it to be a perfectly legitimate and legal presidential act.

Notwithstanding that the "Russia" investigation was never hampered in any way during or after Comey's firing—the president did nothing to limit its reach or funding—the "Trump's abuse of power" narrative persists in the media. However, the fact is that the Trump administration's use of executive power has hardly been abusive. Indeed, it has been unexceptional and even tame.

Again, perspective and context are important, given how reporters cover the president today. Hence, a brief look at history is warranted.

For example, David Burnham, formerly a *New York Times* investigative reporter, in 1989 authored the book *A Law Unto Itself,* in which he provides numerous accounts and extensive evidence of, among other things, the use of the Internal Revenue Service (IRS) to target political opponents—both individuals and organizations—by past presidents and administrations. Take the presidency of the much-celebrated great progressive, Franklin Roosevelt. Burnham writes that "confidential government documents prove . . . that . . . Roosevelt and the officials around him did not hesitate to mobilize the IRS in efforts to destroy the careers of individuals they had decided were enemies. The records even show that on one occasion an inquiry from Eleanor Roosevelt prompted Treasury Secretary [Henry] Morgenthau to order a tax investigation of a conservative newspaper publisher who had become one of the Roosevelt administration's leading critics."[63]

Roosevelt was particularly hostile toward Andrew Mellon, a former Republican Treasury secretary and successful businessman. "Probably the single most brazen display of the Roosevelt administration's willingness to use the tax agency for political purposes," declares Burnham, "was its attack on Andrew Mellon, the millionaire capitalist who served as the Republican secretary of the treasury from 1921 to 1932. . . . Elmer L. Irey, the first director of what is now called the Criminal Investigation Division, acknowledged that Treasury Secretary . . . Morgenthau ordered him to develop serious tax charges against Mellon even though he knew that the just-retired treasury secretary was innocent. It seems unlikely that Morgenthau would have mounted such a campaign without the approval of FDR."[64]

Mellon was harassed for years, with false charge after false charge filed against him. In the end, "all criminal and civil fraud penalties the Roosevelt administration had brought against him" were dismissed.⁶⁵

Burnham explains that Roosevelt "was a driven man who did not hesitate to adopt questionable tactics to maintain his power." "The Mellon case was hardly the only occasion on which the Roosevelt administration mobilized the tax agency for political purposes. From his very first moments as the Democratic presidential candidate in 1931, for example, Roosevelt had understood that Huey Long . . . represented a genuine political threat." "The administration's deep concern about Long was translated into action exactly three days after Morgenthau became Roosevelt's treasury secretary . . . , when Morgenthau ordered . . . Irey, the man he had instructed to go after Mellon, to launch a second campaign against Long."⁶⁶

"Just how important the Long case had become to the Roosevelt administration," wrote Burnham, "is indicated by the direct involvement of the president in an important last-minute aspect of the effort to crush Long: the selection and recruiting of a lawyer to handle the actual prosecution. The story of FDR's direct intervention in the case was told by Irey. . . ."⁶⁷ The investigation effectively ended when Long was assassinated and died on September 10, 1935.

According to former Hillsdale College professor Burton Folsom Jr., "Roosevelt marveled at the potential of the IRS for removing political opponents. Newspaper publisher William Randolph Hearst also found himself under investigation when he began opposing Roosevelt's political programs."⁶⁸ In fact, as Burnham recounts, Eleanor Roosevelt sicced the IRS on "conservative newspaper publisher Frank Gannett, who at the time was also vice chairman of the Republican National Committee."[69]

Hearst and Gannett were not the only newspaper publishers the Roosevelts targeted. "Moses 'Moe' Annenberg . . . also drew an IRS audit—with 35 agents working for two and one-half years to prosecute him," explains Folsom. Annenberg had just bought the *Philadelphia Inquirer*, which would become hostile to Roosevelt's agenda. "Annenberg quickly became immersed in Republican politics, writing against the New Deal in general and competing against the *Philadelphia Record* in particular. David Stern was the editor of the *Philadelphia Record* and Stern enjoyed playing chess with Morgenthau and high stakes politics with Roosevelt—who appreciated Stern's successful efforts to elect more Democrats in Pennsylvania. Annenberg's conservative politics and his entrepreneurial spirit made him an effective Republican competitor in the newspaper and political wars. . . . Annenberg's aggressive advertising and news reporting helped the *Inquirer* sharply increase its subscriptions and sales, and helped cause Stern's *Record* to decline in sales and market share. On the political side, that meant more readers were absorbing Annenberg's pungent editorials against the New Deal in general and Roosevelt in particular. . . . What made things so awful for Stern, Roosevelt, and the Pennsylvania Democrats was that Annenberg was selling his ideas effectively, making money for the *Inquirer*, and helping lead the Republicans to a stunning victory in the 1938 mid-term election . . . Stern was losing money at the *Record* and he turned to the government for help; in desperation, for example, he was able to get the Federal Trade Commission to prosecute Annenberg for selling advertising at rates too low. . . . The Roosevelt administration had a better idea: an IRS investigation of Moe Annenberg. Unlike Mellon, who as secretary of treasury knew tax law inside out, Annenberg was careless and paid little attention to his taxes."[70]

After the massive investigation was completed, it was determined that Annenberg owed the federal government $8 million, which he offered to pay with fines and penalties. But Roosevelt wanted Annenberg imprisoned. "As . . . Irey told Morgenthau, 'They are not going to have the opportunity to pay the tax [and avoid prison].' When Morgenthau and Roosevelt had lunch over the matter on April 11, 1939, Morgenthau asked Roosevelt if he could do something for the president. 'Yes,' Roosevelt said, 'I want Moe Annenberg for dinner.' Morgenthau responded, 'You're going to have him for breakfast—fried.'"[71] The goal was to remove the *Inquirer*'s owner as a political influence in the state by putting him in prison and end the *Inquirer*'s harsh criticism of Roosevelt's policies. It worked.

Folsom also describes how Roosevelt intervened in investigations to protect his political allies. For example, writes Folsom, "[Frank] Hague was the undisputed boss of Jersey City. He initially backed Al Smith for president in 1932, but quickly shifted to Roosevelt after the Democratic convention; Hague promised the swing state of New Jersey to Roosevelt and gave the future president a spectacular parade with 100,000 present in Sea Girt, New Jersey, the largest Roosevelt saw anywhere during the entire campaign. . . . Hague used his patronage wisely and controlled his city with an iron hand. . . . Even with the torrent of federal funds cascading into New Jersey, and charges of corruption rampant, the IRS never made a serious investigation of Hague."[72]

Nonetheless, the time came when Hague needed Roosevelt's

intervention, and he got it. Folsom explains that "Roosevelt was embarrassed by Hague, and never included him in his inner circle, but Hague was needed if New Jersey was to remain in the president's column. Roosevelt was firm on that and proved it when James Farley discovered Hague had a crony at the post office who was opening and reading all mail to and from major political opponents. Tampering with the U.S. mail was a federal offense and some of Huey Long's henchmen went to jail for misusing the post office. Farley, in fact, came to Roosevelt for instructions on how to prosecute Hague. The president, however, stopped Farley in his tracks: 'Forget prosecution. You go tell Frank to knock it off. We can't have this kind of thing going on. But keep this quiet. We need Hague's support if we want New Jersey.'"[73]

Roosevelt helped a loyal Texas congressman by the name of Lyndon Johnson. "Johnson himself became an IRS target for failing to properly report income from his campaigns," explains Folsom. "On January 13, 1944, just as six IRS agents were winding up their 18-month investigation of Johnson, President Roosevelt had an emergency meeting with Johnson. That day, the president contacted . . . Irey and began the process of halting the investigation of Johnson. . . . Johnson was not harmed at all. He had proven himself too valuable to the president to lose."[74]

The Kennedy administration was also notorious for misusing confidential IRS and FBI information, as well as authorizing the FBI to spy on Martin Luther King Jr.

Recall earlier what Jeff Himmelman revealed in his book about Ben Bradlee, *Yours in Truth*, when "Pierre Salinger, Kennedy's press secretary, negotiated to have Ben [Bradlee] come up to Newport, Rhode Island (where Jackie's family had an enormous water-

front estate, Hammersmith Farm), to review FBI files that would prove that organizations spreading the rumors about Kennedy were shady themselves. This would discredit the opposition and advance a story line that the administration wanted to advance."[75]

In his own book *Conversations with Kennedy,* Bradlee writes that "we [President Kennedy and Bradlee] talked about taxes and who pays how much. The president stunned us all by saying that J. Paul Getty, the oil zillionaire who was reputedly the richest man in the world, paid exactly $500 in income taxes last year, and that H. L. Hunt, the Texas oil zillionaire who must be one of the next richest, paid only $22,000 in income taxes last year, he said.... I asked him, since he had obviously done some research on the tax payments of millionaires, how much Daniel Ludwig had paid, referring back to the owner of the yacht that had failed to salute the commander in chief last month in Newport. He smiled but he didn't bite, and then said that all this tax information was secret, and it was probably illegal for him to know or at least for him to tell me. I told him if he ever wanted to give a tax reform bill the last little push, all he had to do was let me publish this kind of information...."[76]

Burnham explains further that there was a regular process in place for the White House to receive confidential IRS information. "On May 23, 1961, [Mortimer M.] Caplin, then serving as Kennedy's brand-new IRS commissioner, had written a long memorandum explaining that a few months before he had allowed Carmine Bellino, a special consultant to President Kennedy, to inspect IRS files 'without a written request.'" Vernon (Mike) Acree, an IRS official, explained: "Right after Kennedy was elected, I got called down to Caplin's office. He introduced me to Bellino. Caplin said Bellino was a special assistant to the president and could have any-

thing. One of my assistants set Bellino up in a little office in the IRS headquarters building. I remember that one day during the Kennedy years that my assistant provided Bellino a stack of tax records about ten inches high that had been submitted by *The New York Times*. We weren't told why the White House wanted to see the *Times*'s returns and didn't ask." "The tax information I made available to Kennedy and Nixon was not unusual." Acree added, "I had provided the same service to the White House people under Truman, Eisenhower, and Johnson."[77]

Furthermore, after being nudged by President Kennedy, and with his knowledge and that of Attorney General Robert Kennedy, Caplin instituted an audit program aimed at groups on the "right" that were critical of the president and his policies. In April 1976, the Senate Select Intelligence Committee reported: "By directing tax audits at individuals and groups solely because of their political beliefs, the Ideological Organizations Audit Project [as the 1961 Kennedy program was known] established a precedent for a far more elaborate program of targeting 'dissidents.'"[78]

The abuses also reached into the FBI. Indeed, the FBI tracked virtually every move of Martin Luther King. CNN reported, in an interview with author David Garrow, that "the FBI began secretly tracking King's flights and watching his associates. In July 1963, a month before the March on Washington, FBI Director J. Edgar Hoover filed a request with Attorney General Robert Kennedy to tap King's and his associates' phones and to bug their homes and offices. In September, Kennedy consented to the technical surveillance. Kennedy gave the FBI permission to break into King's office and home to install the bugs, as long as agents recognized the 'delicacy of this particular matter' and didn't get caught installing them. Kennedy added a proviso—he wanted to be personally informed of any pertinent information."[79]

President Kennedy even had installed a secret recording system in the Oval Office and Cabinet Room as well. He personally ordered Secret Service agent Robert Bouck to undertake the task. In his book *The Tunnels,* author Greg Mitchell wrote: "Three previous presidents had installed listening devices, but they had used them sparingly. Franklin Roosevelt made a few recordings in 1940; Harry Truman and Dwight Eisenhower left behind less than a dozen hours of tapes each. Kennedy's plan would give him far more opportunity than that. JFK aimed to document face-to-face conversations with aides and visitors, for his own use and/or the historical record. Without telling anyone why . . . At Kennedy's direction, he installed the Oval Office microphones under the President's desk and in a coffee table. Kennedy could activate them with the discreet push of a button on his desk. The microphones in the Cabinet Room were hidden behind drapes and could be turned on and off by a button at the head of the table where Kennedy sat."[80]

Widespread domestic espionage and tax investigations only got worse under Kennedy's successor, President Lyndon Johnson.

Like several of his predecessors, but even more so, Johnson used the IRS and the FBI, as well as the CIA, for unconstitutional and unlawful purposes. For example, the Heritage Foundation's Lee Edwards, who had served as director of information for the 1964 Barry Goldwater presidential campaign, tells how Johnson used the CIA and FBI to spy on the Goldwater campaign.

"Former intelligence officer E. Howard Hunt, best known for his role as an orchestrator of the Watergate bugging," wrote Edwards, "told a Senate committee in 1973 that his CIA superior ordered him to infiltrate the Goldwater campaign. Hunt claimed to have questioned the order, only to be told that it had been a personal request of President Johnson and that the information he received would be delivered to a White House aide. CIA Director William Colby confirmed the White House's role in the illegal surveillance while addressing a congressional hearing in 1975. That the CIA is prohibited by law from operating within the U.S. didn't matter to the Johnson campaign. The Goldwater people never suspected that one of them was a spy for the Democrats."[81]

Edwards explained that "the FBI arranged for widespread wiretapping of the Goldwater campaign. Sure enough, campaign reporters could soon be heard asking specific questions about the candidate's travel plans that had only been discussed by Goldwater aides behind closed doors. To protect themselves, Goldwater staffers began using pay phones outside their headquarters. . . . Johnson also illegally ordered the FBI to conduct security checks of Goldwater's Senate staff. . . . In 1971 Robert Mardian, who had been regional director in the Goldwater campaign, became assistant attorney general for internal security. During a two-hour briefing with [J. Edgar] Hoover, Mardian asked about the procedures for electronic surveillance. To Mardian's amazement, Hoover confessed that in 1964 the FBI had wired the Goldwater campaign plane, under orders from the White House. When Mardian asked Hoover why he had complied, the director answered, 'You do what the president tells you to do.'"[82]

The focus of Johnson's espionage was not just his presidential opponent but his own Democratic Party convention months before, when he feared the Kennedys might challenge his legitimacy, and he wanted complete control of the process. Hence Johnson called in the FBI to surveil his own party's convention. As Professor Robert Dallek, author of *Flawed Giant—Lyndon Johnson and His Times 1961–1973*, explains: "To keep track of [Robert] Kennedy's doing and bottle him up, Johnson asked the FBI to send a team of men to Atlantic City. Ostensibly, the thirty agents assigned to the squad were 'to assist the Secret Service in protecting President Johnson and to ensure that the convention itself would not be marred by civil disruption.'"[83]

The then-attorney general, Robert Kennedy, knew nothing of this, nor was he the only subject of the FBI's monitoring. "For seven days . . . ," writes Dallek, "the squad kept 'the White House apprised of all major developments during the Convention's course.' Using 'informant coverage . . . various confidential techniques,' a wiretap on [Martin Luther] King's hotel room, and 'a microphone surveillance of the SNCC [Student Nonviolent Coordinating Committee] and CORE [Congress of Racial Equality],' and 'infiltration of key groups through use of undercover agents, and . . . agents using appropriate cover as reports,' [FBI deputy Cartha] DeLoach provided [Walter] Jenkins [one of Johnson's top cronies] with '44 pages of intelligence data' and 'kept Jenkins and [Bill] Moyers [another top Johnson crony] constantly advised by telephone of minute-by-minute developments.'"[84]

In fact, Dallek writes that when Vice President Hubert Humphrey would later receive the Democratic Party's nomination for president in 1968, "to keep close tabs on the inner workings of Hubert's campaign, Johnson had the FBI tap Humphrey's phones. If Humphrey were going to come out against the [Vietnam] war, Johnson wanted advance notice and a chance to dissuade him."[85]

Johnson also put the IRS to maximum political use. Burnham

observed that "[d]uring the Johnson administration . . . the focus of the IRS's never-acknowledged effort at political control swung from the right-wing to individuals and organizations concerned with racial matters or with opposing the U.S. presence in Vietnam. Unlike the Kennedy period, no evidence has yet emerged that directly links President Johnson to what became increasingly frenetic efforts by the FBI and the IRS to defang and declaw the critics of his administration. However, not too much should be made of this lack of documentary evidence. On January 1, 1967, Cartha DeLoach, J. Edgar Hoover's deputy, wrote a memorandum to Hoover stating that the White House had informed him that 'the President does not want any record made' that would prove his direct involvement in FBI intelligence operations directed at war critics. . . . The record contains a great deal of information, however, proving that the IRS, the FBI, and several other federal agencies were involved in a large number of such projects during the years that LBJ occupied the White House."[86]

Johnson also outdid Kennedy in secretly recording discussions in the White House. Dallek explains that "[t]he record of Johnson's presidency hardly suggests a man who was fastidious about constitutional guarantees of privacy or excessive government intrusion into private conversations and behavior. During his five-plus years in office Johnson secretly recorded over 10,000 conversations without the knowledge of other parties on the telephone or in his White House offices. . . ."[87]

As the Democratic party-press has extensively reported for decades, President Richard Nixon and his administration used the various federal investigative, enforcement, and security agencies to harass, monitor, and deter political and policy opponents. And

Nixon famously used the taping system in the Oval Office as well. However, in Nixon's case, unlike his predecessors, he faced real consequences for these activities.

In July 1974, the House Judiciary Committee charged Nixon with various impeachable acts, including abuse of power in Article II. It stated, in part:

> Using the powers of the office of President of the United States, Richard M. Nixon, in violation of his constitutional oath faithfully to execute the office of President of the United States and, to the best of his ability, preserve, protect, and defend the Constitution of the United States, and in disregard of his constitutional duty to take care that the laws be faithfully executed, has repeatedly engaged in conduct violating the constitutional rights of citizens, impairing the due and proper administration of justice and the conduct of lawful inquiries, or contravening the laws governing agencies of the executive branch and the purposed of these agencies.[88]

In Section 1 of this charge, Nixon is said to have "act[ed] personally and through his subordinates and agents, endeavored to obtain from the Internal Revenue Service, in violation of the constitutional rights of citizens, confidential information contained in income tax returns for purposed not authorized by law, and to cause, in violation of the constitutional rights of citizens, income tax audits or other income tax investigations to be initiated or conducted in a discriminatory manner."[89]

In Section 2, Nixon is said to have "misused the Federal Bureau of Investigation, the Secret Service, and other executive personnel, in violation or disregard of the constitutional rights of citizens, by directing or authorizing such agencies or personnel to conduct or continue electronic surveillance or other investigations for purposes unrelated to national security, the enforcement of laws, or any other lawful function of his office; he did direct, authorize, or permit the use of information obtained thereby for purposes unrelated to national security, the enforcement of laws, or any other lawful function of his office; and he did direct the concealment of certain records made by the Federal Bureau of Investigation of electronic surveillance."[90]

Post-Nixon, the most egregious abuse of power involving the politicization of the IRS occurred during the Obama administration, when hundreds of Tea Party groups were targeted by the IRS. Some were investigated, some were audited, and some had their tax-exempt status questioned or applications for tax-exempt status delayed.

President Obama had denied any knowledge of the IRS's activities and, ultimately, he dismissed the scandal as phony. In a December 2013 interview with MSNBC's Chris Matthews, Obama said, in part: "If . . . you've got an office in Cincinnati, in the IRS office that—I think, for bureaucratic reasons, is trying to streamline what is a difficult law to interpret about whether a nonprofit is actually a political organization, deserves a tax-exempt agency. And they've got a list, and suddenly everybody's outraged."[91]

After initial attention and curiosity, most newsrooms and journalists lost interest as well. Their attitude can best be summed up by far-left website *Salon*'s political reporter, Alex Seitz-Wald, who wrote on July 9, 2013: "The first few days of the IRS scandal that would consume Washington for weeks went like this: Conserva-

tives were indignant, the media was outraged, the president had to
respond, his allies turned on him . . . and only *then,* the Treasury
Department's inspector general released the actual report that had
sparked the whole controversy—in that order. It's a fitting micro-
cosm of the entire saga, which has gone from legacy-tarnishing
catastrophe to historical footnote in the intervening six weeks, and
a textbook example of how the scandal narrative can dominate
Washington and cable news even when there is no actual scandal."
Ironically, Bill Moyers, among President Johnson's most reliable
and effective hatchet men, was so impressed with Seitz-Wald's
piece that he posted it on his own website.[92]

In October 2017, as reported by Stephen Dinan in the *Washington Times*: "The Trump administration agreed Thursday to pay
$3.5 million to tea party groups snared by IRS targeting during
the Obama administration, saying the intrusive scrutiny was illegal and cannot be allowed to happen again. The government also
reversed its tune on former IRS senior executive Lois G. Lerner.
Instead of being a hero who tried to stop the targeting—as the
Obama administration concluded in 2015—the Justice Department and IRS now say she failed to stop her employees and hid
the bad behavior from her bosses for two years. Attorney General
Jeff Sessions, who announced the settlements, offered an apology
to more than 450 groups that were part of two lawsuits against the
IRS. As part of the agreements, the government admitted that the
IRS forced tea party groups into illegal delays and unconscionable
scrutiny, including questions about their political beliefs, plans to
run for office and names of financial backers."[93]

Rather than recognizing that the Trump administration ear-
nestly acted to right a very serious wrong involving an abuse of

power by the IRS during the Obama administration, the reaction from most of the mass media was a collective and cynical yawn. Moreover, there is not a hint that President Trump or his administration have illegally used the IRS, FBI, or CIA, as did several earlier presidents and administrations.

CHARACTER

Whatever President Trump may or may not have done in his personal life before becoming president—which has been of intense interest to the Democratic party-press—there has not been any credible glimmer of moral improbity or faithlessness during his service in the Oval Office. Not so with several of his more recent predecessors, John Kennedy and Lyndon Johnson tops among them, which was ignored by the mass media.

President Kennedy had scores of extramarital flings and affairs both before and *while he was president*—with actresses, secretaries, married women, friends, a mobster's girlfriend, etc. Perhaps two of the most concerning such instances involved an alleged East German spy and a nineteen-year old intern.

As Professor Larry Sabato details: "In July 1963, FBI director J. Edgar Hoover informed Bobby Kennedy that he knew about the president's past relationship with an alleged East German spy named Ellen Rometsch. The wife of an army officer who had been assigned to the West German embassy, Rometsch supplemented her income by turning tricks for Washington's best and brightest. Her pimp was a high-profile Senate aide named Bobby Baker, who had close ties to Lyndon Johnson. In late August 1963, Rometsch was flown back to Germany on a U.S. Air Force transport plane at the behest of the State Department. According to author Seymour Hersh, she was accompanied by LaVern Duffy, one of Bobby Kennedy's colleagues from his days on the McClellan Committee. Records related to Rometsch's deportation have either vanished or were never created in the first place."[94]

Then there was Kennedy's seduction of a young intern who had just arrived at the White House. "The well-supported story of Mimi Alford," writes Sabato, "a nineteen-year-old White House intern at the time of her involvement with JFK, is impossible to overlook. Initiated into JFK's sexual world just four days into her internship, Alford lost her virginity to Kennedy as he conducted what can only be called a deeply inappropriate affair with a young charge; it even included a Kennedy-directed episode of oral sex with aide Dave Powers while Kennedy watched. This behavior, barely hidden from others within the White House and involving government resources to shuttle Alford to and from the traveling president, has caused some to question Kennedy's basic fitness for the highest office. Many have tried to reconcile JFK's high-minded, skilled public persona with his sleazy, reckless private self. It is simply impossible to match up the two sides rationally, and it is certainly inadequate to say that the rules of his time or a sometimes empty marriage permitted or justified these escapades. Any private citizen with modest responsibilities would be condemned for them, and as president, JFK risked his White House tenure, the welfare of his party, his policy goals, and everyone he supposedly held dear."[95]

Lyndon Johnson was no better. Dallek writes that "[a]lthough Johnson had a reverential regard for the presidency ... he didn't see his personal crudeness as demeaning the office. As throughout his Senate and vice-presidential years, he remained an exhibitionist and a philanderer who didn't mind flaunting his conquests. When a woman reporter at a private session with several journalists asked him a tough question, he 'reached down and pulled his crotch and said, "Well . . . I don't know." And he was scratching himself. It was terrible.' During his vice presidency, the press called his Senate office 'the nooky room.' . . . [H]e wanted beautiful women working for him and viewed them as fair game. . . . Lady Bird shut her eyes and ears to some of this behavior. What she didn't know or acknowledge preserved her from painful offenses. . . ."[96]

Next, Dallek makes this salient point when it comes to the press. "Almost all of Johnson's outrageous personal behavior was hidden from the public. In the sixties, journalists largely kept their knowledge of presidential transgressions of the sort Johnson committed to themselves. And not just because current mores dictated such journalistic restraint; reporters and publishers, who had been a partisan force against Goldwater, were reluctant to undermine someone as progressive as LBJ. True, privately, he was sometimes a Neanderthal whose crudeness offended them, but in public he was an unflinching advocate of social reforms that promised large improvements in the lives of all Americans, particularly minorities and women. . . ."[97]

Of course, this goes a long way in explaining the disparate media treatment Kennedy and Johnson received vis-à-vis Trump. Kennedy and Johnson were both Democrats and both progressives. In particular, Johnson launched the Great Society, the greatest expansion of federal welfare programs and entitlements since Franklin Roosevelt's New Deal. Moreover, Kennedy and Johnson had defeated Republican candidates who were much hated by the media—Richard Nixon and Barry Goldwater, respectively. While the Democratic party-press turned on Johnson over the Vietnam War, they did much to protect his private life and Kennedy's from public scrutiny.

Although President Bill Clinton did not receive the kind of kid-gloves media treatment enjoyed by Kennedy and Johnson in their extramarital affairs while serving as president, it was Matt Drudge who broke the Monica Lewinsky story that *Newsweek* spiked at the last moment. As Drudge reported on January 17, 1998:

> At the last minute, at 6 p.m. on Saturday evening, NEWSWEEK magazine killed a story that was destined to shake official Washington to its foundation: A White House intern carried on a sexual affair with the President of the United States!
>
> The DRUDGE REPORT has learned that reporter Michael Isikoff developed the story of his career, only to have it spiked by top NEWSWEEK suits hours before publication. A young woman, 23, sexually involved with the love of her life, the President of the United States, since she was a 21-year-old intern at the White House. She was a frequent visitor to a small study just off the Oval Office where she claims to have indulged the president's sexual preference. Reports of the relationship spread in White House quarters and she was moved to a job at the Pentagon, where she worked until last month. . . .
>
> Ironically, several years ago, it was Isikoff that found himself in a shouting match with editors who were refusing to publish even a portion of his meticulously researched investigative report that was to break Paula Jones. Isikoff worked for the WASHINGTON POST at the time, and left shortly after the incident to build them for the paper's sister magazine, NEWSWEEK.[98]

There were also serious questions raised about NBC's reporting on rape allegations against Clinton dating to the time when he was attorney general of Arkansas. As *Breitbart* reported: "After filming the 1999 interview [with Juanita Broaddrick by correspondent Lisa Myers], NBC waited 35 days until finally airing the exclusive. The timeline is critical. The Senate voted to acquit Clinton in the impeachment case on Feb. 12. NBC's interview, conducted January 20, 1999, did not run until Feb. 24, and the network placed it opposite the highly-rated Grammy Awards."[99]

Although NBC denied any nefarious motive in delaying the show's airing, "[s]ome have questioned NBC's motivation in waiting to air Broaddrick's charge of rape. 'The 35-day interval between tape and air is now one of the legends of the impeachment process. Why didn't the American public get to hear Mrs. Broaddrick before the Senate voted to acquit Mr. Clinton on Feb. 12?' wrote Philip Weiss in the *Observer* in 1999."[100]

Compare these examples not only to the press coverage received by President Trump, but the tawdry reporting surrounding the confirmation hearings of Brett Kavanaugh for associate justice of the Supreme Court. As was reported by news outlets, Kavanaugh was accused of exposing himself, participating in drugging and gang-raping girls, raping a woman on a boat, being in a bar fight, drinking heavily in high school, and committing perjury, among other things.[101] Kavanaugh, a sitting federal appellate judge, had two strikes against him—he was nominated by President Trump and was widely considered (rightly or wrongly) another originalist vote on the Supreme Court should he be confirmed. Therefore, the Democratic party-press abandoned all professional journalistic standards in a failed but disgraceful spectacle in assisting Senate Democrats to destroy Kavanaugh's character and prevent his confirmation.

A STANDARDLESS PROFESSION

IN THE DAYS leading up to and during the American Revolution, the patriots who ran the printing presses and produced the pamphlets and newspapers were intent on establishing a nation founded on republican ideals of liberty, private property rights, representative government, freedom of speech, etc. They were open and transparent about their purpose. Indeed, they were often leaders in the revolutionary cause, making the intellectual, emotional, and factual arguments for independence. Later, the party-press, in which newspapers aligned publicly with political parties and candidates, made no bones about their intentions. Newspapers and newsmen were advocates for a particular party, candidate, or policy, and were clear about their allegiances.

At the turn of the last century, during the rise of the Progressive Movement, the mass media claimed to desire a "scientific" and "professional" approach to news gathering and reporting, one centered on "objectivity," and they sought to distance themselves from the identity media. But even the idea and definition of objectivity became a point of debate and dispute, and remains so today. The word "objective" itself, and its application to the news, is used in a way that overlooks or excuses a news outlet's or reporter's overt fidelity to ideological progressivism and Democratic Party partiality. The contention is that the vetting of the news requires objective uniformity and standards, not the person or newsroom themselves. Consequently, in the last hundred years or so, the attitude has been that journalists need not be objective in their own thinking or politics or seek objectivity in their own thinking or politics, as long as they are objective in their analytical method of gathering and reporting the news.

Turning again to Bill Kovach and Tom Rosenstiel and their book, *The Elements of Journalism*, they make the point this way: "A stronger, more unified, and more transparent method of verifying the news would . . . be the single most important step that those who practice journalism could take to address and, if necessary, correct the rising perception that the work of journalists is marred by bias. . . . What would this journalism of objective *method*—rather than aim—look like? What should citizens expect from the press as a reasonable discipline of reporting?"[1]

Kovach and Rosenstiel provide five "intellectual principles of a science of reporting":

1. Never add anything that was not there.
2. Never deceive the audience.
3. Be as transparent as possible about your methods and motives.

4. Rely on your own original reporting.

5. Exercise humility.[2]

However, it is quite clear that this interpretation of objectivity, while seemingly alluring, has proved impossible for most newsrooms and journalists. The reason is that most partisans are unable or unwilling to put aside their personal ideological and political perspectives or, even worse, they consider them essential to moving and improving society through activism. This is the fundamental nature of the modern media. For the most part, the objectivity of *methods* has become the partisanship of ideological and political results.

The examples of ideologically and politically motivated stories are voluminous. And they lead to flat-out media fabrications and deceit. A few of the most notorious recent examples include:

- the *Rolling Stone* story defaming a University of Virginia dean in a false campus rape story;[3]
- the false allegations of rape against members of the Duke lacrosse team;[4]
- Dan Rather's discredited report about George W. Bush's military record;[5]
- the smear of Brett Kavanaugh;[6]
- the smear of the Covington Catholic students;[7]
- the seemingly endless list of false reports about President Trump, including collusion;[8] and on and on.

In 1897, Adolph S. Ochs, the owner of *the New York Times*, created the famous slogan "All the News That's Fit to Print." It still appears on the masthead of the newspaper today. He wrote the slogan as a declaration of the newspaper's intention to report the news impartially.[9] But the *Times*, which is considered the gold standard of journalism by other newsrooms and journalists and a guide star for news stories and leads, has a wretched history of deceit and untruthfulness virtually unmatched by any other news organization. Having botched miserably the coverage of Adolph Hitler's genocide against the Jews and Joseph Stalin's genocide against the Ukrainians, either of which should have forever tainted the integrity and reliability of the *Times*, today it self-servingly and arrogantly portrays itself as leading the collective media rampart for freedom of the press. Yet, is not the newspaper a well-known bastion of progressivism, which frequently distorts its reporting? And do not such misrepresentations about its true purpose pervert the role and purpose of journalism and a free press? Circumspection is not the media's strong point. And rather than clean up their act with serious self-policing by reforming their practices and standards, the *Times* and other media outlets pound their chests with self-righteous adoration, as they proclaim themselves the defenders of a free press.

As recently as February 20, 2019, current *Times* publisher Arthur Gregg Sulzberger (Ochs's great-great grandson), responding to President Trump referring to the newspaper as "the enemy of the people"—as the president was frustrated with yet another "news" story, this time an "investigative report" filled with allegations and innuendos about him and his administration from anonymous sources—publicly lectured the president and the nation about the importance of a free press. He wrote:

America's founders believed that a free press was essential to democracy because it is the foundation of an informed, engaged citizenry. That conviction, enshrined in the First Amendment, has been embraced by nearly every American president. Thomas Jefferson declared, "The only security of all is in a free press." John F. Kennedy warned about the risks to "free society without a very, very active press." Ronald Reagan said, "There is no more essential ingredient than a free, strong and independent press to our continued success."

All these presidents had complaints about their coverage and at times took advantage of the freedom every American has to criticize journalists. But in demonizing the free press as the enemy, simply for performing its role of asking difficult questions and bringing uncomfortable information to light, President Trump is retreating from a distinctly American principle. It's a principle that previous occupants of the Oval Office fiercely defended regardless of their politics, party affiliation, or complaints about how they were covered.

The phrase "enemy of the people" is not just false, it's dangerous. It has an ugly history of being wielded by dictators and tyrants who sought to control public information. And it is particularly reckless coming from someone whose office gives him broad powers to fight or imprison the nation's enemies. As I have repeatedly told President Trump face to face, there are mounting signs that this incendiary rhetoric is encouraging threats and violence against journalists at home and abroad.

Through 33 presidential administrations, across 167 years, *The New York Times* has worked to serve the public by fulfilling the fundamental role of the free press. To help people, regardless of their backgrounds or politics, understand their country and the world. To report independently, fairly and accurately. To ask hard questions. To pursue the truth wherever it leads. That will not change.[10]

Despite this deprecatory and hyperbolic statement against the president, who simply dared to harshly condemn the *Times* and its reporting, it is a fact that the *Times* frequently does not pursue the truth wherever it leads. And this is certainly true today in its coverage of the Trump presidency, where it has been predictably and aggressively hostile.

Indeed, former ABC News anchor and longtime journalist Ted Koppel—no Trump supporter or conservative—expressed his profound concern about the state of journalism, and particularly reporting at the *Times*, during a March 7, 2019, discussion with Marvin Kalb at the Carnegie Endowment for International Peace. He stated, in part:

We have things appearing on the front page of the *New York Times* right now that never would have appeared fifty years ago. Analysis, commentary on the front page. I remember sitting at the breakfast table with my wife during the campaign after the *Access Hollywood* tape came out and the *New York Times*—I will not offend any of you here by using the language but you know exactly what words they were and they were spelled out on the front page of the *New York Times*.

So [President Trump's] perception that the establishment press is out to get him—doesn't mean that great journalism is not being done. It is. But the notion that most of us look upon Donald Trump as being an absolute fiasco . . . He's not mistaken in that perception, and he's not mistaken when so many of the liberal media, for example, describe themselves as belonging to the Resistance. What does that mean? That's not said by people who consider themselves reporters, objective reporters. That's the kind of language that's used by people who genuinely believe, and I rather suspect with some justification, that Donald Trump is bad for the United States and they're betting that the sooner he's out of office, the better they will like it. Whether that happens by virtue of indictment, impeachment, or election, we'll see. . . .

We are not the reservoir of objectivity I think we were.[11]

However, rather than accept responsibility for the low credibility in which the *Times* and other media outlets are held by the public, as a consequence of their own record and behavior, the *Times* and many other newsrooms conveniently blame President Trump for the distrust and cynicism they, themselves, have sowed with the citizenry.

As discussed earlier, unlike certain of the president's predecessors, Trump has taken no official governmental steps to silence news organizations or journalists. Although Sulzberger mentioned Jefferson, Kennedy, and Reagan as defenders of the press despite their complaints about it, a group in which Trump should actually be included for these purposes, Sulzberger omits that Adams, Lincoln, Wilson, FDR, and Obama did, in fact, use the power of the federal government against news outlets and journalists with whom they disagreed. Sulzberger's rhetoric about

Trump is dishonest and a deflection from his own failure as a newspaper publisher.

Sulzberger is also less than forthcoming when describing the role of his journalists as truth seekers digging for the facts. In an April 25, 2004, opinion piece by the newspaper's public editor, Daniel Okrent, the role of a journalist is described this way:

> With very few exceptions, the longer you've been here, or the higher you've risen in the organization, the less likely you are to believe *The Times* is, or should be, the paper of record. Metro columnist Clyde Haberman told me that in his 27 years at *The Times*, "I have never heard anyone inside the paper refer to it that way"; reporter Richard Pérez-Peña, an 11-year veteran, said, "I don't think I've ever heard my colleagues here use the phrase except rarely, in an ironic, almost self-mocking tone."
>
> I think that's because they recognize both the impossibility of fulfilling the role and the deadening effect it could have on the paper. Katherine Bouton, deputy editor of the paper's Sunday magazine, said: "We understand now that all reporting is selective. With the exception of raw original source material, there really isn't anything 'of record,' is there? . . ."
>
> Here's another way of stating it: In a heterogeneous world, whose record is one newspaper even in the position to preserve? And what group of individuals, no matter how talented or dedicated, would dare arrogate to itself so godlike a role? If you rely on *The Times* as your only source of news, you are buying into the conceptions, attitudes and interests of the people who put it out every day. It cannot be definitive, and asking it to be is a disservice to both the staff and the readers. I

mean no disrespect to *The Times*, but what discriminating citizen can really afford to rely on only one source of news? . . .[12]

Of course, Okrent was right that news organizations, like the
Times, have "conceptions, attitudes and interests of the people who
put it out every day," which speaks to the *Times'* frequent and obvious interchangeable use of its news and editorials pages in service
to the progressive ideology and the Democratic Party program,
like so many media organizations these days. Moreover, he and the
colleagues with whom he spoke acknowledge further that they are
not in the business of simply reporting the news, for it would have
a "deadening effect" on the newspaper. Thus they neither seek nor
deliver objectivity in their news reporting. Its role is news with
social activism, agenda-driving, interpretation, analysis, etc., as a
siren for the progressive cause.

Jim Rutenberg, a *Times* news correspondent turned columnist, is even more blunt. He asserts that if you are a journalist
who despises Trump, as so many in the Democratic party-press
do, and consider him some kind of a threat to the nation, you can
hardly be expected to report objectively about him. On August 7,
2016, Rutenberg explained the mindset at the newspaper and the
media at large, writing: "If you're a working journalist and you
believe that Donald J. Trump is a demagogue playing to the nation's worst racist and nationalistic tendencies, that he cozies up
to anti-American dictators and that he would be dangerous with
control of the United States nuclear codes, how the heck are you
supposed to cover him? . . . [I]f you believe all of those things, you
have to throw out the textbook American journalism has been
using for the better part of the past half-century, if not longer,

and approach it in a way you've never approached anything in your career. If you view a Trump presidency as something that's potentially dangerous, then your reporting is going to reflect that. You would move closer than you've ever been to being oppositional. That's uncomfortable and uncharted territory for every mainstream, non-opinion journalist I've ever known, and by normal standards, untenable. . . . But the question that everyone is grappling with is: Do normal standards apply? And if they don't, what should take their place? . . . It may not always seem fair to Mr. Trump or his supporters. But journalism shouldn't measure itself against any one campaign's definition of fairness. It is journalism's job to be true to the readers and viewers, and true to the facts, in a way that will stand up to history's judgment. To do anything less would be untenable."[13]

The abandonment of objective truth and, worse, the rejection of the principles and values of America's early press and revolutionaries, is not new for the *Times*. It long predates the Trump presidency. And it has led the *Times* and other media outlets into a very bleak and dark place, destructive of the press as a crucial institution for a free people. If newsrooms and journalists do not act forthwith and with urgency to "fundamentally transform" their approach to journalism, which, sadly, is highly unlikely, their credibility will continue to erode and may well reach a point soon where it is irreparably damaged with a large portion of the citizenry—and rightly so. The media will not only marginalize themselves, but *they* will continue to be the greatest threat to freedom of the press today—not President Trump or his administration, but the current practitioners of what used to be journalism.

Therefore, as I said at the opening, this book is intended to, among other things, "jump-start a long overdue and hopefully productive dialogue among the American citizenry on how best to deal with the complicated and complex issue of the media's collapsing role as a bulwark of liberty, the civil society, and re-publicanism."

ACKNOWLEDGMENTS

Writing a book is a family effort. It involves very long hours, at all times of the day and night, including weekends and holidays. I am blessed to have a very tolerant and understanding family, starting with my amazing wife, Julie. She not only endures my crazy hours and the mood swings authors experience during the research and writing process, but she is an indispensable partner and sounding board for my thoughts and ideas. Julie is a brilliant lawyer in her own right, and she not only made this a better book, but she came up with the title!

I cannot say enough about our wonderful children and grandchildren: Lauren, Chase, David, Jenna, Nick, Sloane, and Asher. They are outstanding human beings in every way and bring us much joy. I could not be prouder of each and every one of them. To my big brother, Doug, you are one of the most decent and kind people I have ever had the honor to know. You are an inspiration to everyone who knows you. And to our dear Sylvia, of the greatest generation, whom we adore and who inspires all of us with her wisdom, energy, and kindness.

Finally, I posthumously thank my beloved parents, Jack and

Norma, who recently passed from this life to the next, just four months apart, and who will be forever together and loved in perpetuity by their family. So, too, Leo Strauss, who left an indelible mark on his children and grandchildren, and who will always be a shining light.

Notes

INTRODUCTION: UNFREEDOM OF THE PRESS

1 U.S. Constitution, Preamble.

1. NEWS AS POLITICAL AND IDEOLOGICAL ACTIVISM

1 Hutchins Commission, "A Free and Responsible Press," 1947, in *The Journalist's Moral Compass, Basic Principles*, Steven R. Knowlton and Patrick R. Parsons, eds. (Westport, CT: Praeger, 1995), 209.

2 Ibid., 210

3 Ibid.

4 Jeffrey M. Jones., "U.S. Media Trust Continues to Recover from 2016 Low," Gallup, October 12, 2018, https://news.gallup.com/poll/243665/media-trust-continues-recover-2016-low.aspx (March 16, 2019).

5 Ibid.

6 "Mike Drop" interview with Lara Logan, February 15, 2019, iHeart Radio, https://www.iheart.com/podcast/867-mike-drop-29170721/episode/023-lara-logan-30567470 (March 16, 2019).

7 Ibid.

8 Lara Logan, appearing on *Hannity*, February 20, 2019, Fox News Corp.

9 Hutchins Commission, "A Free and Responsible Press," 218–19.

10 Knight Foundation, "Public trust in the media is at an all-time low.

231

Results from a major new Knight-Gallup report can help us understand why," Medium.com, January 15, 2018, https://medium.com /trust-media-and-democracy/10-reasons-why-americans-dont-trust -the-media-d0630c125b9e (March 16, 2019).

11 Ibid.

12 Ibid.

13 Ibid.

14 Hutchins Commission, "A Free and Responsible Press," 221–22.

15 Bill Kovach and Tom Rosentiel, *The Elements of Journalism* (New York: Three Rivers Press, 2007), 5.

16 Ibid., 5–6.

17 Ibid., 6.

18 Ibid., 7.

19 Ibid., 240,

20 Ibid., 82.

21 Ibid., 81.

22 Ibid., 82.

23 Ibid., 83.

24 Tim Groseclose, *Left Turn: How Liberal Media Bias Distorts the American Mind* (New York: St. Martin's Griffin, 2011), vii.

25 Ibid., 111.

26 Ibid., 111–12.

27 American Press Institute, "Understanding Bias," https://www .americanpressinstitute.org/journalism-essentials/bias-objectivity/under-standing-bias (March 16, 2019).

28 Lars Willnut and David H. Weaver, "The American Journalist in the Digital Age," Indiana University School of Journalism, 2014, http:// archive.news.indiana.edu/releases/iu/2014/05/2013-american-journalist -key-findings.pdf (March 16, 2019).

29 Hadas Gold, "Survey: 7 Percent of Reporters Identify as Republican," *Politico,* May 6 2014, https://www.politico.com/blogs/media/2014/05 /survey-7-percent-of-reporters-identify-as-republican-188053 (March 16, 2019).

30 Media Research Center, "The Liberal Media: Every Poll Shows Journalists Are More Liberal than the American Public—and the Public Knows

It," https://www.mrc.org/special-reports/liberal-mediaevery-poll-shows
-journalists-are-more-liberal-american-public-—-and (March 16, 2019).

31 Andrew C. Call, Scott A. Emett, Eldar Maksymov, and Nathan Y. Sharp,
    "Meet the Press: Survey Evidence on Financial Journalists as Information
    Intermediaries," December 27, 2018, https://papers.ssrn.com/sol3/papers
    .cfm?abstract_id=3279453 (March 16, 2019).

32 Dave Levinthal and Michael Beckel, "Journalists Shower Hillary Clinton
    with Campaign Cash," Center for Public Integrity, October 18, 2016,
    https://www.publicintegrity.org/2016/10/17/20330/journalists-shower
    -hillary-clinton-campaign-cash (March 16, 2019).

33 Elspeth Reeve, "Rick Stengal Is at Least the 24th Journalist to Work for
    the Obama Administration," *Atlantic*, September 12, 2013, https://www
    .theatlantic.com/politics/archive/2013/09/rick-stengel-least-24-journalist
    -go-work-obama-administration/310928/ (March 16, 2019).

34 Paul Farhi, "Media, Administration Deal with Conflicts," *Washington
    Post*, June 12, 2013, https://www.washingtonpost.com/lifestyle/style
    /media-administration-deal-with-conflicts/2013/06/12/e6f98314-ca2e
    -11e2-8da7-d274bc611a47_story.html?utm_term=.630777c069c4
    (March 16, 2019).

35 Jack Shafer and Tucker Doherty, "The Media Bubble Is Worse than You
    Think," *Politico*, May/June 2017, https://www.politico.com/magazine
    /story/2017/04/25/media-bubble-real-journalism-jobs-east-coast-215048
    (March 16, 2019).

36 Ibid.

37 Thomas E. Patterson, "News Coverage of Donald Trump's First 100
    Days," Harvard Kennedy School, Shorenstein Center on Media, Politics,
    and Public Policy, May 18, 2017, https://shorensteincenter.org/news
    -coverage-donald-trumps-first-100-days (March 16, 2019).

38 I am the host of *Life, Liberty & Levin*, which airs Sunday nights on Fox.

39 Thomas E. Patterson, "News Coverage of Donald Trump's First 100 Days."

40 Pew Research Center, Project for Excellence in Journalism, "Obama's
    First 100 Days: How the President Fared in the Press vs. Clinton and
    Bush," April 28, 2009, http://www.journalism.org/2009/04/28/obamas
    -first-100-days (March 16, 2019).

41 Media Research Center, "Media Bias 101," January 2014, http://www.mrc

.org/sites/default/files/uploads/documents/2014/MBB2014.pdf (March 16, 2019).

42 Jay Rosen, "Donald Trump Is Crashing the System. Journalists Need to Build a New One," *Washington Post*, July 13, 2016, https://www .washingtonpost.com/news/in-theory/wp/2016/07/13/donald-trump-is -crashing-the-system-journalists-need-to-build-a-new-one/?noredirect= on&utm_term=.6dfd02937907 (March 16, 2019).

43 Ibid.

44 Alicia C. Shepard, "The Gospel of Public Journalism," *American Journalism Review*, September 1994, http://ajrarchive.org/Article.asp?id= 1650 (March 16, 2019), 28–34.

45 Ibid.

46 Amitai Etzioni, *The Spirit of Community: Rights, Responsibilities, and the Communitarian Agenda* (New York: Crown, 1993), 2.

47 John Dewy, *Liberalism and Social Action* (New York: Prometheus Books, 1991), 65–66.

48 Ibid., 66.

49 Walter Lippmann, *Public Opinion* (New York: Renaissance Classics, 2012), 299 (chapter 27, "The Appeal to the Public," section 1).

50 Ibid., 300.

51 Ibid., 302.

52 Charles R. Kesler, "Faking It," *Claremont Review of Books*, Summer 2018, https://www.claremont.org/crb/article/faking-it/ (March 16, 2019).

53 Ibid.

54 Jay Rosen, *What Are Journalists For?* (New Haven, CT: Yale University Press, 1999), 19–20.

55 John Dewey, *The Public and Its Problems* (Athens: Ohio University Press, 1927), 179–80.

56 Ibid., 180–81.

57 Matthew Pressman, *On Press* (Cambridge, MA: Harvard University Press, 2018), 1–2.

58 Ibid., 23.

59 Ibid., 23–24.

60 Thomas Edsall, "Journalism Should Own Its Liberalism," *Columbia Journalism Review*, October 8, 2009, https://archives.cjr.org/campaign _desk/journalism_should_own_its_libe.php (March 16, 2019).

61 Art Swift, "Six in 10 in U.S. See Partisan Bias in News Media," Gallup, April 5, 2017, https://news.gallup.com/poll/207794/six-partisan-bias -news-media.aspx (March 16, 2019).

62 Edsall, "Journalism Should Own Its Liberalism."

63 Ibid.

64 Ibid.

65 Kovach and Rosentiel, *The Elements of Journalism*, 235.

66 Kesler, "Faking It."

2. THE EARLY PATRIOT PRESS

1   Isaiah Thomas, *The History of Printing in America* (London: Forgotten Books, 2012), 14.

2   Ibid., 15.

3   Ibid., 15–16.

4   Ibid., 17.

5   Ibid., 18.

6   Ibid., 136.

7   Ibid., 136–39.

8   David A. Copeland, *The Idea of a Free Press* (Evanston, IL: Northwestern University Press, 2006), 206–7.

9   Ibid., 207 (spelling, italics, and capitalizations in original).

10 Carol Sue Humphrey, *The American Revolution and the Press* (Evanston, IL: Northwestern University Press, 2013), 3–4.

11 Ibid., 5.

12 Ibid.

13 Copeland, *The Idea of a Free Press*, 15.

14 Bernard Bailyn, *Pamphlets of the American Revolution* (Cambridge, MA: Harvard University Press, 1965), 8.

15 Ibid., viii.

16 Ibid., 17–19.

17 Ibid., 19.

18 Bernard Bailyn, *The Ideological Origins of the American Revolution* (Cambridge, MA: Harvard University Press, 1992), 8.

19 National Constitution Center, "How Thomas Paine's other pamphlet saved the Revolution," December 19, 2018, https://constitutioncenter.org

/blog/how-thomas-paines-other-pamphlet-saved-the-revolution (March 16, 2019).

20 Thomas Paine, *Common Sense*, February 14, 1776, http://www.ushistory .org/paine/commonsense/ (March 16, 2019).

21 Ibid.

22 Ibid.

23 Ibid.

24 Ibid.

25 Ibid.

26 Ibid.

27 Ibid.

28 Humphrey, *The American Revolution and the Press*, 12.

29 Ibid., 15.

30 Ibid., 202–3.

31 Woodrow Wilson, "Fourth of July Address on the Declaration of Independence," appearing in *Classics of American Political & Constitutional Thought*, vol. 2, (Cambridge, MA: Hackett, 2007), 318 (italics added).

32 Ibid.

3. THE MODERN DEMOCRATIC PARTY-PRESS

1 Charles L. Ponce De Leon, "Press and Politics," in *The Concise Princeton Encyclopedia of American Policy History* (Princeton, NJ: Princeton University Press, 2011), 399.

2 Ibid.

3 Jim A. Kuypers, *Partisan Journalism* (Lanham, MD: Rowman & Littlefield, 2014), 18.

4 Peter Onuf, "Thomas Jefferson: Campaigns and Elections," University of Virginia Miller Center, https://millercenter.org/president/jefferson /campaigns-and-elections (March 16, 2019).

5 Ibid.

6 "Candidacy," Andrew Jackson's Hermitage, https://thehermitage.com /learn/andrew-jackson/president/candidacy (March 16, 2019).

7 Ibid.

8 Kuypers, *Partisan Journalism*, 21.

9 Ibid., 22–23.

10 Ibid., 23.

11 Harold Holzer, *Lincoln and the Power of the Press* (New York: Simon & Schuster, 2014), Introduction, xxi.

12 Andrew Malcolm, "Media's Anti-Trump Addiction Amps Up the Outrage and Fuels the Public's Suspicion," *Miami Herald*, January 15, 2019, https://www.miamiherald.com/article224535145.html (March 16, 2019).

13 Ibid.

14 Ibid.

15 Matthew Continetti, "How Trump Survives," *National Review*, September 1, 2018, https://www.nationalreview.com/2018/09/trump-survives -thanks-to-economy-and-detractors/ (March 16, 2019).

16 Jennifer Harper, "Media Mulled Impeaching Trump Even Before He Was Elected," *Washington Times*, December 9, 2018, https://www.washington times.com/news/2018/dec/9/inside-the-beltway-media -mulled-impeaching-trump-b (March 16, 2019).

17 Bill D'Agostino, "CNN, MSNBC Say 'Impeachment' 222 Times in One Day," MRC NewsBusters, August 23, 2018, https://www.newsbusters.org /blogs/nb/bill-dagostino/2018/08/23/cnn-msnbc-say-impeachment-222 -times-one-day (March 16, 2019).

18 Letter from Attorney General William Barr to House and Senate Committees on the Judiciary, March 24, 2019, available on Lawfare, https://lawfareblog.com/document-attorney-general-barr-letter-mueller -report (March 28, 2019).

19 Michael W. Chapman, "What the Liberal Media Actually Say About Trump, a.k.a. 'Hitler, Madman, Dictator, Racist,'" cnsnews.com, October 29, 2018, https://www.cnsnews.com/blog/michael-w-chapman/what -liberal-media-actually-say-about-trump-aka-hitler-mussolini-white (March 16, 2019) (emphasis added).

20 John Nolte, "List: 24 Pieces of MSM Fake News in 5 Days," *Daily Wire*, January 31, 2017, https://www.dailywire.com/news/13001/omg-list -last-week-msm-spread-much-fake-news-john-nolte (March 16, 2019).

21 Daniel Payne, "16 Fake News Stories Reporters Have Run Since Trump Won," *Federalist*, February 6, 2017, http://thefederalist.com/2017/02/06

/16-fake-news-stories-reporters-have-run-since-trump-won/ (March 16, 2019).

22 Sharyl Attkisson, "75 Media Mistakes in the Trump Era: The Definitive List," Sharylattkisson.com, March 3, 2019, https://sharylattkisson.com/50-media-mistakes-in-the-trump-era-the-definitive-list/ (March 16, 2019).

23 Jason Leopold and Anthony Cormier, "President Trump Directed His Attorney Michael Cohen to Lie to Congress About the Moscow Tower Project," BuzzFeednews.com, January 18, 2019, https://www.buzzfeednews.com/article/jasonleopold/trump-russia-cohen-moscow-tower-mueller-investigation (March 16, 2019).

24 Ibid.

25 See, generally, https://www.newsbusters.org/media-places/buzzfeed?page=0%2C1 (March 16, 2019).

26 Amber Athey, "CNN and MSNBC Repeatedly Floated Impeachment Over Disputed BuzzFeed Report," *Daily Caller*, January 18, 2019, https://dailycaller.com/2019/01/18/cnn-msnbc-impeach-trump-buzzfeed-mueller/ (March 16, 2019).

27 Curtis Houck, "Networks Spend Over 27 Minutes on Dubious BuzzFeed Trump Story," mrcNewsBusters, January 19, 2019, https://www.newsbusters.org/blogs/nb/curtis-houck/2019/01/19/networks-spend-over-27-minutes-dubious-buzzfeed-trump-story (March 16, 2019).

28 Chris Mills Rodrigo, "Special counsel issues rare statement disputing explosive Cohen report," *The Hill*, Jan. 18, 2019, https://thehill.com/homenews/administration/426128-special-counsel-issues-rare-statement-disputing-buzzfeeds-cohen (March 28, 2019).

29 Phil McCausland, "Democratic Bill Lays Groundwork to Remove Trump from Office," NBCNews.com, July 3, 2017, https://www.nbcnews.com/news/us-news/democratic-bill-lays-groundwork-remove-trump-office-n779171 (March 16, 2019).

30 Brandy Lee, *The Dangerous Case of Donald Trump* (New York: St. Martin's Press, 2017), 8.

31 Ibid., xii, xiii, xiv.

32 Annie Karni, "Washington's Growing Obsession: The 25th Amendment," *Politico*, January 3, 2018, https://www.politico.com/story/2018/01/03/trump-25th-amendment-mental-health-322625 (March 16, 2019).

33 Jonathan Easley, "Reporter Asks Questions on Trump's 'Mental Fitness' at WH Press Briefing," *The Hill*, January 3, 2018, https://thehill.com /homenews/administration/367289-reporter-questions-trumps-mental -fitness-at-white-house-press (March 16, 2019).

34 U.S. Constitution, Twenty-Fifth Amendment.

35 Ralph Ginzburg, "1,189 Psychiatrists Say Goldwater Is Psychologically Unfit to Be President," *Fact*, September–October, 1964, https://www .scribd.com/document/322479204/Fact-Magazine-Goldwater-1964 (March 16, 2019), 3, 4.

36 Ibid., 24.

37 APA's Principles of Medical Ethics with Annotations Especially Applicable to Psychiatry, 7.3.

38 Bobby Azarian, "The Psychology Behind Donald Trump's Unwavering Support," *Psychology Today*, September 13, 2016, https://www.psychology today.com/us/blog/mind-in-the-machine/201609/the-psychology-behind -donald-trumps-unwavering-support (March 16, 2019).

39 Ibid.

40 Ibid.

41 Will Rahn, "The Unbearable Smugness of the Press," CBSNews.com, November 10, 2016, https://www.cbsnews.com/news/commentary-the -unbearable-smugness-of-the-press-presidential-election-2016 (March 16, 2019).

42 Jeff Himmelman, *Yours in Truth* (New York: Random House, 2012).

43 Roger Yu, "Ben Bradlee, Legendary 'Washington Post' Editor, Dies," *USA Today*, October 21, 2014, https://www.usatoday.com/story/news/nation /2014/10/21/ben-bradlee-obituary/16640515/ (March 16, 2019).

44 Himmelman, *Yours in Truth*, 78.

45 Ibid., 82–83.

46 Ibid., 83

47 Ibid., 83.

48 Ibid., 83–84.

49 Ibid., 87.

50 Ibid.

4. THE REAL THREAT TO PRESS FREEDOM

1 Bob Salsberg, "Newspaper Calls for War of Words Against Trump Media Attacks," Associated Press, August 10, 2018, https://apnews.com /1381b7918b8a40baa182a72ae618c3f1 (March 16, 2019).

2 Claire Atkinson, "Newspapers Across the Country Denounce Trump's Media Attacks with Coordinated Editorials," NBC News, August 16, 2018, https://www.nbcnews.com/business/business-news/newspapers-across -u-s-decry-trump-s-media-attacks-coordinated-n901211 (March 16, 2019).

3 Editorial Board, "Journalists Are Not the Enemy," *Boston Globe*, August 15, 2016, https://www.bostonglobe.com/opinion/editorials/2018/08/15 /editorial/Kt0NFFonrxqBI6NqqennvL/story.html (March 16, 2019).

4 Kalev Leetaru, "Measuring the Media's Obsession with Trump," *RealClearPolitics*, December 6, 2018, https://www.realclearpolitics.com /articles/2018/12/06/measuring_the_medias_obsession_with_trump _138848.html (March 16, 2019).

5 Ibid.

6 Thomas E. Patterson, "News Coverage of Donald Trump's First 100 Days," Harvard Kennedy School, Shorenstein Center on Media, Politics and Public Policy, May 18, 2017, https://shorensteincenter.org/news -coverage-donald-trumps-first-100-days (March 16, 2019).

7 Editorial Board, "Journalists Are Not the Enemy," *Boston Globe*, August 15, 2016.

8 Jenn Topper and Amelia Nitz, "New Report Shows American Voters Overwhelmingly Support Press Freedom but Are Missing Signs It's Under Threat," Committee for Freedom of the Press, September 5, 2018, https:// www.rcfp.org/new-report-shows-american-voters-overwhelmingly -support-press-freedo/ (March 16, 2019).

9 Ibid.

10 Ibid.

11 Editorial Board, "Journalists Are Not the Enemy," *The Boston Globe*, August 15, 2016.

12 Richard Buel, Jr., "Freedom of the Press in Revolutionary America: The Evolution of Libertarianism, 1760–1820," in *The Press & the American Revolution*, Bernard Bailyn and John B. Hench, eds. (Worcester, MA: American Antiquarian Society, 1980), 61.

13 Sedition Act, July 14, 1798, http://www.constitution.org/rf/sedition
    _1798.htm (March 16, 2019).

14 Buel, "Freedom of the Press in Revolutionary America," 61.

15 Ronald G. Shafer, "The Thin-Skinned President Who Made It Illegal to
    Criticize His Office," *Washington Post*, September 8, 2018, https://www
    .washingtonpost.com/news/retropolis/wp/2018/09/08/the-thin-skinned
    -president-who-made-it-illegal-to-criticize-his-office/?utm_term=
    .ef3e3de112ea (March 16, 2019).

16 Buel, "Freedom of the Press in Revolutionary America," 89.

17 Ibid., 95.

18 Harold Holzer, *Lincoln and the Power of the Press* (New York: Simon &
    Schuster, 2014), 335–36.

19 Ibid., 336–37.

20 David T. Z. Mindich, "Lincoln's Surveillance State," *New York Times*,
    July 5, 2013, https://www.nytimes.com/2013/07/06/opinion/lincolns
    -surveillance-state.html?_r=0 (March 16, 2019).

21 Holzer, *Lincoln and the Power of the Press*, 489–90.

22 Abraham Lincoln, "Executive Order—Arrest and Imprisonment of
    Irresponsible Newspaper Reporters and Editors," May 18, 1864, available
    online by Gerhard Peters and John T. Woolley, American Presidency
    Project, http://www.presidency.ucsb.edu/ws/?pid=70018 (March 16,
    2019).

23 Holzer, *Lincoln and the Power of the Press*, 492, 495.

24 Sedition Act of 1918, Encyclopedia.com, https://www.encyclopedia.com/
    politics/legal-and-political-magazines/sedition-act-1918 (March 16, 2019).

25 "U.S. Congress passes Sedition Act, May 16, 2018," History.com, https://
    www.history.com/this-day-in-history/u-s-congress-passes-sedition-act
    (March 16, 2019).

26 Christopher B. Daly, "How Woodrow Wilson's Propaganda Machine
    Changed American Journalism," *The Conversation*, April 27, 2017,
    https://theconversation.com/how-woodrow-wilsons-propaganda
    -machine-changed-american-journalism-76270?xid=PS_smithsonian
    (March 16, 2019).

27 Gale Group, "Civil Liberties, World War I," Encyclopedia.com, https://
    www.encyclopedia.com/defense/energy-government-and-defense
    -magazines/civil-liberties-world-war-i (March 16, 2019).

28 Daly, "How Woodrow Wilson's Propaganda Machine Changed American Journalism."

29 Gil Troy, "America's First Minister of Propaganda," *Daily Beast*, March 27, 2016, https://www.thedailybeast.com/americas-first-minister-of -propaganda (March 16, 2019).

30 David Beito, "FDR's War Against the Press," *Reason*, April 5, 2017, https:// reason.com/archives/2017/04/05/roosevelts-war-against-the-pre/print (March 17, 2019).

31 Ibid.

32 Ibid.

33 Ibid.

34 Ibid.

35 David Beito, "The New Deal Witch Hunt," *National Review*, July 30, 2013, https://www.nationalreview.com/2013/07/new-deal-witch-hunt-david-t -beito/ (March 17, 2019).

36 Ibid.

37 Graham J. White, *FDR and the Press* (Chicago: University of Chicago Press, 1979), 17.

38 James E. Pollard, *The Presidents and the Press* (New York: Macmillan, 1947), 797.

39 Ibid., 798.

40 Ibid., 839.

41 Ibid., 840.

42 Leonard Downie Jr., "In Obama's War on Leaks, Reporters Fight Back," *Washington Post*, October 4, 2013, https://www.washingtonpost.com /opinions/in-obamas-war-on-leaks-reporters-fight-back/2013/10/04 /70231e1c-2aeb-11e3-b139-029811dbb57f_print.html (March 17, 2019).

43 Oliver Knox, "Obama Administration Spied on Fox News Reporter James Rosen," Yahoo.com, May 20, 2013, https://www.yahoo.com/news/blogs /ticket/obama-admin-spied-fox-news-reporter-james-rosen-134204299 .html (March 17, 2019).

44 Joanna Walters, "James Risen Calls Obama 'Greatest Enemy of Press Freedom in a Generation,'" *Guardian*, August 17, 2014, https://www .theguardian.com/world/2014/aug/17/james-risen-obama-greatest -enemy-press-freedom-generation (March 17, 2019).

45 Calvin Woodward and Christopher Rugaber, "AP Fact Check: Obama

Doesn't Always Tell the Straight Story," Associated Press, September 12, 2018, https://www.boston.com/news/politics/2018/09/12/ap-fact-check -obama-doesnt-always-tell-the-straight-story (March 17, 2019).

46 "Gov't Obtains Wide AP Phone Records in Probe," Associated Press, May 13, 2013, https://www.ap.org/ap-in-the-news/2013/govt-obtains-wide -ap-phone-records-in-probe (March 17, 2019).

47 Matt Margolis, "The Top Five Ways Obama Attacked the Free Press," PJ Media, September 11, 2018, https://pjmedia.com/trending/the-top-five -ways-obama-attacked-the-free-press (March 17, 2019).

48 Jack Shafer, "Spare Me Your Hypocritical Journalism Lecture, Mr. President," *Politico*, March 29, 2016, https://www.politico.com/magazine /story/2016/03/obama-hypocritical-journalism-lecture-213775 (March 17, 2019).

49 Ibid.

50 Ibid.

5. NEWS, PROPAGANDA, AND PSEUDO-EVENTS

1 Edward Bernays, *Propaganda* (New York: IG, 1928), back cover.

2 Christopher B. Daly, "How Woodrow Wilson's Propaganda Machine Changed American Journalism," *Smithsonian*, April 28, 2017, https:// www.smithsonianmag.com/history/how-woodrow-wilsons-propaganda -machine-changed-american-journalism-180963082/ (March 17, 2019).

3 Bernays, *Propaganda*, 27–28.

4 Ibid., 50–51.

5 Ibid., 51–52.

6 Ibid. 52.

7 Ibid.

8 Ibid., 55.

9 Ibid., 57.

10 David Samuels, "The Aspiring Novelist Who Became Obama's Foreign-Policy Guru: How Ben Rhodes Rewrote the Rules of Diplomacy for the Digital Age," *New York Times*, May 8, 2016, https://www.nytimes.com/2016 /05/08/magazine/the-aspiring-novelist-who-became-obamas-foreign -policy-guru.html (March 17, 2019).

11 Ibid.

12 Ibid.

13 Ibid.

14 Ibid.

15 Ibid.

16 Ibid.

17 Chuck Todd, *Meet the Press*, January 2, 2019, video and transcript available at https://www.realclearpolitics.com/video/2019/01/02/chuck _todd_im_not_going_to_give_time_to_climate_deniers.html (March 17, 2019).

18 Joe Weisenthal, "The 10 Most Respected Global Warming Skeptics," *Business Insider*, July 30, 2009, https://www.businessinsider.com/the-ten -most-important-climate-change-skeptics-2009-7 (March 17, 2019).

19 "Estimated 40 Percent of Scientists Doubt Manmade Global Warming," National Association of Scholars, Press Release, January 3, 2011, https:// www.nas.org/articles/Estimated_40_Percent_of_Scientists_Doubt _Manmade_Global_Warminghttps://www.nas.org/articles/Estimated_40 _Percent_of_Scientists_Doubt_Manmade_Global_Warming (March 17, 2019).

20 Ibid.

21 Patrick Michaels, "Global Warming Scientists Scrap Real Science, Bow Before President Obama Instead," *Forbes*, March 27, 2014, https://www .forbes.com/sites/patrickmichaels/2014/03/27/global-warming-scientists -scrap-real-science-bow-before-president-obama-instead/#59cf119f6d0e (March 17, 2019).

22 Richard Lindzen, biography, Cato Institute, https://www.cato.org/people /richard-lindzen (March 17, 2019).

23 Maria Tadeo, "Greenpeace Co-founder Patrick Moore Tells U.S. Senate There Is 'No Proof' Humans Cause Climate Change," *Independent*, February 28, 2014, https://www.independent.co.uk/environment/climate -change/greenpeace-co-founder-patrick-moore-tells-us-senate-there-is-no -proof-humans-cause-climate-change-9159627.html (March 17, 2019).

24 Roy Spencer, biography, drroyspencer.com, http://www.drroyspencer .com/about (March 17, 2019).

25 Warner Todd Huston, "Dr. Roy Spencer: Science Knows 'Almost Nothing' About Global Warming," *Breitbart*, July 10, 2014, https://www.breitbart

.com/politics/2014/07/10/dr-roy-spencer-science-knows-almost-nothing
-about-global-warming/ (March 17, 2019).

26 Ibid.

27 Ibid.

28 Chuck Todd, *Meet the Press*, January 2, 2019, video and transcript
available at https://www.realclearpolitics.com/video/2019/01/02/chuck
_todd_im_not_going_to_give_time_to_climate_deniers.html (March 17,
2019).

29 H. Sterling Burnett, "Time to Clear Out the Obama Holdovers and the
Climate Propaganda They Spread," Heartland Institute, December 28,
2018, https://www.heartland.org/news-opinion/news/time-to-clear-out
-the-obama-holdovers-and-the-climate-propaganda-they-spread (March
17, 2019).

30 Daniel J. Boorstin, *The Image: A Guide to Pseudo-Events in America* (New
York: Vintage Books, 1961), 8–9.

31 Ibid., 14.

32 Ibid., 33–34.

33 Letter from Attorney General William Barr to House and Senate
Committees on the Judiciary, March 24, 2019, http://judiciary.house.gov
/sites/democrats.judiciary.house.gov/files/documents/AG%20March%20
24%202019%20Letter%20to%20House%20and%20Senate%20
Judiciary%20Committees.pdf (March 29, 2019).

34 Rich Noyes, "Fizzle: Nets Gave Whopping 2,284 minutes to Russia
Probe," *NewsBusters*, March 25, 2019, http://www.newsbusters.org/blogs
/nb/rich-noyes/2019/03/24/fizzle-nets-gave-whopping-2284-minutes
-russia-probe (March 29, 2019).

35 Michael Calderone, "Pulitzer Prizes honor reporting on Trump-Russia,
sexual misconduct scandals," *Politico*, April 16, 2018, http://www.politico
.com/story/2018/04/16/2018-pulitzer-prize-winners-526854 (March 29,
2019).

36 Amy Chozick, "After Mueller Report, News Media Leaders Defend Their
Work," *New York Times*, March 25, 2019, http://www.nytimes.com/2019
/03/25/business/media/mueller-report-media.html (March 29, 2019).

37 Joshua Caplan, "Jeff Zucker: No Regrets on CNN's Russia Hoax
Coverage, 'We are not investigators,'" *Breitbart*, March 26, 2019, https://

www.breitbart.com/the-media/2019/03/26/jeff-zucker-no-regrets-on
-cnns-russia-hoax-coverage (March 29, 2019).

38 Chozick, "After Mueller Report, News Media Leaders Defend Their
Work."

39 Ken Meyer, "ABC's Jon Karl Defends Media Coverage of Mueller Probe:
'How could reporters not cover that?'" *Mediaite,* March 25, 2019,
http://www.mediaite.com/tv/abcs-jon-karl-defends-media-coverage
-of-trump-russia-probe-how-could-reporters-not-cover-that/ (March
29, 2019).

40 Carlos Garcia, "Brit Hume says collusion story is the 'worst journalistic
debacle' of his lifetime in scathing commentary," *The Blaze,* March 25,
2019, http://www.theblaze.com/news/brit-hume-slams-media-on
-collusion (March 29, 2019).

41 Boorstin, *The Image,* 33–34.

42 Anonymous, "I Am Part of the Resistance Inside the Trump Administration—I work for the president but like-minded colleagues and I have
vowed to thwart part of his agenda and his worst inclinations," *New York
Times,* September 5, 2018, https://www.nytimes.com/2018/09/05
/opinion/trump-white-house-anonymous-resistance.html?module=
inline (March 17, 2019).

43 Ibid.

44 Boorstin, *The Image,* 35.

45 *Washington Times* staff, "Trump v. CNN's Jim Acosta: The Full
Exchange," *Washington Times,* November 7, 2018, https://www
.washingtontimes.com/news/2018/nov/7/trump-vs-cnns-jim-acosta
(March 17, 2019).

46 Katie Pavlich, "Mexican Citizens: Trump Is Right, This Caravan Is
Absolutely an Invasion," Townhall.com, November 19, 2018, https://
townhall.com/tipsheet/katiepavlich/2018/11/19/mexican-citizens-this
-caravan-is-absolutely-an-invasion-n2536171 (March 17, 2019).

47 Ami Horowitz, "The Truth Behind the Caravan," *Daily Wire*, video report
available on YouTube, November 12, 2018, https://www.youtube.com
/watch?v=quz5A87Oqgc (March 17, 2019).

48 Curtis Houck, "Adorable: Fake News Jim to Publish Book to Make Us
Feel Bad for Him," MRCNewsbusters, January 24, 2019, https://www

.newsbusters.org/blogs/nb/curtis-houck/2019/01/24/adorable-fake-news
-jim-publish-book-make-us-feel-bad-him (March 17, 2019).

49 Ibid.

50 Boorstin, *The Image*, 35.

51 Ibid.

52 Ibid., 6.

53 Ibid., 29.

6. THE *NEW YORK TIMES* BETRAYS MILLIONS

1 Deborah E. Lipstadt, *Beyond Belief: The American Press & the Coming of the Holocaust 1933–1945* (New York: Free Press, 1986), 10.

2 David S. Wyman, *The Abandonment of the Jews* (New York: New Press, 1984), 321.

3 Ibid., 62.

4 Andrew Buncombe, "Allied Forces Knew About Holocaust Two Years Before Discovery of Concentration Camps," *Independent*, April 18, 2017, https://www.independent.co.uk/news/world/world-history/holocaust -allied-forces-knew-before-concentration-camp-discovery-us-uk-soviets -secret-documents-a7688036.html (March 17, 2019).

5 Wyman, *The Abandonment of the Jews*, 62.

6 Ibid., 321.

7 Ibid.

8 Ibid., 321–22.

9 Lipstadt, *Beyond Belief*, 244–45.

10 Ibid., 245–46.

11 Ibid., 252.

12 Ibid., 251.

13 Ibid.

14 Ibid.

15 Ibid., 245–46.

16 Laurel Leff, *Buried by the Times* (New York: Cambridge University Press, 2005), back cover.

17 Ibid., 5.

18 Ibid.

19 Ibid., 6–7.

20 Ibid., 13.

21 Ibid., 13–14.

22 Ibid., 14.

23 Ibid., 15–16.

24 Ibid., 237.

25 Ibid.

26 Max Frankel, "150th Anniversary: 1851-2001; Turning Away from
    the Holocaust," *New York Times*, November 14, 2001, https://www
    .nytimes.com/2001/11/14/news/150th-anniversary-1851-2001
    -turning-away-from-the-holocaust.html?mtrref=www.google
    .com&gwh=5EF060B0F36492EA97FC390DED59E112&gwt=pay
    (March 17, 2019).

27 Ibid.

28 Ibid.

29 Ibid.

30 Ibid.

31 Neil A. Lewis, "Israel in *The New York Times* Over the Decades: A
    Changed Narrative and Its Impact on Jewish Readers," Joan Shorenstein
    Center on the Press, Politics, and Public Policy, Harvard University,
    Spring 2011, https://shorensteincenter.org/wp-content/uploads/2012/03
    /d69_lewis.pdf (March 17, 2019).

32 Frankel, "150th Anniversary: 1851-2001."

33 Ed Koch, "The New York Times' Anti-Israel Bias," *RealClearPolitics*, June
    1, 2006, https://www.realclearpolitics.com/articles/2006/06/the_new
    _york_times_antiisrael.html (March 17, 2019).

34 Matti Friedman, "What the Media Gets Wrong About Israel," *Atlantic*,
    November 30, 3014, https://www.theatlantic.com/international/archive
    /2014/11/how-the-media-makes-the-israel-story/383262 (March 17,
    2019).

35 Ibid.

36 Ibid.

37 Ibid.

38 Ambassador David Friedman, "Liberal Media Sides with Hamas over
    Trump," Fox News, May 20, 2018, https://www.foxnews.com/opinion/us

-ambassador-to-israel-david-friedman-liberal-media-sides-with-hamas
-over-trump (March 17, 2019).

39 Ibid.

40 Vivan Yee and Hwaida Saad, "Christmas in Lebanon: 'Jesus Isn't Only
    for the Christians,'" *New York Times*, December 24, 2018, https://www
    .nytimes.com/2018/12/24/world/middleeast/christmas-lebanon.html
    ?smtyp=cur&smid=tw-nytimesworld (March 17, 2019).

41 Ibid.

42 Ibid.

43 "Hezbollah," Counter Extremism Project, https://www.counterextremism
    .com/threat/Hezbollah (March 17, 2019).

44 Gilead Ini, "The 'Times' and Israel: A Review of 2018," *Commentary*
    magazine, Feb. 2019, https://www.commentarymagazine.com/articles
    /the-times-and-israel-a-review-of-2018/, April 5, 2019.

45 Bruce Bartlett, "The Shame of the Times," *Human Events*, July 5, 2006,
    http://humanevents.com/2006/07/05/the-shame-of-the-times (March 17,
    2019).

46 Ibid.

47 S. J. Taylor, *Stalin's Apologist* (New York: Oxford University Press, 1990),
    205.

48 Robert Conquest, *The Harvest of Sorrow* (New York: Oxford University
    Press, 1986), 308–9.

49 Walter Duranty, "Russians Hungry, but Not Starving," *New York Times*,
    March 31, 1933.

50 Ibid.

51 Walter Duranty, "Big Ukraine Crop Taxes Harvesters," *New York Times*,
    September 18, 1933.

52 Lubomyr Luciuk, "It's Time Journalism's 'Greatest Liar' Lost His Prize,"
    Montreal Gazette, May 1, 2003, http://www.ukemonde.com/news/duranty
    .html (March 17, 2019).

53 Conquest, *The Harvest of Sorrow*, 320.

54 Arnold Beichman, "Pulitzer-Prize Winning Lies," *Weekly Standard*, June
    12, 2003, https://www.weeklystandard.com/arnold-beichman/pulitzer
    -winning-lies (March 17, 2019).

55 Douglas McCollam, "Should This Pulitzer Be Pulled," *Columbia*

Journalism Review, November/December 2003, http://www.uncg.edu
/~jwjones/russia/378readings/durantypulitzer.html (March 17, 2019).

56 Ibid.

57 Jacques Steinberg, "Times Should Lose Pulitzer from 30s, Consultant
Says," *New York Times*, October 23, 2003, https://www.nytimes.com/2003
/10/23/us/times-should-lose-pulitzer-from-30-s-consultant-says.html
(March 17, 2019).

58 Ibid.

59 James William Crowl, *Angels in Stalin's Paradise* (New York: University
Press of America, 1982), 140–41.

60 Helen Roche, *Bloodlands: Europe Between Hitler and Stalin* (New York:
Basic Books, 2010), 56.

7. THE TRUTH ABOUT COLLUSION, ABUSE OF POWER, AND CHARACTER

1 Olivia Gazis, "Richard Burr on the Senate Intelligence Committee's Russia
Investigation, 2 Years On," CBS News, February 7, 2019, https://www
.cbsnews.com/news/richard-burr-on-senate-intelligence-committees
-russia-investigation-2-years-on/ (March 17, 2019).

2 Ken Dilanian, "Senate Has Uncovered No Direct Evidence of Conspiracy
Between Trump Campaign and Russia," NBC News, February 12, 2019,
https://www.nbcnews.com/politics/congress/senate-has-uncovered
-no-direct-evidence-conspiracy-between-trump-campaign-n970536
(March 17, 2019).

3 Sean Davis, "Obama's Campaign Paid $972,000 to Law Firm That
Secretly Paid Fusion GPS in 2016," *Federalist*, October 29, 2017, http://
thefederalist.com/2017/10/29/obamas-campaign-gave-972000-law-firm
-funneled-money-fusion-gps/ (March 17, 2019).

4 John Solomon, "How the Clinton Machine Flooded the FBI with Trump
-Russia Dirt . . . until Agents Bit," *The Hill*, January 22, 2019, https://
thehill.com/opinion/white-house/426464-how-the-clinton-machine
-flooded-the-fbi-with-trump-russia-dirt-until (March 17, 2019).

5 John Solomon, "FISA Shocker: DOJ Officials Warned Steele Dossier
Was Connected to Clinton, Might Be Biased," *The Hill*, January 16, 2019,

https://thehill.com/opinion/white-house/425739-fisa-shocker-doj-official
-warned-steele-dossier-was-connected-to-clinton (March 17, 2019).

6 William Cummings, "Reporter Who Broke Steele Dossier Story Says
ex-British Agents' Claims 'Likely False,'" *USA Today*, December 18, 2018,
https://www.usatoday.com/story/news/politics/2018/12/18/steele-dossier
-michael-isikoff/2347833002 (March 17, 2019).

7 John Solomon, "The Mueller Probe's Troubling Reliance on Journalists as
Sources," *The Hill*, September 5, 2018, https://thehill.com/opinion/white
-house/405242-the-mueller-probes-troubling-reliance-on-journalists-as
-sources (March 17, 2019).

8 Ibid.

9 Ibid.

10 Ibid.

11 Ibid.

12 Ibid.

13 Ibid.

14 Kelly Cohen, "Former Top FBI Lawyer James Baker Under Criminal
Investigation for Media Leaks," *Washington Examiner*, January 15, 2019,
https://www.washingtonexaminer.com/news/former-top-fbi-lawyer-james
-baker-under-criminal-investigation-for-media-leaks (March 17, 2019).

15 Eric Scheiner, "Unfactual: AP Walks Back Several Trump-Russia Stories,"
Media Research Center, July 2, 2017, https://www.mrctv.org/blog/unfactual
-ap-walks-back-several-trump-russia-stories (March 17, 2019).

16 Mollie Hemingway, "18 Questions CNN Needs to Answer After Getting
Busted for Fake News," *Federalist*, December 8, 2017, http://thefederalist
.com/2017/12/08/18-questions-cnn-needs-to-answer-after-getting-busted
-for-fake-news/ (March 17, 2019).

17 Rowan Scarborough, "FBI-Debunked Russia-Trump Story Helped New
York Times win Journalism Award," *Washington Times*, March 1, 2018,
https://www.washingtontimes.com/news/2018/mar/1/fbi-debunked
-russia-trump-story-helped-new-york-ti (March 17, 2019).

18 Mollie Hemmingway, "Tips for Reading *Washington Post* Stories About
Trump Based on Anonymous Leaks," *Federalist*, May 16, 2017, https://
thefederalist.com/2017/05/16/tips-for-reading-washington-post-stories
-about-trump-based-on-anonymous-leaks/ (March 17, 2019).

19 Rowan Scarborough, "Robert Muller's Warning: 'Many' News Stories
    on Trump Russia Probe Are Wrong," *Washington Times*, April 16, 2018,
    https://www.washingtontimes.com/news/2018/apr/16/robert-mueller
    -many-news-stories-trump-russia-prob/ (March 17, 2019).

20 Chuck Ross, "NPR Falsely Accuses Don Jr. of Lying in Senate Testimony,"
    Daily Caller, November 30, 2018, https://dailycaller.com/2018/11/30/npr
    -false-donald-trump-jr/ (March 17, 2019).

21 *60 Minutes*, "Andrew McCabe: The Full 60 Minutes Interview," February
    17, 2019, https://www.cbsnews.com/news/andrew-mccabe-interview
    -former-acting-fbi-director-president-trump-investigation-james-comey
    -during-russia-investigation-60-minutes/ (March 17, 2019).

22 Ibid.

23 Ibid.

24 Joseph A. Wulfsohn, "CNN's Jeffrey Toobin Calls Andrew McCabe
    'Patriotic,' 'Not Treasonous' for Handling of President Trump," Fox News,
    February 18, 2019, https://www.foxnews.com/entertainment/cnns
    -jeffrey-toobin-calls-andrew-mccabe-patriotic-not-treasonous
    -for-handling-of-president-trump (March 17, 2019).

25 Ben Brantley, "Review: Young Rebels Changing History and Theater,"
    New York Times, August 6, 2015, https://www.nytimes.com/2015/08/07
    /theater/review-hamilton-young-rebels-changing-history-and-theater
    .html (March 17, 2019).

26 Ibid.

27 Lance Benning, "Republican Ideology and the French Revolution: A
    Question of Liberticide at Home, in *Responses of the Presidents to Charges
    of Misconduct*, C. Vann Woodward, ed., (New York: Delacorte Press,
    1974), 11.

28 Ibid., 11–12.

29 Peter Robinson, "Ted Kennedy's Soviet Gambit," *Forbes*, August 28, 2009,
    https://www.forbes.com/2009/08/27/ted-kennedy-soviet-union-ronald
    -reagan-opinions-columnists-peter-robinson.html#3bb23c0f359a
    (March 17, 2019).

30 Paul Kengor, "The Kremlin's Dupe: Ted Kennedy's Russia Romance,"
    American Spectator, April 12, 2018, https://spectator.org/the-kremlins
    -dupe-ted-kennedys-russia-romance/ (March 17, 2019).

31 Ibid.

32 Ibid.

33 Ibid.

34 Robinson, "Ted Kennedy's Soviet Gambit."

35 Paul Kengor, *The Crusader: Ronald Reagan and the Fall of Communism* (New York: Harper Perennial, 2006), 205–6.

36 Kengor, "The Kremlin's Dupe."

37 Logan Act defined at https://legal-dictionary.thefreedictionary.com /Logan+Act (March 17, 2019)

38 Byron York, "When a Foreign Adversary Meddled in a Presidential Election," *Washington Examiner*, September 9, 2018, https://www .washingtonexaminer.com/opinion/columnists/byron-york-when-a -foreign-adversary-meddled-in-a-presidential-election (March 17, 2019).

39 William C. Rempel, Henry Weinstein, and Alan C. Miller, "Testimony Links Top China Official, Funds for Clinton," *Los Angeles Times*, April 4, 1999, http://articles.latimes.com/1999/apr/04/news/mn-24189 (March 17, 2019).

40 Ibid.

41 Ibid.

42 Ibid.

43 York, "When a Foreign Adversary Meddled in a Presidential Election."

44 Rempel, Weinstein, and Miller, "Testimony Links Top China Official, Funds for Clinton."

45 Ibid.

46 Ibid.

47 York, "When a Foreign Adversary Meddled in a Presidential Election."

48 Associated Press, "Pelosi Shrugs Off Bush's Criticism, Meets Assad," NBC News, April 4, 2007, http://www.nbcnews.com/id/17920536/ns/world _news-mideast_n_africa/t/pelosi-shrugs-bushs-criticism-meets-assad /#.XFhF_PZFxcY (March 17, 2019).

49 Ibid.

50 Tom Rogan, "Why Pelosi's Syria Visit Remains Indefensible," *National Review*, March 16, 2015, https://www.nationalreview.com/2015/03/why -pelosis-syria-visit-remains-indefensible-tom-rogan (March 17, 2019).

51 Sara Fritz, "President and Wright Clash on Nicaragua: Speaker's Meetings

with Ortega, Obando Draw Reagan's Ire," *Los Angeles Times*, November 17, 1987, http://articles.latimes.com/1987-11-17/news/mn-21965_1 _daniel-ortega (March 17, 2019).

52 Ibid.

53 Ibid.

54 Philip Rotner, "Trumps' Abuse of Power," *HuffPost*, July 27, 2017, https://www.huffingtonpost.com/entry/trumps-abuse-of-power_us _5978c1d9e4b01cf1c4bb74cc (March 17, 2019).

55 Ibid.

56 David Rutz, "The Strongest Media Reactions to Trump's Firing of James Comey," *Washington Free Beacon*, May 10, 2017, https://freebeacon.com /politics/strongest-media-reactions-trumps-firing-of-james-comey (March 17, 2019).

57 Ibid.

58 Ibid.

59 Steven T. Dennis, "Schumer Says He Lost Confidence in FBI's Comey Over E-Mail Probe," Bloomberg, November 2, 2016, https://www .bloomberg.com/news/articles/2016-11-02/schumer-says-he-lost -confidence-in-fbi-s-comey-over-e-mail-probe (March 17, 2019).

60 Nancy Cordes, "Tensions Boil Up Between Democrats and FBI Director," CBS News, January 13, 2017, https://www.cbsnews.com/news/democrats -angry-james-comey-john-lewis-maxine-waters-hank-johnson/ (March 17, 2019).

61 "FBI Director James B. Comey's Termination: Letters from the White House, Attorney General," *Washington Post*, http://apps.washingtonpost .com/g/documents/politics/fbi-director-james-b-comeys-termination -letters-from-the-white-house-attorney-general/2430/ (March 17, 2019).

62 Jim Sciutto, "First on CNN: In ltr to FBI staff, Comey says he's 'long believed a president can fire an FBI director for any reason or no reason at all,'" Twitter, May 10, 2017, https://twitter.com/jimsciutto/status /862461497401909248 (March 17, 2019).

63 David Burnham, *A Law Unto Itself* (New York: Random House, 1989), 228–29.

64 Ibid., 229.

65 Ibid., 230.

66 Ibid., 231.

67 Ibid., 232.

68 Burton W. Folsom Jr., "FDR and the IRS," Hillsdale College, https://www
.hillsdale.edu/educational-outreach/free-market-forum/2006-archive
/fdr-and-the-irs/ (March 17, 2019).

69 Burnham, *A Law Unto Itself*, 236.

70 Folsom, "FDR and the IRS."

71 Ibid.

72 Ibid.

73 Ibid.

74 Ibid.

75 Jeff Himmelman, *Yours in Truth* (New York: Random House, 2017), 87.

76 Benjamin C. Bradlee, *Conversations with Kennedy* (New York: Norton,
1975), 218.

77 Burnham, *A Law Unto Itself*, 244.

78 Ibid., 272.

79 Jen Christensen, "FBI Tracked King's Every Move," CNN, December 28,
2008, http://www.cnn.com/2008/US/03/31/mlk.fbi.conspiracy (March
17, 2019).

80 Greg Mitchell, *The Tunnels* (New York: Broadway Books, 2016), 95.

81 Lee Edwards, "The FBI Spied for LBJ's Campaign," Heritage Foundation,
June 7, 2018, https://www.heritage.org/crime-and-justice/commentary
/the-fbi-spied-lbjs-campaign (March 17, 2019).

82 Ibid.

83 Robert Dallek, *Flawed Giant: Lyndon Johnson and His Times, 1961–1973*
(New York: Oxford University Press 1998), 161–62.

84 Ibid., 162.

85 Ibid., 576.

86 Burnham, *A Law Unto Itself*, 273.

87 Dallek, *Flawed Giant*, 407.

88 House Judiciary Committee, "Articles of Impeachment," July 27, 1974,
http://watergate.info/impeachment/articles-of-impeachment (March 17,
2019).

89 Ibid.

90 Ibid.

91 Brendan Bordelon, "Obama Dismisses IRS Targeting of Conservatives:
    'They've Got a List, and Suddenly Everybody's Outraged,'" *Daily Caller*,
    December 6, 2013, https://dailycaller.com/2013/12/06/obama-dismisses
    -irs-targeting-of-conservatives-theyve-got-a-list-and-suddenly
    -everybodys-outraged/ (March 17, 2019).

92 Alex Seitz-Wald, "How the Media Outrageously Blew the IRS Scandal,"
    BillMoyers.com, July 9, 2013, https://billmoyers.com/2013/07/09
    /how-the-media-outrageously-blew-the-irs-scandal/ (March 17, 2019).

93 Stephen Dinan, "Justice Department Admits IRS Wrongdoing, Agrees
    to $3.5 million Settlement with Tea Party Groups," *Washington Times*,
    October 26, 2017, https://www.washingtontimes.com/news/2017/oct/26
    /tea-party-groups-targeted-irs-get-35-million-settl/ (March 17, 2019).

94 Larry Sabato, *The Kennedy Half Century* (New York: Bloomsbury, 2013),
    129.

95 Ibid., 129–30.

96 Dallek, *Flawed Giant*, 186–87.

97 Ibid., 188.

98 Matt Drudge, "Newsweek Kills Story on White House Intern," Drudge
    Report Archives, January 17, 1998, http://www.drudgereportarchives
    .com/data/2002/01/17/20020117_175502_ml.htm (March 17, 2019).

99 Aaron Klein, "Juanita Broaddrick: NBC Skipped 'Perfect Opportunity' to
    Ask Bill Clinton About Rape Allegations," *Breitbart*, June 4, 2018, https://
    www.breitbart.com/the-media/2018/06/04/juanita-broaddrick-nbc
    -skipped-perfect-opportunity-to-ask-bill-clinton-about-rape-allegations/#
    (March 17, 2019).

100 Ibid.

101 Alexandra Desanctis, "The Worst Moments in Media Coverage of the
    Kavanaugh Confirmation Fight," *National Review*, October 11, 2018.

EPILOGUE: A STANDARDLESS PROFESSION

1 Bill Kovach and Tom Rosenstiel, *The Elements of Journalism* (New York:
   Three Rivers Press, 2007), 88–89.

2 Ibid., 89.

3 Ashley Collman, "Rolling Stone Found GUILTY of Defaming University

of Virginia Dean in False Campus Rape Story," *Daily Mail*, November 4, 2016, https://www.dailymail.co.uk/news/article-3906362/Rolling-Stone -GUILTY-defaming-University-Virginia-dean-false-campus-rape-story .html (March 17, 2019).

4 Mary Katherine Ham, "Fantastic Lies: 10 Appalling Moments from the Duke Lacrosse Case," *Federalist*, March 16, 2016, http://thefederalist .com/2016/03/16/fantastic-lies-10-appalling-moments-from-the-duke -lacrosse-case (March 17, 2019).

5 William Campenni, "The Truth About Dan Rather's Deceptive Reporting on George W. Bush," *Daily Signal*, October 30, 2015, https://www.daily signal.com/2015/10/30/the-truth-about-dan-rathers-deceptive-reporting -on-george-w-bush (March 17, 2019).

6 Lisa Boothe, "The Media's Orchestrated Smear of Brett Kavanaugh," Fox News, October 30, 2018, https://www.foxnews.com/opinion/the-medias -orchestrated-smear-of-brett-kavanaugh (March 17, 2019).

7 Matt Walsh, "4 Lessons We Can Learn from the Despicable Smear Campaign Against the Covington Catholic Students," *Daily Wire*, January 21, 2019, https://www.dailywire.com/news/42418/walsh-4-lessons-we-can -learn-despicable-smear-matt-walsh (March 17, 2019).

8 John Lott Jr., "The Media Just Can't Stop Lying About Trump," *The Hill*, June 21, 2018, https://thehill.com/opinion/campaign/393553-the-media -just-cant-stop-lying-about-trump (March 17, 2019).

9 http://www.readwritethink.org/classroom-resources/calendar-activities /york-times-used-slogan-20412.html (March 17, 2019).

10 A. G. Sulzberger, "New York Times Publisher A.G. Sulzberger Responded to President Trump's Continued Attacks on a Free Press," *New York Times*, February 20, 2019, https://www.nytco.com/press/new-york -times-publisher-a-g-sulzberger-responded-to-president-trumps -continued-attacks-on-a-free-press/ (March 17, 2019).

11 P. J. Gladnick, "Ted Koppel: Trump's 'Not Mistaken' That Liberal Media Are Blatantly 'Out to Get Him,'" NewsBusters, March 18, 2019, https:// www,newsbusters.org/blogs/nb/pj-gladnick/2019/03/18/ted-koppel -trump-not-mistaken-about-biased-liberal-media.

12 Daniel Okrent, "The Public Editor; Paper of Record? No Way, No Reason, No Thanks," *New York Times,* April 25, 2004, https://www.nytimes.com

/2004/04/25/weekinreview/the-public-editor-paper-of-record-no-way
-no-reason-no-thanks.html (March 17, 2019).

13 Jim Rutenberg, "Trump Is Testing the Norms of Objectivity in
    Journalism," *New York Times*, August 8, 2016, https://www.nytimes.com
    /2016/08/08/business/balance-fairness-and-a-proudly-provocative
    -presidential-candidate.html (March 17, 2019).